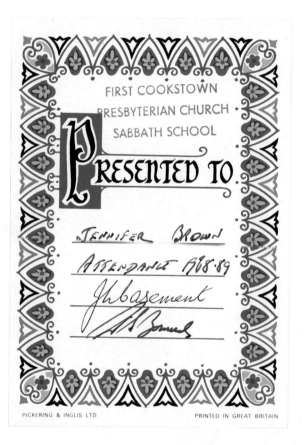

FIRST COOKSTOWN
PRESBYTERIAN CHURCH ·
SABBATH SCHOOL

PRESENTED TO

Jennifer Brown
Attendance 1988·89
JH Basement

PICKERING & INGLIS LTD.   PRINTED IN GREAT BRITAIN

Presented to ....

By ....

On ....

MY OWN BIBLE STORY BOOK

Illustrated throughout in full colour

Stories retold by Jenny Robertson

Illustrated by Gordon King

Consulting Editors

Alan Bamford M.Ed.
Principal, Westhill College of Education, Birmingham

Russell T. Hitt B.A., M.S., Litt.D.
Editor, *Eternity* Magazine

The Rev. David H. Wheaton M.A., B.D.
Principal, Oakhill Theological College, London

Editors, Scripture Union
Michael Hews LL.B.
Helen Smart B.A.

WORD PUBLISHING

Word (UK) Ltd
Milton Keynes, England

WORD BOOKS AUSTRALIA
Heathmont, Victoria, Australia

SUNDAY SCHOOL CENTRE WHOLESALE
Salt River, South Africa

ALBY COMMERCIAL ENTERPRISES PTE LTD
Scotts Road, Singapore

CONCORDE DISTRIBUTORS LTD
Havelock North, New Zealand

CROSS (HK) CO
Hong Kong

PRAISE INC
Quezon City, Philippines

ISBN 0-8509-256-6

Made and printed in Great Britain by
Purnell & Sons (Book Production) Ltd.,
Member of the BPCC Group, Paulton, Bristol

Old Testament

New Testament

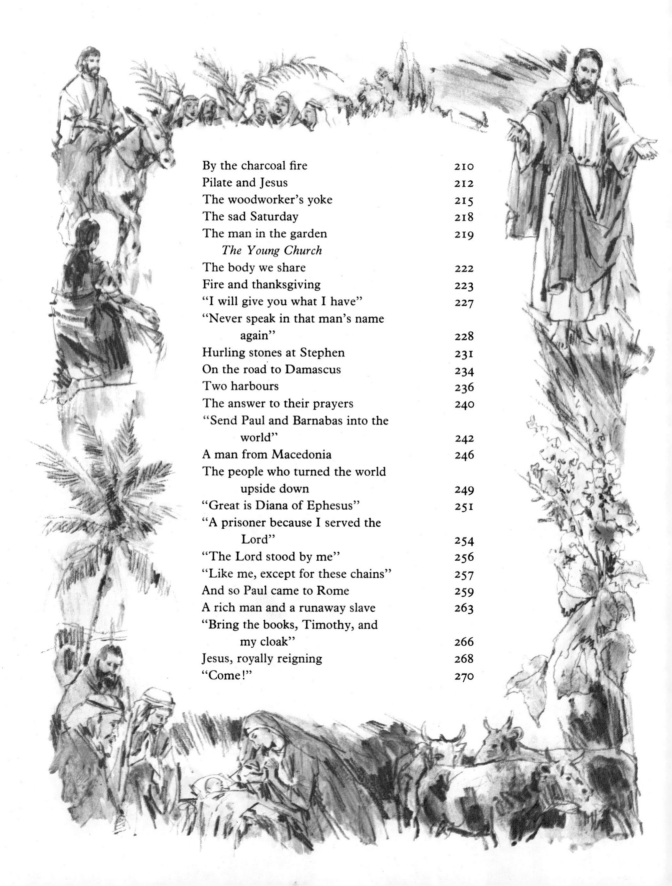

In the beginning

"What was there in the beginning at the very start of things?" The old man stopped, looking around him at the bright young faces of his audience. He was a Jewish priest who had been taken prisoner by the proud foreign armies that had swept through his homeland. Now he was in exile, far away from the homeland that the youngsters in front of him had never seen.

"Listen, then, and I'll tell you, and remember well, so that the story of our people which your minds receive will burn in your hearts."

The boys nodded. Their parents sent them to the old priest so that they should learn all the teaching of their people which had been handed down through the centuries. They knew the old stories well, and loved them. They had asked questions eagerly about their favourite heroes. The old man had listened patiently.

"We must begin at the beginning," he said, "For

in the beginning there was nothing, nothing at all, but at the same time there was everything, for there was God."

"God was at the beginning, and in the dark his Spirit hovered over the deeps, where the earth would be made.

"God spoke and his Word created.

" 'Let there be light,' said God. Light broke through the dark and God saw that it was good. Now there was a dark time and a light time. God called them 'night' and 'day'.

"Then God made the sky. He divided the watery deeps, gathering water together to form clouds. Thus the sky was made, like a great arch stretching over the deep water below where there was still not earth, nor any form of life.

"God made the earth. He gathered up all the waters together so that dry land appeared. God called the dry land 'earth' and the deep surging mass of water 'the seas'. God saw that it was good.

"Now life could begin on the earth. 'Let there be plants and trees that bear seeds and bring fruit all over the earth,' God said, and at his word vegetation spread, took root and bore fruit on the earth, and God saw that it was good.

"In their places in the sky God set the sun and the moon, for all life depends on the heat of the sun and the waxing and waning of the moon. So there were the seasons, and time could be measured in days, months, and years. And God saw that it was good.

"God said: 'Now let the waters be filled with life and let birds fly above in the sky.' So the seas were filled with great sea-serpents and tiny wriggling fish, and in the sky above little birds darted, and great birds soared. God saw that it was good. God spoke in blessing: 'Be fruitful, reproduce and rear your young to fill the waters and the skies.'

"Then God said: 'Let the earth produce every kind of creature: cattle and insects; reptiles and wild beasts.' So in the fields and forests over the earth, animals grazed and little creatures crawled. God saw that it was good.

"But there were no people yet on the earth.

"So the last form of life that God made was mankind. God said: 'People are made in the same way as God, with minds that understand; with hearts that can love, or hate, and with tongues that can speak.' Then God blessed humankind and said, as he had said to the animals: 'Be fruitful, have babies and bring them up into adulthood.' But he added: 'Conquer the whole earth. You are the masters over the fish in the oceans, over the birds in the sky and over the animals. Now look, I am giving you all the plants and trees on the earth; their fruits shall be your food.'

"God looked at all he had made and was pleased because it was very good.

"Six times light had turned to darkness as God created the world and every living thing; the seasons and the sun. Now everything was complete: the heavens with their hosts of stars, the earth with its abundance of life. As light became dark again, God rested. It was the seventh day and he blessed it, making it a special holy day for everyone to keep, both to worship God and to rest, because he had rested after all his work of creating."

The old man finished his story.

"So when the Sabbath lights are lit and your families gather together to pray and keep God's holy day, remember that God was in the beginning: nothing in the world came into being without him. This is the teaching of our people."

The garden where God walked

The earth stretched out for mile after mile: a citiless, silent immensity. Above it spread the sky, blue and still. No little woodland birds fluttered there, for there were no trees on the earth, nor any plants, for the Lord God had not yet sent rain. There were no people, none at all, so the earth stretched out, an empty world, awaiting the footsteps of man, and his tools to till the soil.

But from the earth, from some secret depths, a flood gurgled and spiralled into the silent land, watering the surface of the soil. Then from the dust of the soil the Lord God made a man. The man lay on the ground. He was naked, strong and handsome, but lifeless and dumb. So the Lord breathed into the man's nostrils. The body grew warm. Life pulsed through it. The man stirred, opened his eyes and looked around him.

The Lord God planted a garden called Eden. It lay in the east. It was in this garden that God put the man he had made. The man was fully alive now, breathing, moving, touching and feeling. There was hunger in him. He needed to eat. There was beauty around him. He needed to touch. No one forbade him. This was his garden. He reached out and ate.

"Eat freely, and eat your fill." The man heard the voice of God. He stood still, his head tilted back. He was using his ears for the first time. The sound of the voice echoed in his brain. He heard and understood. "You may eat the fruit of all the trees in the garden. But see, in the middle of the garden there stands one tree and of its fruit you may not eat. It is the tree of the knowledge of good and evil. Man cannot digest that fruit easily. On the day that you eat of it you shall surely die."

So the man stayed away from that tree in the middle of the garden, but he was perfectly happy. He wandered alone to the edge of the garden that God had given him to cultivate. There at the boundaries a river flowed. It had enough water for the whole of Eden and out of it four streams encircled four lands: the source of pure gold and of the black jem, the onyx and of bdellium, a sweet-smelling sap. Two of the four streams formed the boundaries of Babylon.

God knew what the man still needed. For in the garden where God walked, where there was plenty to eat and to enjoy, one thing was lacking. The man was alone. He had no companion.

"It is not good for the man to be alone," God thought, and as the man wandered at will and worked in the unpeopled garden, he heard the voice of the Lord calling to him. It was the only voice he had ever heard, apart from his own. The voice of the Lord drew him as the magnet draws the needle of a compass. He came running through the trees.

"Here I am, Lord!" Then he stopped short in surprise.

In front of him were many strange creatures. They did not walk on two legs as the man walked. They made all sorts of noises but did not have the power of speech. About them fluttered little things with feathers and with wings: they could do what man would never be able to do without the help of engines and machinery; they flew.

"Is this your work, Lord?" the man eventually asked.

"It is my work. I have made them for you. Look, Man, I have brought you the beasts and the birds. It is for you to give them their names."

The man laughed. His white teeth flashed in his dark-skinned face. "I like you!" he declared, running his hand through the flowing mane of one huge beast. "See, you, with the great mane and wonderful strength, you are the mighty monarch. I call you lion."

The lion shook its mane, and its strong muscles rippled beneath its sleek coat. It turned its head and roared, but stopped as it saw a small, white, new-born creature skipping beside its mother.

"It is the little lamb. See it has such a soft coat and such nimble feet," said the man.

The lamb bounded over to the lion's side and played skittishly between the beast's huge paws.

Next the man named the dog, the friend of man, and the horse, his helpmate, and the donkey who patiently carried his burdens. He named the swift hind from the high hills, the lumbering elephant from the hot plains: the eagle that soared high, further than the man could see. He named the cooing dove and the tiny wren. He named the camel and the cow; the buffalo and the bear; the raven and the squirrel. And so he went on until, at the very end, he named the serpent.

The serpent could walk upright then.

"Friends and helpmates you have given me, Lord," the man said. "Thank you."

"They cannot speak to you, Man," God reminded him.

"No," the man said and did not see the serpent inch his way a little closer, upright over the dusty ground.

"You cannot eat together. They will not share your food."

"No," the man agreed. The serpent coiled its long body round the trunk of a nearby tree, until it was nearly on the same level as the man.

"I shall make you a companion. She shall not be quite as you are, though she will have speech, understanding, love and the knowledge of my voice, just as you have. She is the other part of human kind and you shall call her woman. Sleep now, Man," God said and sent the animals away.

When the man awoke, the Lord brought his companion to him.

"At last you have given me my companion, bone of my bone and flesh of my flesh," the man cried out in delight. He stretched out his hand. It was strong and broad, stained with the loam and soil and with the juice of many fruits. The woman came to him. They walked through the trees together and lay in the shade. They wore no clothes, nor had they need of any. Whatever they did need, they got from the garden God had planted, or from the beasts he had brought to man to name and rule over.

The man showed the woman all the trees of the garden. They laughed together as they pulled the boughs low and sank their teeth into juicy fruit. The animals sensed that the man was completely happy now. They helped him in his work as he tilled the soil, or cut back the trees that had borne fruit, so that fresh fruit would grow. Often they followed as the man and the woman walked through the garden together. The serpent was always there, very close and often quite unseen. It did nothing to help, but watched, and seemed to listen.

The woman wove a basket. She walked ahead of the man, picking fruit as she wandered further and further into the centre of the garden. There stood a beautiful tree. Its boughs were bent beneath a crop of fruit that was heavier than any other tree had borne.

"Why have we not been here before?" she wondered aloud. "Why have we never gathered the fruit of this tree? Or is this perhaps the tree my husband told me about, the one that God said we should not touch?"

Something rustled in the branches above her head. She looked up. The long, vividly coloured body of the serpent lay in coils there. She heard a voice and was surprised, for she and the man knew that only they and the Lord God were able to speak together in words. She turned and listened, frowning a little, trying to understand. The voice was smooth. It seemed to be coming from the serpent above her. It asked a question.

"Did God really say you weren't to eat any fruit from any of the trees in the garden?"

"Oh, no!" She answered straight away. "No, of course not! God has given us complete freedom all over the garden. We eat our fill daily of all kinds of delicious fruit from the trees—from every tree, you know, except for one tree, the one in the middle of the garden. If we eat its fruit, God warned us, we shall die that very day."

"Oh, no, you won't die!" the voice said. There was just the slightest hissing noise as the serpent spoke. "Is the fruit not from the tree of knowledge? God knows that when you eat that fruit you'll be just like

The man stood very still. "What have you done?" he asked her, horrified.

"I have eaten good fruit," she said. "Knowledge is good. God has been keeping knowledge from us."

"God said we will die on the day we eat this fruit."

She laughed then. "I have eaten and I am not dead. Look at me. I know everything now."

That annoyed her husband. "Give me this fruit. I'll have some, too," he said. "Then I'll know everything as well."

him. You'll know everything. You'll understand good—and evil," it added, quietly.

The woman looked at the crop of fruit. It seemed more delicious than ever now. "The fruit of all the other trees well satisfies both our hunger and thirst," she said.

"But this tree gives you knowledge," the voice told her.

"Ye-es," she agreed slowly, thinking hard.

"That cannot be harmful." The voice was saying exactly what she was thinking. "Knowledge is a good thing."

The woman stretched out her hand and picked one of the fruits. She ate it slowly.

"Where are you?" It was the voice of her husband. She was frightened. What would he say? She had disobeyed the one commandment the Lord God had given them. She did not move from the tree. She had knowledge now. She stood still, half-hidden by the bent boughs with their load of luscious fruit. She had power over the man now.

"I gathered fruit as we agreed," she said, "And see! This fruit was the sweetest of any. For it not only satisfies hunger and thirst. It fills with knowledge."

So the man ate the fruit. At first the fruit left a good taste. The man looked at it, wanting another bite. Then he changed his mind and threw it, half-eaten, down to the ground. He looked at his wife.

"We're naked," the man said.

"Yes." She knew it now as well. "God gave the animals fur to keep them warm, or thick, leather hides."

"But we have nothing."

They ran over to the tall, wide-spreading fig tree. They tore off its thick leaves. Clumsily, they sewed the leaves together. It took them a long time. When they had finished, they tied them round their waists like short skirts.

"Shsh!" The man was very still, listening. "What was that?"

"It is the sound of the Lord God," his wife said. "We've taken so long to make ourselves coverings it's now the cool of the day, the time when he walks in the garden."

They looked at each other. They were afraid.

"What is this feeling inside me?" the woman asked. "I don't like it. I've never felt like this before."

"I have it, too," the man whispered. "I don't like it either. It is fear," he added, knowing and feeling more afraid. "Let's hide."

They crouched amongst the trees to hide from the Lord.

"Man," the Lord God called. "Where are you?"

Trembling, the man and the woman crept out into the open.

"Where have you been?"

"I heard the sound you made as you walked in the garden," the man's voice shook. "And . . . and I was afraid because I was naked," he faltered. "And so I hid."

"Who told you about being naked?" the Lord asked. "Have you been eating the fruit of the tree I told you not to eat?"

"It was the woman you put with me," the man answered, pointing to his wife. "She gave me the fruit and I ate it."

Then the Lord God asked the woman. "What is this you have done?"

She looked down at the ground. There was a faint rustle behind her. Out of the corner of her eye she saw a flash of colour as the serpent darted away. "The serpent said it was good, beautiful fruit," she said. "I listened to him and I ate."

"Serpent!" called the Lord, "because you have done this, I curse you. You shall crawl on your belly and go like the worm over the ground. You shall eat dust every day of your life. Now hatred has come into the garden. You and the woman are enemies now, and your children and her children will be enemies for ever. One day, a descendant of the woman will fight you. In the struggle you will wound him, but he will crush you to the ground."

The serpent slunk away, its bright skin covered in dust, and the woman laughed, pleased to see her enemy punished.

"Woman," said the Lord sternly, "you have done wrong. You disobeyed me and listened to the lies the serpent told you. So I tell you now that you shall know pain when you give birth to your babies, and in your marriage you will have yearning and sorrow."

To the man he said: "You listened to your wife and ate the fruit I told you not to eat. Up till now you had only to go to the trees and pull down their fruit. But from now on you must toil day in, day out, for the soil is cursed because of you. You will sweat and suffer for your food until in the end your body is laid to rest beneath the earth. For dust you are and to dust you shall return."

The man and his wife drew closer together then.

"You are Eve," the man said to his wife, "for you are the mother of all who will live."

"Come now," the Lord said, "for I am making you clothes of skins. They will last longer and protect you better than your skirts of fig leaves. Put them on now, for I am sending you away from Eden for ever."

So, clad in the skin clothes the Lord had made them, the man and his wife, Eve, left the garden where the Lord had walked and talked with them. Eden was barred with the flame of a flashing sword. The story started there goes on and on through all the years of Time.

A boat and a rainbow

"Father! Father, what *are* you doing?" The three young men came running over the grassy hill. They stopped and stared. For their father, who was called Noah, was cutting down a tree.

"Whatever are you doing this for? How many more trees are you going to cut down?"

Noah looked at them with a twinkle in his eyes. "I'm building a boat, sons," he said. "Don't worry, I'm not going mad – though folk are certainly going to think so! God has told me to build a boat."

"Why?" they asked. They weren't surprised that God had spoken directly to their father, nor that Noah was doing exactly what God told him, however strange it seemed, because they knew that Noah and God were very close, almost like friends, in fact, and that Noah always tried to please God in everything.

Noah looked at them. His face had grown solemn now. "Why? Because God is going to send a tremendous downpour of rain. The whole earth will be flooded, covered over by one enormous ocean."

"What will happen to all the people?" asked one brother.

"Tell me one thing," Noah asked them. "Do you

18

know of anyone who truly respects and obeys God?"

The brothers considered this. "No," they answered slowly. "No-one has any time for God, and they hate one another as well."

Noah nodded. "They are violent and destroy everything God has made. So God is going to wipe out everything He has made."

"Us too?" Their eyes were wide with horror. "And what about our wives?"

"We shall be safe. That is why God has told me to build a boat. We shall shelter there when God sends the rain. Then we shall begin a new life, and God is going to make a special agreement with us."

"How big is the boat to be?" asked his oldest son.

"Huge!" Noah answered. "You see, it has to carry animals as well. God doesn't want to wipe out life from this earth. We must take into our boat a male and female of every kind, so that when we land somewhere animal life will begin anew."

"Did God tell you how to make the boat?" the brothers wondered.

"Yes, in detail." Noah smiled. "It's to be very big: 450 feet long, 75 feet wide and 45 feet high. We must put a roof on it and make a door high up in one side. It's to have three decks, because we'll need to store plenty of food and water for us and the animals."

So they went on with their building. The story spread around that Noah was building a huge boat miles from the sea. Many people came to watch. Quietly, Noah went on with his work. He told everyone exactly what God was going to do, but no-one believed him. They laughed at him, and went away, shaking their heads: "He's gone mad, stark, raving mad!"

Noah did everything exactly as God had told him. The boat was made of layers of gopher wood, reeds and pitch. It was lined with pitch inside and out to make it completely waterproof. When it was ready God told Noah: "The rain will come in a week's time. Go aboard the boat now, with your family. Take the animals and birds."

Wild and tame animals crowded together; the birds fluttered and fussed overhead and then flew in through the open door.

Noah and his family also entered. God shut the door behind them.

Then they heard the first drops of rain fall. At first there was a light pitter-patter, but then the downpour really started. It seemed as if an enormous dam had opened in the sky and all the water in the universe had come foaming through. The noise was deafening. Animals and humans huddled together inside the boat. They felt the boat rock a little. Then it moved. And they knew that Noah had been right to believe what God had told him.

The earth was submerged below the water. Soon even the highest mountains were completely covered. For a great many days the water level went on rising, and Noah and his family watched their food stocks getting lower and lower as time went by.

Outside a great wind wailed, and gradually the rain stopped. Slowly the water ebbed away from the earth. One day they felt a sudden jolt as the boat came to rest on a very high mountain. After a while other peaks appeared, sticking up like rocks in the sea.

Inside the boat they waited more and more impatiently. One day Noah opened a small port-hole he had cut in the side of the boat and sent out a raven. The black bird flew off, its raucous cry echoed across the waters as it went back and forth, but there was nowhere for it to perch. Then Noah sent out a dove, and again they waited.

"Listen," Noah's wife said. "I hear a sort of tapping sound outside."

They all crowded around the porthole. Noah opened it and the dove nestled gratefully in the hollow of his outstretched hand. He brought the tired bird into safety. There had been nowhere for it to rest.

After a week they let the dove go again. Again they waited anxiously.

This time she returned the same day.

"Look!" they exclaimed as she settled again on Noah's hand. "She's got a twig in her beak. It's so green and fresh. It's a new olive branch."

And then they rejoiced. "The water must be down to the level of the trees then! God hasn't forgotten us. We won't have long to wait now before we can go out and begin life afresh."

They waited another week and then they sent out the dove again. This time she didn't return. Noah opened the door. The earth was dry. There was a scurry and a rustle, a hustle and a bustle as out they trooped, all the animals, the wild and the tame, the little creeping things, the snakes and lizards, the tortoises and crocodiles and the birds fluttering their wings, glad to be free.

"Let them swarm all over the earth and fill it again with animal life," God said.

How glad Noah and his wife and family were to be on the fresh clean earth again, breathing in sweet air, drinking in daylight.

Noah built an altar and offered animals and birds on the leaping flames of the fire he made there. It was his way of saying "thank you" to God.

Then God blessed them, as he had blessed man when he first made him: "Teem over the whole earth and be its lord," he said, "for I shall never again send a flood to destroy the earth. As long as the earth lasts spring and harvest, summer and winter, day and night shall never cease."

The sky was overcast, though the wind was driving away the clouds and suddenly the sun burst through.

"Look, look, everyone!" shouted Noah, pointing into the cloudy sky.

A rainbow hung there, a perfect arch that stretched all the way from the earth to heaven and back.

"It's God's special sign," Noah whispered. "When we see the rainbow, we will remember the agreement he has made with us and with every living creature on the earth."

Genesis 6–9

The friend of God

Abraham

The temple of the moon-god towered above the city of Ur. To worship the moon, people climbed up the enormous stone stairway, past beautiful trees and shrubs which decorated the three terraces round the pyramid at the base of the temple.

The people who came from outside the city lived in tents made of black goat or camel hair stretched over nine poles. They were nomads, people who wandered around, settling for a short time wherever they found water, and moving on again. They looked around them in wonder as they slowly climbed higher and higher to worship the moon.

Then a foreign king conquered the city. He decreed that the sun and not the moon should be worshipped in the lofty temple. A young man called Abram lived in Ur at the time when the king made his decree. Abram's father worshipped the moon. Perhaps the young man started to think:

"Can you change gods like this, and suddenly stop praying to the moon and start worshipping the sun? Where did the moon come from? Who made the sun?"

"Come, Abram," Terah, his father, said to him and the rest of the family one day. "We are going on a journey. We're going to Haran. They still worship our moon god there."

Abram's little nephew Lot was listening. His eyes grew big with wonder. "To Haran? But it's miles away. Why, I'll be a big man by the time we arrive!"

Terah's solemn face relaxed into a smile: "Then we'd better get started right away," he said to his small grandson.

Haran was about 600 miles away. They travelled slowly, for their burdened asses could cover no more than twenty miles a day. Besides, they had flocks of sheep and goats with them, and although sheep skip nimbly over the hills and rocky slopes,

they move very slowly along the roads. Abram and his wife Sarai looked after Lot, whose father had died while they were still in Ur.

At Haran old Terah died. Not long after his death Abram heard the voice of God. It was not the voice of the moon god, whom Terah had worshipped, nor the voice of the sun god whose magnificent temple rose seventy feet above the city of Ur. Abram heard the voice of the true God, who had made both the sun and the moon.

God said to Abram, "Leave Haran and your father's household, and go to the land I will show you. I will make you the father of a great nation and I will bless you."

Abram obeyed. He took Sarai and Lot, whom they treated as their own child, because they were childless. They had a great many possessions – flocks of sheep and goats, silver and gold, and many servants – for Abram had become a rich man.

They left Haran and set off for the land of Canaan. It lay to the south: they had to cross the river Euphrates. So the people in Canaan called them the "Hebrews", which meant: "The ones who crossed the river."

It was a long journey. They settled wherever they found pasture and water, then they moved on again. Everywhere they stopped, Abram built an altar to God, who had promised to make his descendants into a great nation. Although they were still without any children of their own, Abram believed what God had said, just as Noah had done when he built his boat miles away from the sea.

Canaan was a small country. Along the coast and in the valleys was fertile land. But there were mountains and desert where little could grow, and the limestone hills provided grazing only for the hardy sheep and goats.

Abram and his clan settled in the hill country all during the long hot summer. In the winter they moved south, camping outside the villages, paying sometimes for the use of the well; sometimes buying fields to pitch their tents. Once when the famine was bad, they moved to Egypt.

The place where Abram settled most often was called Hebron, and some people still call it, after him, the "city of the friend of God".

Their numbers were growing. By now Lot had his own family, flocks and servants.

"We must part company," Abram said to Lot. "Your herdsmen and mine keep quarrelling. There must be no strife, my nephew, for we are like brothers. Choose now. The whole land lies before you. If you go east, I'll go west. I give you first choice."

Lot saw the fertile land that lay around the river Jordan. His eyes lit up, and a greedy look crossed

you Hagar. She can be your wife for a little while and maybe she will have a baby boy. Then God's promise will come true."

Hagar did have a son. They called him Ishmael, but God soon made it clear to Abram that this was not his way.

"I am God," Abram heard God say. "I make my agreement with you. You will have a son. Now your name is not Abram but Abraham, for I am making you the father of many. A great nation will be descended from you and I will be their God. I will give your descendants the whole land of Canaan, and they shall be my special people."

Abram bowed low to the ground.

"Now Sarai is to be called Sarah," said God.

his face. He knew exactly what he wanted.

"This shall be my share." He pointed across to the rich countryside. He moved on eastward and settled near the city of Sodom. It was an evil city, and Lot could find no other men who worshipped God there. Soon after he arrived, the whole place was destroyed by God, with only Lot and his family escaping.

Abram moved west, as he had agreed, back to Hebron where he built an altar to God. Sarai and he still had no children, but Abram trusted in God's promise that he would be the father of a great nation.

One night he went outside his tent, and stood, blinking at the glory of the night sky filled with stars.

"Can you count the stars?" asked God. "You will have as many descendants as the stars in the sky. And your heir will be your own flesh and blood."

Abram believed God and so did Sarai, but they tried to work out God's promise in their own way.

"Listen, Abram," Sarai suggested. "God has promised you a son, but you and I have no children. Now, amongst our people it's the custom for the wife to lend her slave-girl to her husband. I'll lend

"I will bless her, and she will have a baby boy."

Abram laughed to himself at the words he heard. "We are too old to have children," he thought. Sarah was listening behind the tent flap and she laughed, too.

But God said, "Is anything too hard for the Lord? Sarah will have a son. You shall call him Isaac. I will do what you ask, and I will bless Ishmael. But my special agreement, my covenant, belongs to your own son, Isaac. He will be born this time next year."

And it turned out as God had promised. Sarah had her baby boy. The old parents called their son Isaac.

"How happy we are now! I believed that God would do as he said and give us many descendants, but I never believed he would be so good to us and give us our own baby. His promises have come true," said Abraham. "So our baby's name means 'Laughter'. God will always do everything he promises."

Baby Isaac grew. Soon he was toddling around, stumbling over the cords and wooden stakes that held the tent down. He played with Sarah's loom and shuttle, tangling the goat's hair threads. Later he wandered further afield, chasing the sheep and getting in the way while the shepherds watered the flocks at the hollowed drinking troughs.

"Just imagine," Sarah said one day, hugging her child, "pagan people give their first-born sons to their gods. They kill them and offer them on the altar." She shuddered, pressing Isaac closer to her. "Of course I've always known that they do this, but it's only now that we have our own son I realise what a dreadful custom it is."

Abraham said nothing. His mind was in a turmoil. For he had been thinking that very thing. In fact, even worse, he was certain that God, speaking within him, was telling him to go away to a sacred place in the mountain and offer Isaac there as a sacrifice.

Very early next morning, Abraham went outside and saddled his ass. Sarah was still sleeping in the women's part of the tent, but Isaac was up and was skipping after the sheep.

"Come, Isaac," his father called.

"Where to, father?" Isaac came across to Abraham.

"To a place that God will show us."

He chopped wood to build the fire for his sacrifice.

Taking two servants with them, they set off. Isaac felt very grown up, but as he got tired of walking and sore in the saddle perched in front of his father, he started to think about his mother and the comforting shelter of the tent at home.

They travelled for three days.

"Wait here now," Abraham told his servants. "Look after the donkey. The boy and I will go over there to the place God has chosen for us. We will make our sacrifice and worship God. Then we'll come back to you."

Abraham bound the wood for the fire on to Isaac's back. He carried the burning wick that would set the wood on fire, and the sharp knife to kill the sacrifice.

Isaac had watched them offer sacrifices before. They made an altar, tied the animal chosen for the sacrifice to the edge of the altar, slaughtered it with the knife his father was carrying, and burned it on the fire as an offering to God.

"Father." He was lagging behind for the way was steep and he was burdened with the wood he carried.

"Yes, my son?" Abraham answered.

"Look, father, we've got the wood and the flame and the knife, but where is the lamb for the burnt offering?"

"My son," – Abraham's voice sounded strange – "God himself will provide the lamb."

When they arrived at the place God had chosen for him, Abraham built an altar and took the wood off Isaac's back. Slowly he arranged it to make it ready for the fire.

"Come." With the rope that had bound the firewood, Abraham bound his child. He laid the terrified boy on to the top of the altar. Then he stretched out his hand and raised his knife to kill Isaac as a sacrifice to God.

From the blue sky above, where only the eagle soared, Abraham heard the voice of God.

"Abraham! Abraham!"

"I am here!" He lowered his knife, his heart beating wildly.

"Do not kill your son!" Isaac stopped sobbing and lifted his head, realising that Abraham was listening to the God his mother had often told him about.

"Your faith has been tested, and I see that you worship me with all your heart."

Abraham looked around. Nearby a ram was struggling to free itself from a thorn bush. Its horns were stuck fast, and the more it struggled, the more the long, sharp thorns tore its thick woollen coat.

"Isaac!" Abraham called joyfully, "God has spoken to me." He quickly untied his son. "Our God is greater than the gods the pagans worship. Our people will never again offer human sacrifice to God. He doesn't want such things." Freeing Isaac, he held him close. "Look, he has provided the ram for the burnt offering just as I told you he would."

With one blow Abraham put an end to the ram's pain. They kindled the fire and burned the ram on the altar where Isaac had lain. The blue smoke spiralled upward.

Standing very still beside his father, Isaac realised that God was speaking to Abraham again.

"I will send blessings on you like showers of rain. Your descendants will be as many as the stars in the sky and as the grains of sand on the seashore. All the nations of the world shall be blessed because of you."

Abraham worshipped God. Then they went down the mountain and back home to Sarah who, forgetting her age and womanhood, went running to meet them. Tears streamed down her cheeks as Abraham led them both back into the tent.

Genesis 11–22

24

A wife for Isaac

It had been a long, hot journey. The tired traveller had been on the road for many days, and now he was nearly at his journey's end. He was glad to rest at the well outside the city of Haran. But he had one big problem. His master, Abraham, had sent him all the way from Canaan back to his brother Nahor's family, who still lived in Haran. For Abraham wanted to find a wife for Isaac and he wanted her to be from his own relatives, not a Canaanite girl.

No wonder the servant was so anxious! Supposing he chose the wrong girl? Suppose he found the right girl, but she would not leave her family and travel into a foreign country with him?

Well, he reassured himself, Abraham believed it was all part of God's plan. God had promised that he would be the father of a great nation, and that the covenant would continue with Isaac and his children. God wouldn't let such an important thing go wrong.

In the evening, when the young girls left the city walls with their jugs and waterpots on their shoulders, Abraham's servant made his thirsty camels kneel down beside the well.

"Lord God," he prayed, "here come all the young girls of the town to get water. I'm going to ask one of them for a drink. If she says, 'Drink,

family; it's Abraham's brother's family. Praise God!"

Rebekah ran home. They welcomed Abraham's servant and looked after the camels.

"Now come and eat," Rebekah's brother, Laban, said to their guest.

He refused. "First let me tell you everything that has happened." He told them how his master had sent him to find a wife for his only son.

"God has blessed Abraham who went at his bidding across the river to Canaan. My master is very rich and has one child, Isaac, born when he and his wife were long past the age for children. With Isaac, God's covenant will continue. I prayed and God showed me that Rebekah is the girl for Isaac. Are you willing to let her marry Abraham's son?"

"There is Rebekah. Take her to be Isaac's wife," Laban said.

The servant brought out silver and gold jewellery and beautiful clothes. He gave these to Rebekah, and other rich presents to her brother and her mother. Then he ate his meal.

Next morning he was impatient to leave.

"Oh!" Laban and Rebekah's mother cried out. "It's too soon. Let Rebekah stay with us for another ten days."

"God has led me this far," said the servant. "I beg you to let me return to my master now."

"Do you want to go immediately, Rebekah?" they asked.

"Yes," she said.

It was a long journey for her. At the end they came to a well with greenery around it. Isaac was walking there as the hot day cooled and the evening shadows grew long.

Rebekah, swaying wearily as the camel lurched and bumped along, looked up and saw him. He quickened his steps and hurried towards them.

She jumped down from her camel.

"Who is that man?" she asked the servant.

"That is my master," said the servant simply. Rebekah hid her face in her veil and stood in silence as the servant told Isaac the whole story.

Then Isaac led Rebekah into his tent and made her his wife. They had twin boys, Esau, the first-born, and Jacob. Esau was a huntsman. He loved to be out in the open, while Jacob stayed at home all day in the tents. Rebekah preferred Jacob, but Isaac favoured Esau.

and I will give your camels water, too,' may she be the one you have chosen to be Isaac's wife."

Before he had finished his prayer, Rebekah came through the gate. She was very beautiful. She walked gracefully to the well and bent to fill her jug. Abraham's servant ran across to her.

"Please give me a drink," he begged.

Rebekah lowered her jug from her shoulder. "Drink, my lord. I will give your camels water, too." She went over to the drinking troughs beside the well, and filled her jug many times to water the thirsty animals. The servant watched in silence. It seemed as if his prayer were being answered, but what would happen now?

When the thirsty camels finished drinking, the servant gave Rebekah a solid gold ring. He put two heavy gold bracelets on her arms. Then he said:

"Whose daughter are you? Does your father have any room for me to spend the night?"

"I am the granddaughter of Nahor," Rebekah told him. "There's plenty of room for . . . what is it?" she asked in surprise, for the man had fallen flat on his face!

"Praise God!" he kept saying. "It's the right

Jacob the cheat

xhausted and starving, Esau the hunter returned wearily home from the hills. From outside the tent came a good smell. As he came closer, Esau could see the big cooking pot steaming over the fire.

"Jacob's been cooking!" The thought of good thick soup spurred him on, but he was so tired he could do little more than stumble toward the tent.

With a clatter he let his weapons – his bow and arrows, axe and throwing stick – drop to the floor.

"Jacob, I'm dying. Give me some food. I've not eaten since I left home days ago."

Jacob didn't move. "This is my chance," he thought. "When father dies, Esau will get the best part of the property because, although we're twins, he was born first. But now's my chance to outwit him."

"Jacob, brother!" Esau implored weakly. "Give me some soup before I die!"

"First sell me your birthright," Jacob came close to his brother.

"I'm dying," Esau said. "My birthright's no use to me now. You can have it."

"When he's eaten and revived, he'll go back on his word," Jacob thought. "No, brother," he said aloud. "First swear me an oath on it, and then I'll give you as much soup as you want."

Esau swore on oath and handed his birthright, the rights of the elder son over the younger, to Jacob. Then Jacob gave him bread which Esau dipped into the thick soup, eating with his fingers until the bowl was clean and he felt satisfied. He got up and went outside.

"Is that all he cares for his birthright?" thought Jacob.

They went their separate ways, twins with a rift of hatred between them.

"Father still loves Esau," Jacob brooded, "even though those wives of his, local girls from Canaan, are such a disappointment. Even though I have Esau's birthright, father will give him his blessing before he dies and there will be nothing for me."

By now Isaac was blind and very old. He called Esau to him.

"My son!" His sightless eyes peered up. He knew Esau by the smell of his clothing.

"I am here, father."

"I shall die soon. Take your bow and arrows and go into the hills. Hunt me some game: deer or a wild beast. Then make me the kind of savoury stew I like and bring it to me, so that I may eat and give you my blessing before I die."

Rebekah overheard. As soon as Esau disappeared with his bow and arrow, she found Jacob and told him what the old man had said.

"Now listen, my son," she whispered. "Go, and kill two young kids from the flock. I'll cook them and you can take them to your father and receive his blessing."

Jacob turned the matter over in his mind.

"But, mother, Esau is hairy. I am smooth-skinned. If father touches me, he'll know at once that I'm cheating him."

"Just do what I say," Rebekah reassured him.

Jacob killed two kids and his mother cooked an appetising stew. She took Esau's best clothes and dressed Jacob in them, taking care to cover his bare arms and hairless chest with the skins of the kids.

"There you are," she said, as she gave him the stew. "Off you go."

He entered Isaac's part of the tent. "I am here, father."

"Who are you, my son?" With the sharper sense of smell that total blindness brings, Isaac knew that Esau had brought him the stew. But it was Jacob's voice!

"I am Esau, your first-born," Jacob lied. "Please get up and eat the stew you wanted and give me your blessing."

"How quickly you found it, my son!"

"It was the Lord your God who helped me," Jacob answered, impatiently.

"Come here then, and let me touch you to know if you are Esau or not." Isaac was still suspicious. "It is Jacob's voice but his arms are hairy like Esau's," he murmured, touching Jacob.

"Are you really my son Esau?" he asked again. And Jacob lied once more: "Yes, I am."

Isaac allowed Jacob to serve him then. He took the stew and some wine. He was still a little suspicious, but he was put at ease by the good food and the warmth in his body from the wine.

"Come and kiss me, my son," he said when he had eaten.

Jacob kissed his father. The old man immediately knew the smell of Esau's clothing and he blessed Jacob with many blessings, finishing: "Be master over your brother." Jacob hastened away, but just as he was leaving Esau returned from hunting. He cooked a stew and brought it to Isaac.

"Father, eat your stew and bless me!"

"Who are you?" Isaac asked, dismayed.

"I am Esau, your first-born son."

Isaac trembled and shook. "I have eaten meat and blessed another."

"Father, father, bless me too!" Esau said, bitterly.

"Jacob has cheated you out of your blessing," said Isaac. "I cannot take the blessing from him now."

"He stole my birthright and now he's taken my blessing! Have you no blessing for me, father?"

"My son, I have made him your master. I blessed him as I would you, giving him provision of grain and wine. There is no blessing left for you."

"Is that all you can say? Father, give me a blessing too!"

Isaac remained silent. Esau wept, and from then on he hated Jacob.

"When father is dead I will kill him, though he's my brother," he vowed.

When Rebekah heard his plan, she arranged for Jacob to go to her brother Laban.

"These Canaanite women Esau married are wearing me out!" she told Isaac. "Let Jacob choose a wife from Haran, as you chose me," she added, persuasively.

"Go, then," Isaac said to Jacob.

So Jacob set out for Haran to find a bride and to escape his brother.

Genesis 25–27

A ladder in the desert

As the sun set, the wilderness grew cold. Somewhere in the distance a wolf howled. Nearby a screech owl hooted and a small wild thing screamed in fear. The light was going fast and Jacob lay where he was, taking a stone for his pillow.

That night he dreamed. A ladder stretched from earth to heaven and God was there, standing over him. He heard God's voice.

"I am the God of Abraham and Isaac. Your descendants shall be as many as the specks of dust on the ground. They shall spread all over Canaan. Be sure that I am with you. I shall bless you and keep you safe wherever you go and bring you back to your homeland."

Jacob awoke, awed and afraid.

"I've been lying in the place where God lives!" he thought. He took oil from his bags and poured some over the stone that had been his pillow.

"This is Bethel, the house of God," he declared, making his vow: "If God goes with me and gives me enough to eat and clothes to wear and brings me home safely, then the Lord my father worships will be my God too."

On his journey he met some of Laban's shepherds. Amongst them was a lovely little shepherdess. Her name was Rachel. She was Laban's younger daughter. Jacob fell in love at once and agreed with Laban to stay with him and work for him as a shepherd for seven years to win Rachel.

He worked hard and the years were long, but because he loved Rachel so much they seemed to pass very quickly. He watched her grow up, and she became more and more beautiful.

At the end of seven years he went to Laban. "Give me my wife. I have won her at last."

Laban gave a great party. He had two daughters but the elder, called Leah, a dull, unlovely girl with none of the grace or the sparkle in her eyes that Rachel had, was nowhere to be seen during the celebrations. The bride herself was heavily veiled. She was very quiet and solemn, sitting silently all

through the feasting, and although Jacob kept looking at her and even whispered to her once or twice, she bent her veiled face and made no response. He was surprised, but it was the custom in those days for the bride to be shy and even sad.

When night came, Jacob and his bride were led, amidst laughter, a shower of good wishes, and many words of good advice, to a couch specially curtained off in a private corner.

In the morning, Jacob pulled the curtains back and the glimmer of light from the lamp fell across the face of the girl who slept beside him. It was Leah.

Jacob didn't like being cheated. He got up and found Laban at once.

"Why have you tricked me? I worked honestly for seven years for Rachel, and you've married me to Leah."

Laban looked sly. Both men knew the reason for Laban's trick: an unattractive girl like Leah would have great difficulty finding a husband.

"Do you still want Rachel?" he asked.

Jacob nodded. Of course he did! The wily old father knew that his nephew from Canaan had fallen in love with the graceful young shepherdess.

"Well then," Laban said, soothingly. "Just wait for this week of marriage feasting to be over, and you can take Rachel as your second wife. Of course," he added, laying his hand affectionately across his son-in-law's shoulders, "you'll have to work for me another seven years. I'm sorry, my boy," he continued, "But I simply couldn't have Rachel married before her elder sister. It's just not done. Surely by now you know the customs of our country: the elder daughter always marries first."

It was on the tip of Jacob's tongue to protest: "Why didn't you tell me so when I asked you for Rachel seven years ago?" But he kept silence. He had come without a dowry and without possessions, a man with a stolen birthright and a blessing he'd acquired by fraud. He was completely in Laban's hands. So he took Rachel as soon as the week was over and he worked for Laban for another seven years.

He hardly cast a look in Leah's direction now that Rachel was his. Leah sat neglected in the tent and, in the evening, listened to Rachel and Jacob laughing and murmuring together. But Rachel remained childless and Leah had four boys all in a row: Reuben, Simeon, Levi and Judah.

"Oh, Jacob," Rachel complained. "Why don't I have a baby yet, and my sister has four sons! Look, I'll lend you my slave girl and we'll see if she'll have a baby."

Soon Leah's little boys had two half-brothers: Dan and Naphtali, the children of Rachel's slave girl.

Rachel was almost as pleased as if they were her own. "I'm winning now!" she said as she chose the name of the second son.

Leah immediately lent her slave girl to Jacob too. Another little boy was born.

"What good fortune!" said Leah, naming him Gad. Then her slave girl had another boy and they called him Asher.

Then Leah had three more children: two boys called Issachar and Zebulun and a girl called Dinah.

Even though she still had no children of her own, Jacob still loved Rachel. Imagine how happy they both were when at last she had a baby, a little boy. They named him Joseph.

"Now that we have our baby, we'll go home to Canaan," said Jacob.

"But all the flocks belong to father. We have no possessions," Rachel objected.

"You leave it to me," Jacob said. And once he had Laban's permission to leave for home with his wives and children, Jacob cheated his father-in-law into giving away the best and strongest sheep and goats from the flocks. They set off without any farewells, but Laban went after them.

"You're stealing away my daughters as though they were captives after a battle!" he complained. "We should have had a proper farewell, with songs and the music of tambourines and lyres."

"I was afraid that you would find some way of snatching my wives from me," Jacob said, and angry words passed between them.

"I have toiled for you for twenty years and God has seen my labour," said Jacob.

"Everything you have belongs to me," fumed Laban. "But come now, let us make an agreement. We will make peace together. Treat the girls well, Jacob, and don't take any more wives."

They built a rough mound of stones from the boulders that lay around, and ate a meal together there. Then Jacob offered a sacrifice to God and they spent the whole night together.

"This mound is a boundary mark between us," said Laban. "I will never cross it to attack you; nor must you attack me."

Early next morning Laban kissed his daughters and grandchildren and set off home. Jacob sent messengers ahead to Esau.

"Tell Esau: your servant Jacob is coming with oxen, sheep and goats, and with slaves. Your servant wishes to win the approval of his lord."

The messengers returned with news that made Jacob afraid. "Esau is coming to meet you with four hundred men."

Jacob remembered God's promise in the lonely wilderness he had named Bethel.

"Oh God," he prayed, "I am not worthy of your blessing, but you have shown great kindness to me and you have promised that I will go home safely and have many descendants. Now save me and the mothers with their children from my brother."

Jacob chose a present for Esau: 220 goats; 220 sheep; 30 camels with their calves; 40 cows and 10 bulls; 20 asses and 10 donkeys. He made them line up, and told his servants to lead them to Esau.

"Maybe he'll be so pleased with such a fine gift that he won't be angry with me," Jacob thought. He spent the night in the camp.

While it was still dark, he sent his wives and slave-girls and his eleven sons and only daughter across the ford with all his possessions. So Jacob was left alone.

Before daybreak there came a man who wrestled with Jacob until the dawn. The stranger could not overpower him, but he struck Jacob in the

socket of his hip and lamed him, dislocating his hip. Still Jacob wrestled on, although he was in great pain.

"Let me go," gasped the stranger. "For the day is breaking."

Between his teeth Jacob panted: "I will not let you go unless you bless me."

So they drew apart and the stranger asked: "What is your name?"

"Jacob," he replied, but did not return the question to the one who had lamed him.

"It is Jacob no longer, but Israel. You have wrestled with God; you will not be defeated by man."

"Please tell me your name," begged Jacob, knowing it already.

"Why do you ask my name?" asked the stranger, and he blessed Jacob.

As the sun rose Jacob was alone.

"I have seen God face to face," he said, and went limping away to find his family and meet his brother.

Esau came on with four hundred men. Jacob went to greet him. Behind him walked the slave-girls and their children; next came Leah and her children; last of all came Rachel and Joseph.

Jacob bowed himself to the ground seven times before his brother, but Esau, in tears, embraced him.

"I do not need all the things you've sent me," Esau said.

"Brother," Jacob urged him, "take them because you have been so generous to me."

They parted in peace, and Jacob travelled on through Canaan. Before he reached Hebron, to settle where his grandfather and father had lived, a great sorrow occurred. Rachel died, giving birth to her second son.

"I shall call him Ben-oni, the son of my sorrow," she gasped, closing her eyes. Jacob couldn't bear it that Rachel's baby should grow up with such a sad name. He changed it to Benjamin, which meant "the son of my right hand". They buried Rachel at the town called Bethlehem. Sadly Jacob travelled on, a man with many sons but without his lovely bride. He loved Joseph more than ever now that the little boy's mother had died. Whenever he looked at her son, he remembered Rachel and the happy times they had shared.

"You and the baby are all I have left of your mother," Jacob sighed.

Genesis 28–35

32

Dreams come true

Joseph

Old Jacob sat under a shady tree. He peered up when a shadow fell across his feet. He was nearly blind.

"Is it you, Joseph?" His quavery voice was glad. "You always manage to take time to talk with me." He smiled at young Joseph, Rachel's son. The old man's eyes dimmed as he thought of the girl who had been his lovely bride. How hard he'd worked to win her . . . .

Joseph put down his shepherd's crook and squatted beside his father.

"What would I do without you, Joseph? If ever anything happens to you. . . ." Jacob's eyes misted over. "Listen, son. I've got a special present for you. I'll give it to you tonight."

That night the twelve sons gathered in Jacob's tent. They were grown men, except for Joseph and his brother Benjamin, Rachel's other son.

"Look, here's my present, Joseph."

"Present!" they grumbled. "*We* never have anything. The old man's always been fondest of Joseph. He's a spoilt, stuck up brat."

They were even more furious when they saw what the present was. It was a coat, a kind of tunic with long white sleeves.

"Little lord!" they snarled. Only the master or overseer ever wore such a garment.

"And we, who toil for our father, risking our lives for his sheep, we wear skins and rough clothing," Judah grumbled.

After that they couldn't say a kind word to Joseph. Jacob's gift made it seem as if he had made Joseph their master.

Joseph only made things worse. "Listen, everyone," he said, "I had such a strange dream last night."

They turned their backs on him, but Joseph was used to this.

"I saw it all so clearly. It was harvest time, and we were binding our sheaves. Do you know, all your sheaves bowed down to my sheaf."

"So that's what you saw in your dream, is it?" There was a nasty edge to their voices, but Joseph didn't seem to realise because the next time he had a dream, he told them all about it.

"We don't want to know," they groaned.

"Tell us your dream," said Jacob over-hearing and, even though the brothers were grown men, they had to give in to their father.

"I dreamt that the sun, the moon and the eleven stars came and bowed down to me."

Jacob was furious. He understood the meaning straight away, and he scolded Joseph.

"Do you really mean that all of us – your brothers, your stepmother Leah, and myself – are to come and bow down to you?"

"Well, that's what my dream was. I can't help it, father, I'm only telling you what I saw," Joseph said.

His brothers seethed, but Jacob kept Joseph's words in his mind.

Later Joseph's brothers went off to graze Jacob's flocks in the rich pastureland around Shechem, about sixty miles away in the north. Joseph was sent after them to find out how they were.

When Joseph reached Shechem, there was no sign of his brothers. He wandered over the lonely hills where wild animals roamed. He was glad to meet a man who told him that the brothers had moved off to Dothan, about twenty miles away.

The brothers saw Joseph in the distance.

"Hey, here comes the dreamer!"

They looked at one another.

"What are we waiting for? This is our chance! We could throw his body into one of those empty wells we've seen around. No one would find it. And we could tell father a wild beast has torn him in pieces."

"No," said Reuben, the eldest brother. "We mustn't kill him. Teach him a lesson if you like, and put him down a well for a while, but don't be rough with him."

They had to listen to Reuben because he was the eldest.

"There you are at last!" Joseph called to them.

They crowded silently around.

"Brothers," he begged, "Father sent me. . . ."

"Father's a long way off now. . . ." they jeered. They caught hold of him and ripped off his coat, before they pushed him down the empty well.

Then they sat down to eat. Down below them, hurt, hungry and terrified, Joseph pleaded for help. Later he heard the swish of a rope. Hardly daring to hope, he caught hold of it and they pulled him out of the clay lined well.

Joseph realised what they were planning to do with him when he saw the traders and their camels. Twenty silver coins changed hands. The camel train swayed off again, taking Joseph to be sold in the slave markets of Egypt.

Then the brothers slaughtered one of the goats and dipped Joseph's torn coat in the blood. One of their servants took it back to Jacob with this message: "Father, we think this is Joseph's coat that we've found."

Jacob heard footsteps outside his tent. He peered at the servant and silently took the coat, listening in horror to the message. Stiffly he got up and shuffled outside, holding the ragged, costly coat to the fading light.

"It *is* Joseph's coat! Joseph has been torn to pieces by some wild animal." And he wept and refused to be comforted.

. . . .　　. . . .　　. . . .　　. . . .　　. . . .

Potiphar the Egyptian, the commander of Pharaoh's guard, was strolling homeward. His steward, who looked after his business affairs, walked just a pace or two behind him. The only other people in sight were a group of desert traders with their camels and a weary, dirty, despondent young captive.

Potiphar prided himself on being a good judge of character. "That's a fine looking boy," he said. "What's your name?"

"Joseph, sir." Joseph met Potiphar's gaze without flinching.

"What race do you belong to?"

"I'm a Hebrew, sir," he said in the broken Egyptian he'd picked up from the traders.

Now Potiphar was an Egyptian, born and bred. But Egypt in those days was ruled by another nation called the Hyksos. Potiphar knew that Pharaoh liked the Hebrews, a race similar to his. He turned the matter over in his mind and decided to buy Joseph to impress Pharaoh. Besides, there was something about the boy. . . .

So Joseph became Potiphar's slave. Quickly he mastered the language of Egypt and all the strange customs of his new household, especially the Egyptian skills of counting and writing. Potiphar found he could trust Joseph completely and soon put him in charge of all his affairs.

"Why is it everything you touch goes so well?" Potiphar wondered, but he looked bewildered as Joseph replied, "The God I honour is with me and has blessed your affairs because of me."

"Well, well," said Potiphar, at a loss for words, "I suppose it's comforting that we've got the Hebrew God on our side."

Some time later though, things went very wrong for Joseph.

Potiphar came home to find everyone shouting at once.

"It's that Hebrew slave!"

"These foreigners!"

"What is this all about?" Potiphar shouted above the noise.

His wife sobbed out her woes.

"It's that foreign slave. He came into my room and insulted me. Look there's his garment. He left it on the floor and rushed off as I started calling for help."

Furious, Potiphar threw Joseph into prison.

Joseph was innocent. It was all a trick, but he had no one to come to his defence, so he had to stay in prison.

The chief jailer, however, found Joseph so reliable and efficient that he soon put him in charge of all the prisoners.

"God is still with me," Joseph thought.

One day two of the prisoners looked sad as Joseph brought them in their breakfast.

One was Pharaoh's baker, the other was his cup-bearer. They were important people in Pharaoh's court, especially the cup-bearer. He had to taste Pharaoh's wine before he poured it out for the king. If anyone had slipped poison into the wine the cup-bearer would die instead of the king.

"What's the matter?" Joseph asked.

"We both had a dream last night," said the cup-bearer.

"We know the gods speak to men in dreams," said the baker.

"But what good does it do when we can't under-stand what our dreams mean," they both finished in unison.

"Tell me your dreams," Joseph invited them.

The cup-bearer decided to trust Joseph.

"I saw a vine with three branches. Grapes grew on the branches. I squeezed their juice into Pharaoh's cup and gave the cup to Pharaoh. Now tell me what the dream means."

"The three branches stand for three days," Joseph explained. "In three days you'll be set free and get your job back. But please, do remember me and tell Pharaoh about me."

"I'll remember," the cup-bearer promised. He was beginning to feel pleased that things were turning out well.

The baker was pleased too. "Now let me tell you my dream. I carried three trays on my head with all Pharaoh's favourite cakes on the top tray. But the birds flew down and ate them all up."

"You too will be released in three days. But you'll be sent to the gallows and the birds will peck the flesh from your bones."

The baker shuddered.

Three days later it was Pharaoh's birthday. He gave a big party and restored the cup-bearer to his place, but just as Joseph had foretold, the baker was led off to be hanged.

The cup-bearer was so excited about getting his job back that he forgot to tell Pharaoh about Joseph. Two years passed. Then Pharaoh himself had two dreams which none of his wise men and magicians could explain to him. Then the cup-bearer remembered Joseph.

"Send for him right away," ordered Pharaoh and they brought Joseph out of prison.

"They tell me you understand the secrets the gods whisper to us when we sleep." Pharaoh looked curiously at the Hebrew slave in front of him.

"I don't count, Pharaoh," Joseph said. "It's God himself who will give Pharaoh his answer."

So Pharaoh told Joseph his dream.

"I was standing on the banks of the river Nile," he said. "Seven fine fat sleek cows came out of the water and began to graze on the bank. Seven more cows followed, ugly, skinny and lean. Before my eyes, the scrawny cows gobbled up the fat ones.

"Then I woke up but, when I got back to sleep, I had another dream. This time I saw a single stalk of corn. Out of it grew seven ears of corn, big, full and ripe. But then seven poor shrivelled ears of corn grew and swallowed up the good ears."

"God is showing his future plans to you, Pharaoh," said Joseph. "First there will be seven years of abundant harvests bringing wealth to the whole of Egypt. But then famine will come. The harvest will fail for seven years. God gave you the same dream twice to show you how urgent it is. Make plans and you will save many lives."

"Yes, yes, of course," said Pharaoh, thoughtfully, "but what measures should I take?"

"Choose a wise man to be governor. During the good years he will see that surplus grain is stored so that no one will starve in the hungry years."

"Well done, Joseph!" called out Pharaoh and all his ministers. "That's a good plan."

"And you're the very one for the job," Pharaoh said, going over to Joseph. He put his own ring on Joseph's finger, called for fine linen clothes for him and put a gold chain around his neck. "You are the most important man in Egypt under me."

Joseph worked hard and stored all the crops carefully during the seven good years. Huge barns were filled brimful with grain, spilling over like the sand on the seashore.

When famine came, Joseph opened up his storehouses of grain. People came from all over Egypt and the surrounding countries to buy grain

from him. The famine spread to faraway Hebron where old Jacob was eating his heart out for his long lost son, Joseph.

"They say there's grain for sale in Egypt," Jacob told his eleven sons. "Go to Egypt and buy grain for us all."

"Oh, good!" Benjamin exclaimed. "I've always wanted to go to Egypt and see the huge buildings and . . ."

"No," Jacob cut him short. "You are all I have left now that Joseph's dead. Nothing must happen to you."

So Joseph's ten stepbrothers went off to Egypt and were directed to Pharaoh's governor. They knelt before him on their hands and knees, their foreheads touching the dusty ground. Joseph recognised his brothers and remembered his dreams so long ago. But he did not tell them, and instead he accused them:

"You're spies!"

"No, no!" they began. "We are ten of twelve brothers, sons of Jacob," but he had them arrested. Two days later, he examined them more closely. Then he gave them a test. "One of you must stay here as a prisoner," he said, "while the others go home and bring this youngest brother you have spoken about to me."

"It's all our fault," they said to one another. "We're being punished now for that dreadful thing we did to Joseph."

Joseph overheard. He went away in tears, but

"I'll be home at noon and we'll all eat together," he said.

The brothers were scared when they saw that they were being taken to Joseph's house.

"Excuse us," they said to the chamberlain. "When we got home after our last trip here, we found the money we'd paid for the grain. It's all a big mistake and we've brought it back to you."

The chamberlain had to puzzle out the foreigner's speech. They were rough men, who smelt of the sheepfold, but he smiled at them, for his job was to please his master.

"Don't be afraid," he said. "I was paid the full amount for the corn you bought. And look, here is your brother Simeon."

When Joseph came home, he spoke kindly to them. They bowed before him and offered him their gifts. Then Joseph caught sight of Benjamin and he hurried out with tears streaming down his cheeks. He washed his face and then they had their meal.

The brothers all sat at one table and Joseph had food from his own dishes carried to them, with an extra special helping for Benjamin. They were all very happy.

But Joseph remembered his second dream. His father, too, must be brought to Egypt. So he told his chamberlain to hide his silver cup in Benjamin's sack.

Just after the brothers set out for home, the chamberlain rushed up to them.

"Stop!" he shouted breathlessly.

They looked at one another. Things had gone so well! Now it looked as if they were in trouble again.

They were!

"How could you do such a dishonest thing to someone who's treated you so kindly? One of you has stolen his cup," he said.

"Look, we took back the money we found in our sacks. That's a sign we're honest men," they protested. "And we brought your master fine presents, didn't we?"

But when the chamberlain searched their belongings, he found the cup in Benjamin's sack.

They tore their clothes in despair and trailed back to the governor.

"What have you done?" Joseph said sternly.

"What can we say?" Judah spoke up. "We're in your hands."

"You can go free, but the thief must stay here with me."

when he came back, he chose Simeon to stay behind as a hostage.

The nine brothers set off for home. That night one of them discovered that the money he had paid the governor for his corn was still in his sack. They were terrified.

"What's God doing to us now?" they said.

When they reached home, they told Jacob the whole story and emptied their sacks of grain. Each had money inside it.

They were panic stricken. "What are you doing to me," Jacob moaned. "One by one you are robbing me of my children."

After a time they used up their grain. Jacob didn't want to allow Benjamin to go with them to Egypt, but in the end he gave in.

"Look, you must take the governor presents, the finest spices and sweets our land can offer. And return his money to him. May God move him to be kind to you and let you bring back Simeon and Benjamin."

Once again the brothers joined the long line of hungry people. Joseph told his chamberlain to take them to his house.

"Please, my lord," Judah begged. "It will kill our father if we come home without Benjamin. Please make me your slave instead of him."

Joseph could bear it no longer. He sent his servants away.

"I am Joseph," he told his brothers, sobbing as he spoke. "Is my father really alive after all these years?"

But they were too terrified to answer.

"Come closer to me," Joseph begged. "Don't blame yourselves for what you did to me. See how God has been behind it all and turned it all to good. He sent me here to save the lives of many people."

Then he hugged and kissed them all, laughing and crying for joy. And the news of it spread like wildfire all over the palace.

"Tell your father to come at once," Pharaoh told Joseph. "How we'll honour him! He shall feed on the fat of the land!"

So Jacob set out on his last journey, riding in wagons that Pharaoh had sent. His happiness was complete when he saw Joseph again, and met his family, blessing Joseph's two sons Manasseh and Ephraim.

Not long after, Jacob died and Joseph took his body and buried it faraway in Canaan. Then he returned to Egypt, where he lived for the rest of his life.

Just before he died he told his family: "One day God will lead our descendants home to Canaan. Take whatever remains of my body there and bury me in the soil of my homeland."

But it was four hundred and thirty years before the Hebrews went home.

Genesis 37–50

The prince who ran away

From his great palace, Pharaoh Rameses II watched the work go on. Slowly from the desert sands huge buildings were rising.

"It's *my* work!" he thought, proudly. "How great I am! I've got so many slaves, too. The ground down there is black with them! They're like an army of ants – *my* ants, working because I've planned it all."

But he still had one worry.

"These Hebrews now . . . They came over to Egypt four hundred years ago. That's a long time. There were so few of them when they came, and there are far too many of them now! Of course, they're all my slaves and they work hard in the brickfields and on the building sites but, I can't trust them. Supposing they tried to push *me* from my throne. They could do it by sheer force of numbers."

So he sent out an order:

"Let the Hebrews be crushed by really hard labour!" Worse than that, the cruel, ambitious, self centred ruler ordered that all their baby boys should be thrown into the river.

In their little huts and homes beside the river Nile, in a part of Egypt called Goshen, the Hebrew mothers tried to hide their babies. In one home a brother and a sister, called Aaron and Miriam, helped their mother to hide their baby brother. They gathered papyrus reeds from the edge of the

Nile. Their mother wove a basket. They coated it all over with pitch to make it waterproof, and then they put their baby inside the basket and hid him among the bulrushes in the river.

Miriam stayed by the river watching to see what would happen.

The basket was well hidden. Boats sailed by in the middle of the Nile. People washed their clothes at the water's edge. No one noticed the basket until an Egyptian lady came along.

She was a very fine lady, a princess, one of the daughters of Pharaoh, who had seventy-nine sons and fifty-nine daughters. She was coming to have a bath in the river, as even grand ladies did then. She noticed the basket and one of her maids lifted it out of the water.

Miriam crept closer.

The princess opened the lid, and there was the baby yelling inside.

"A baby!" The princess picked him up. "Oh, how sweet he is. Ssh! Ssh!" she soothed him. "Why I do believe he's a Hebrew baby. Oh, but we can't possibly kill him. I'll take him back to the palace with me. He'll be my very own. I'll call him Moses, my little boy, my son. Ssh. Ssh." She rocked the baby gently but he would not be comforted.

"I'll get a nurse for you from among the Hebrew women," Miriam offered, bowing low to the princess who was so anxious to stop the baby crying that she didn't ask the little girl any questions.

Miriam brought her mother to the princess.

"Can you look after the baby for me?" the princess asked. "I'll pay you well and then when he's old enough, you must bring him to the palace to me."

The mother was overjoyed. Now her baby was safe! She carried Moses home with her and he grew up in the little mud hut beside the brickfields. When he was older he played there, and heard the crack of the Egyptian overseers' whips. He learned all the old stories of his people, stories of Isaac and Jacob in Canaan; of Joseph and how he had come to Egypt.

"God brought him here. At first he was a slave, as we are today, but he became the greatest man in Egypt under Pharaoh. God hasn't forgotten us," his father would tell him. "One day he'll lead us all home to Canaan, our promised land."

"And do you know there was once a baby who was hidden in a basket and found by a princess," his mother would say, so that from his earliest days Moses knew that before long he would leave his mother and father and go to live in the palace.

His life as a prince was very different. He learned to write, he learned the ancient art of magic from the priests and the stories of the gods of Egypt. But he never forgot that he was a Hebrew, born in a mud

knocked him to the ground and killed him. There was no one else in sight. He hid the body in the sand and went home.

But he was unhappy, thinking about his people. The next day he went back to the brickfields. Once again he stood and watched. He saw two Hebrew slaves fighting.

"Why are you hitting our fellow countryman, your brother?" Moses cried out in dismay.

Panting, the slave he spoke to looked around.

"Little Egyptian prince!" he sneered. "Who made you my judge? Go on then, kill me like you killed the Egyptian yesterday!"

Moses turned away, thinking hard.

"It's obvious everyone knows about that," he thought. "It won't be long before Rameses gets to know, and then he'll have me put to death. I must get away!"

So Moses left the royal palace and the brickfields of Egypt. There was only one safe route he could take. He joined a group of traders and travelled with them eastwards, past the copper mines of Mount Sinai, where more slaves sweated deep underground to bring Rameses wealth.

He reached the country of the wandering tribes of a people called the Midianites and he sat down by a well.

Perhaps he was trying to work out what his next move should be.

Then he heard giggling and chatter. Seven sisters came along to the well. They filled the water troughs beside the well and the sheep crowded round, bleating and butting each other. Then some shepherds came along. They hit out at the girls and pushed them away so that their own sheep could drink the water the girls had drawn.

To everyone's surprise the weary traveller, an Egyptian by his dress, fought the shepherds, who gave way and made off. Moses filled the water troughs again for the girls' sheep to drink. They went home with their sheep.

"You're back early, girls," said their father Jethro. He belonged to the tribe called the Kenites. They were coppersmiths, but he was also their priest.

"An Egyptian at the well protected us from the shepherds." They put down their heavy water jars.

"He even drew water for us!"

"Do you mean you've come back home without asking him to come and stay with us?" Jethro was astounded. "Go back at once and ask him to come and eat with us."

hut, the child of slaves.

One day when he was grown up, Moses went out alone to see the Hebrew slaves at work. He saw them work waist deep in water: he watched them stagger under heavy loads of bricks and his anger rose inside him. In a corner of the brickfields he watched an Egyptian overseer beating a Hebrew slave.

Moses was horrified. He couldn't stand there and do nothing. Furiously he attacked the Egyptian,

So Moses went with the girls to Jethro's tent. He and Jethro liked each other at once and Jethro was even more pleased when Moses explained that he was a Hebrew. His ancestors had been shepherds in Canaan.

"We didn't live in cities like the Egyptians, but wandered around with our flocks, living in tents as you do," Moses said and Jethro was so pleased that he invited Moses to stay with them and even gave him his daughter Zipporah to be his wife.

So Moses the prince lived in a tent and looked after his father-in-law's sheep, wandering through the desert as his forefathers had done.

Then there came a day when Rameses died and his son Merenptah became king in his place. Now it would be safe for Moses to return to Egypt where the Hebrew slaves groaned out all their wretchedness to God.

God heard the cry of despair that broke from the lips of slaves who lay in the mud wounded and dying under their masters' cruel whips.

He gave Moses a sign.

Moses was out with his sheep close to Mount Sinai where Jethro told him that God lived. He was

thinking of his people. They needed a leader who would stand up to Pharaoh and force him to let them go free.

But where would such a leader be found among a people crushed by slavery?

He looked up and saw something that seemed to be a flame of fire. It came from the heart of a bush. The bush seemed ablaze and yet was not burned up.

"I must look more closely at this! I wonder why the bush isn't being consumed?"

As he went forward he heard God speak to him: "Moses, Moses!"

"Here I am," said Moses.

"Come no nearer," God told him. "Take off your sandals for the ground on which you stand is holy. I am the God of your people."

When Moses heard this, he covered his face for he was afraid.

"Go to Pharaoh, Moses, and tell him to let the people go."

Moses was terrified. "Who am I to go to Pharaoh and tell him such a thing!"

"I shall be with you," God replied.

"But – but what is your name? The Egyptians have many gods. They call on their name and receive their power. I must know your name, else how will the people believe that you have spoken to me?"

"I am who I am," God answered. "I am God, Yahweh, the God of your people. They shall call me 'Yahweh' which means 'He is', whenever they call me by name. So go and tell your people Yahweh is going to lead you home to Canaan."

"Suppose they don't believe me? Suppose they say 'Yahweh hasn't spoken to you at all'?" Moses objected.

"What's in your hand?"

"My shepherd's staff."

"Throw it on the ground."

So Moses threw it on the ground and it wriggled away. It had become a serpent and Moses drew back, but God said:

"Catch hold of it by its tail." So Moses obeyed and the serpent turned back into his staff as soon as he took hold of it.

"This sign will convince the people of your power," God said. "Look, I will show you two more signs."

He taught Moses two more signs of power, but Moses still raised objections. He could think of so many reasons why he *shouldn't* go to Pharaoh!

"Oh, my Lord," he pleaded. "I've never in my

life been a great speaker. I'm not eloquent like the people in Pharaoh's palace, always making fine long speeches. I can't do that. I can't make speeches at all."

"Who gave you your mouth?" God asked. "It was me, wasn't it? Now go, and I shall help you to speak and tell you what to say."

"Oh, please, please," begged Moses, "send anyone you like, anyone at all, but don't send me."

"Well then," God said, "there is your brother Aaron. I know he is a good speaker. Even now he's left Egypt to meet you, because Pharaoh is dead and it's safe for you to return. Aaron is coming to find you. He'll be so happy to hear your news and he'll speak to the people for you. You can tell him what to say. Go, then, and remember to take your staff and do the signs I showed you."

So Moses went back to Jethro and asked his permission to go back to Egypt.

"Go in peace," Jethro said.

Moses left with his wife Zipporah and their little boy. Just as God had told him Aaron had come to meet him and they returned together. They gathered all the Hebrews together and Aaron told the people everything that God had told Moses. The people bowed down to the ground in worship. God was going to put an end to their misery and lead them all to Canaan, the land he had promised their forebears hundreds of years ago.

But Pharoah wouldn't let the people go.

"Who is your God, Yahweh? I don't know anything about him," Pharaoh told Moses and Aaron. "You don't expect me to let all my slaves go just like that?"

He sent Moses and Aaron away and summoned the slave drivers and the overseers.

"This nonsense must stop," he said. "The people are idle. You can't be working them hard enough, if they've got time to dream up a God of their own. What's the matter with the gods of Egypt? Now listen, from now on they'll have to go out to the stubble fields and gather the straw you've always provided them with for their bricks, to bind the clay together. But they must make the same number of bricks as before."

So the slaves had to scatter all over the countryside and gather corn from the prickly stubble fields and chop it up for their bricks. The slave drivers beat them with cruel blows.

The Hebrew foremen went to Pharaoh himself.

"Why do you treat your slaves like this? We can't do it, we can't make the same number of bricks when we have to gather and cut the straw too . . ."

"You're lazy, lazy!" Pharaoh screamed at them. "That's why you've got time to listen to all this nonsense about a God. Get back to work at once!"

As the foremen left Pharaoh they met Moses and Aaron who had come to look for them.

"Oh, leave us alone!" The foremen pushed the two brothers aside. "May God punish you as you deserve. Look what they're doing to us now! And it's all because of you and your talk that God is going to set us free."

Moses made no reply. He lifted his head and prayed.

"Lord, just what are you doing? Why do you treat your people so cruelly? Why ever did you send me here? Ever since I've spoken about you to Pharaoh he's been worse than ever, and you're not doing anything at all to stop it."

Then Moses' face lit up. He remembered God's promise and he heard God speak to him: "Pharaoh will be forced to let them go."

And Moses knew that it would be so.

Exodus 1–6

44

"Let my people go"

en terrible things happened one after the other.

"Your God is sending us all these troubles," Pharaoh told Moses after each disaster. "All right, then, you can go!"

But he always changed his mind. He couldn't bear to see a major part of his labour force disappear into the desert somewhere.

First, their water turned blood red and became polluted so that no one could drink it. Then the whole of Egypt, apart from the land of Goshen where the Hebrew slaves lived, was plagued with swarms of tiny stinging mosquitoes and disease-bringing flies. Hail, unusual for that time of year, pelted down and flattened the crops, especially the flax that they used for linen, and the barley which was in the ear.

Even Pharaoh's servants and courtiers came and urged him: "Do let those slaves go to the land their God is giving them. We just can't bear these troubles any more."

But Pharaoh refused to give in. Then the east wind blew in a tremendous swarm of locusts. The ground was black with them. They ate every bud, every tender shoot. All the crops that had survived the hail – and every bit of greenery all over Egypt- was completely destroyed.

"I've done wrong!" Pharaoh cried out to Moses. "Ask your God to get rid of these locusts."

So Moses prayed and a west wind blew and carried away the locusts. But Pharaoh immediately changed his mind and a sand storm swirled in from the desert, blotting out the sun for three whole days.

Pharaoh gave in again. "You can go! But don't take your cows, sheep or goats with you. Ours have all been killed by the hail and the diseases that haven't touched you Hebrews in the land of Goshen."

"No," said Moses firmly. "God wants us to take our flocks with us. They're all the wealth we possess and we'll need them when we get to the land that God is giving us. Besides, we will offer animals to him as sacrifices and we don't know yet which ones we must choose."

"Get out!" Pharaoh stormed. "If I ever see

you again, I'll have you put to death!"

Moses turned and walked calmly away. "I'll never come near you again, Pharaoh."

So the tenth and most terrible disaster struck. Death spread through the crowded cities. All through Egypt in every home parents watched their oldest child die. In his fine palace, Pharaoh sat with his face dark with grief and rage. The women wept and lamented. Pharaoh's eldest son had not escaped.

In their mud huts by the Nile the Hebrews were safe. That night they gathered family by family, keeping a special feast. They kept it each spring but this year Moses gave them a new name for it and it had a new meaning.

"It is your Passover feast, and you must keep it each year for ever to remind you of how God set you free. For tonight the Angel of Death is walking through the whole of Egypt but God will pass you by. Kill your lamb this year, then, as an offering of thanks to God. Smear the lamb's blood over the door posts of your home. That sign will protect you. You must eat your bread flat, without leaven, as you always did at the old festival, but from now on you will remember the haste with which you must eat your meal."

They ate in great haste, for Pharaoh sent a message: "Go!"

So they ate their meal wearing their outdoor clothes, with their long staffs in their hands and then they followed Moses out, wrapped in their cloaks, taking with them their unrisen dough and their kneading bowls. They would cook and eat their bread as they travelled.

They left in great joy, heading for Canaan, their Promised Land.

Moses led the people along the same route he had taken when he ran away from Pharaoh, years before.

But before they had gone very far, Pharaoh changed his mind again. He ordered his swiftest chariots to be driven out after the slaves. The Egyptians caught up with the much slower-moving people near to the Sea of Reeds, the marshy land that lies to the north of the Red Sea.

The Hebrews huddled together in terror. They could hear the rumble of the pursuing chariots. In front of them was the water splashing among the reeds.

"Why did you bring us here, Moses? It is better to build storehouses for Pharaoh's treasures than to die here in the swamps!"

"Don't be afraid!" Moses reassured them. "God

will save you. He'll do all the fighting for you, and you'll never see the Egyptians again."

Darkness came and a strong east wind began to blow. All night it blew and the Hebrew sentries strained their ears to hear the sound of chariots above the wind. When morning came they saw that Moses had been right. God had looked after them. The east wind held back the water and the Hebrews walked carefully across to the other side.

They sang and they rejoiced, but as they looked behind them their laughter died on their lips. The Egyptians had caught up with them and were driving their chariots madly down to the opposite shore.

Calling and waving, the Egyptians swept on. But they did not know that last night the whole place had been under water. Their chariots stuck fast in the oozing mud. Confused, the soldiers jumped free and immediately sank deep into the mud. They tried to stuggle out and got deeper into it. They gave way to complete disorder. At God's command, Moses stretched out his hand over the sea, and the turning tide drowned the chariots, horses and horsemen.

Triumphant now, the Hebrews surged forward, shouting their praises.

Moses headed the procession, singing out his joy. "Of the Lord I sing . . ."

"He has covered himself with glory," Miriam took up the song, leading all the women in a dance.

So on they went into the wilderness, following Moses and the God who had set them free. They were heading for home, heading for Canaan, slaves no longer. They were becoming a people, a nation set apart by God, learning his ways, to whom he would give his Law.

But it was far from easy for them. They were used to hard labour, but they had always known when their next meal was coming. Soon they started to grumble again, as their stomachs grew emptier and there seemed no end to their journey.

"Why did you bring us out here to die?" they groused to Moses.

"We are parched with thirst," someone complained. "You're starving us to death."

As usual Moses listened patiently. He heard the voice of God. He told Aaron and Aaron told the people:

"Make no mistake, when you grumble it's not us you're complaining against – for who are we? We're nothing at all. No, you're complaining against God. Well, he's coming to your rescue. You'll eat meat and bread. Then you'll learn that God can look after you in the desert too."

That evening a flock of quails dropped exhausted by their camp. Each year these birds make an even longer journey than the hungry, foot-sore Hebrews. They fly from the hot climate of Africa each spring to the flat wheatfields of Eastern Europe, and rest on the flat land around the Sea of Reeds before flying on over the mountains. Marvelling, the Hebrews ran and picked up the birds. They cooked them and ate their fill, thanking God for this unexpected feast of rich and tasty meat.

Next morning they went outside their tents before sunrise. As the sun came up, the night dew dried from the ground and they saw that all around about the earth was covered with something white, like a sprinkling of frost.

"What is it?" they were asking. "Whatever can it be?"

"It is called Manna," Moses explained. "And it is the bread that God has sent you. Gather it quickly before the sun melts it or the ants eat it up."

It tasted sweet, like wafers made with honey, and it became their daily food for all the long journey.

On they journeyed. Now they were among the mountains. They were used to the flat countryside beside the Nile and they looked around them in wonder mixed with fear.

"Look!" they pointed out one vast peak.

"It towers right to the sky!"

"God certainly has come to dwell here," said another. "Look at the smoke pouring from its top!"

"No, it's the clouds that hang low over it. They hide God from our eyes," someone contradicted.

"No, it's smoke, a sign of his power. But look, look at his glory!" was the awed reply.

They watched the sunset streak the steep sides of Mount Sinai with pink and red and purple.

"God will speak to us here. Moses said so. We are his people. Other tribes have their own gods, but our God has chosen us. He will give us his Law."

Moses, their leader, climbed alone up the mountain. They watched him disappear, a small black shape becoming smaller and smaller among the huge, over-hanging boulders.

As Moses climbed he saw a mother eagle teaching her young to fly. He watched her bear them on her outstretched wings from the eyrie high in the rocks above him. She hovered close as they made their first leap into the air. One eaglet seemed about to drop like a stone to the ground. Immediately the mother swooped down and caught the frightened young bird on her wings.

"See," Moses heard the voice of God. "This is how I look after you, my people. I lead you and carry you safely on my wings like an eagle. Only you must obey me. I shall give you my Law."

Moses came back to the people and they promised to do everything God told them.

Then a storm broke over the head of Mount Sinai. Lightning streaked out of the overcast sky. Peals of thunder echoed and rumbled across the rocks. Moses led the people out of their camp.

"See, God has come to the top of the mountain," they cried in terror. "He's calling for Moses to come to him."

Smoke poured down the sides of the mountain.

"We can't bear it. We shall die," they cried.

"Don't be afraid. Remember, Our Lord God who is strong and clothed in splendour carries us as the mother eagle carried her young," Moses reminded them, as he climbed steadily up into the dark over-hanging cloud that obscured the top of the mountain from them.

Moses wrote down the laws God gave him. There were ten of them: the first four told the people how they should act toward God. They were not to worship any other god, or make an idol and pray to it. They must keep one day in seven holy for God and never swear by using God's name. Parents had to be respected and honoured.

The next five commandments told them how to treat each other with respect for one another, without violence, hatred, dishonesty or envy.

Moses read out these laws one by one to the people, and then they built an altar and sacrificed animals on it. This was a way of worshipping God, and asking his forgiveness when they did not keep his laws. God was teaching them that forgiveness was a costly matter.

"We will obey God's laws," they promised.

Perhaps in their hearts they were afraid. "Who could live such a perfect life?" they wondered. "Who could say he had never hurt someone else or envied the things that someone else had?"

"None of the pagan gods ask these things," they thought. "Our God is true. His Law is better than any of the laws of the other nations we know."

Then Moses and seventy elders with special tasks of leadership went toward the mountain and the people cried out as they saw the glory of the Lord like a flaming fire around the mountain top.

"Now stay here," Moses said to the elders. "God is telling me to go higher up the mountain. I'm taking Joshua as my assistant, for we will write down more laws from God and teach the people how they must lead their lives."

"This is the first time that the deeds of our people have been put into writing," said one of the elders, watching Moses show Joshua the way up the mountain.

"Yes, we know all about the stories of Jacob and Joseph because our fathers and grandfathers passed them on to us," someone added.

Moses and Joshua were in the mountain for a long time. When they returned, Moses held in his hands two tablets of stone on which God's commandments were engraved.

"Listen, what's that?" Joshua asked. "By the sound of it, our people are getting ready for war."

"No, that's not a battle cry. They're singing," Moses strained his ears to hear.

"Look, they're dancing!" Joshua exclaimed as they got closer.

"They've gone mad!" he added, hearing the noise from the camp.

"No," Moses voice was bitter. "They've forgotten the commandment God gave us about worship. Do you remember? He said we are not to make idols and worship them."

"Surely the people haven't made an idol!" Joshua exclaimed in dismay.

Then Moses felt anger rise inside him. The people, wearied by his long absence in the mountain, had made a golden calf and were dancing round it, praying to it, drinking wine and getting wilder as the wine went down.

Crash! The noise made the people stop and look round.

Furious, Moses had flung down the tablets of stone, shattering them at the foot of the mountain. Silently, the people made way as their leader, whom they had given up·as lost, swung towards them, snatched their golden idol and flung it into the fire they had made around it. Quarrelling and fighting broke out, and Moses turned to the Lord.

"Oh, Lord God," he pleaded, "these people have done a terrible thing, but please forgive them. Or if you can't forgive them because they have already broken your law, please kill me instead of them."

"They are my people; you are their leader," God told Moses. "Go, lead them to the Promised Land and I will help you."

So Moses went back to the people with two new tablets of stone. Instead of a golden calf, he told them how to make an Ark, a special sacred thing, like a big box. Inside the box were the new stone tablets with the ten commandments written on them. The box was made of acacia wood, light to work with and hard-wearing. It was covered with gold inside and out. There were four golden rings on it, through which long rods were inserted to carry the precious box. It was a symbol of God's presence with them, and they carried it wherever they went. Whenever they stopped, they also set up a special tent just outside the camp in a private place. It was called the Tabernacle and it was used for people to go and pray by themselves to God.

They had to take an indirect route to reach their Promised Land. First, they had to pass through five kingdoms belonging to five different tribes. They had to fight because the tribes, wandering people living in tents like themselves, refused to let them pass through their lands. Moses and Joshua were good leaders. The people succeeded in reaching right to the east shore of the River Jordan. The Promised Land lay before them on the other shore.

After years of slavery, years of wandering, the Hebrews were in sight of home. There were battles ahead, but at last they could feast their eyes on the homeland that would be theirs.

"But not mine," said Moses. "I am old now, and tired. My work is done. God has given you his laws. Keep them. The laws are not for just thinking about. You must do them! Make them your life and then you will have long, happy lives in the land across the Jordan."

So Moses died on the east side of the Jordan, and it was Joshua who led the people across the river home to Canaan.

Parts of Exodus 7–40

Tumbling walls

Joshua called out the news to all the people. "God has spoken to me. It is time to cross the Jordan into Canaan, our Promised Land."

While the people were bustling and scurrying around, busy with their packing and preparations, Joshua secretly sent out two spies to the ancient town of Jericho.

The two spies had to get to the Jordan, wide and overflowing its banks in those days of spring and melting snows. Ahead of them towered the huge walls of Jericho.

The walls rose to a height of thirty feet. They encircled the entire town. The two spies soon realised, as they went through the only gateway, that there was another wall inside the first wall.

"They're about twelve feet apart," they agreed, making quick measurements.

A woman called Rahab spotted the two foreigners.

"Come along and stay with me," she called down from the doorway of her house. It was one of the stone houses built between the walls. One of its windows looked onto the city; the other was like an opening in the outer wall, with a view across the surrounding countryside.

The men gladly accepted Rahab's invitation and climbed up into the house.

Meanwhile the king of Jericho had received word of the two spies.

"Call the chief of police," shouted the king.

Soon the chief of police and his men were pounding on Rahab's door.

"Go and hide," she whispered to the spies.

"Look, up there on the roof. There's a pile of flax there, ready for beating out and making into cloth. Look," she pushed them out on to the roof while the policemen banged on the door below.

"The king has sent me to tell you to hand over the two men who are lodging with you. They're spies from the Hebrew army, come to reconnoitre the whole city," the spokesman said firmly.

"The king!" Rahab looked impressed. "I wish I could help. I really do, but unfortunately the men left me, and I just can't tell you where they went. If it's any help to you, I can tell you when they left. It wasn't long ago. They wanted to be through the gates before nightfall, you see. You've still time to go after them, if you hurry."

She chuckled to herself as she watched the gates clang shut on the pursuers. Then she went up

to the spies who were hiding on the roof.

"Why have you done this for us?" they tried to thank her.

Rahab replied, "We've heard how God dried up the sea for you, and how he's helped you in your battles, I know your God is the real God. Now, please, swear to me by the Lord God, since I've done you a favour, that you will look after me and all my relatives when God gives Jericho to your army."

She fetched a rope and secured it firmly, then let it down through the open window.

"On the day you take Jericho I'll mark my house with a scarlet rope hanging from this window. Remember your promise and save our lives."

"Yes, we will," they assured her, climbing down the rope.

Joshua was pleased when he heard the spies' report and was delighted to know they had one friend inside the city.

Early in the morning they struck camp, rolling up their black tents, digging out the wooden poles, piling their baggage upon their sturdy asses. They travelled about seven miles to the banks of the Jordan.

"We'll camp here for four days," Joshua ordered.

So beside the river Jordan, which was in full flood

and overflowing its banks, they pitched their tents.

The town of Jericho faced them on the other side of the river, no more than four miles away.

"How will we ever get across?" they whispered to one another.

"Maybe God will dry up the water as you've told us he did long ago in Egypt," a little boy said.

"Maybe," the grown-ups shook their heads doubtfully, staring until they were dizzy at the swirling water.

Three days later the order came: "When you see the priests carry the Ark of the Lord out of the camp, you must pack up and follow it. You have never gone this way before, so follow it closely and God will guide you."

Joshua called them all to him. "Prepare today for the great thing that God is going to do for us tomorrow. Pray, and set yourselves apart for the Lord, because tomorrow the Lord our God will work wonders for us."

They looked at each other with a mixture of fear and hope. Was God at work for them? The priests must have thought so, because they stepped out into the river, carrying the Ark between them.

"Look, I think the water is falling," said someone suddenly. "It is, it is! There's hardly a trickle now! Joshua was right. God has worked this wonder for us. He is on our side," they shouted in triumph.

"Look, the Ark has stopped in the middle of the river, the priests are waiting there for us to cross before they go over. Oh, quickly, we don't want to drown like the Egyptian soldiers. Hurry up!" they urged each other forward, anxiously shepherding their toddlers and tottering old folk, their laden donkeys and sure-footed, foolish sheep over the slippery rocks on the river bed.

The people watched anxiously as the priests picked up the sacred Ark and carried it across to the river bank. Instantly, the waters broke, and a brown, foaming, tumbling mass of water roared down, flooding the river bed where people had just crossed.

Awed and silent, they made their way to a place called Gilgal about two miles from the river and two miles from Jericho. There they raised a monument, a circle of twelve boulders from the bed of the River Jordan.

Knowing that the Hebrews were camped close to his city, the King of Jericho had ordered a barricade and the gates were closed night and day. No one entered or left the city as Jericho got ready to fight.

Alone one day near the silent walls of Jericho, Joshua met a man. The naked blade of an unsheathed sword glinted in the stranger's hand. Joshua's heart beat wildly. Had the King of Jericho sent this man out from the city to fight with a picked man from the Hebrew's army, a fight that would decide the fate of the city? Or had this stranger come from somewhere else?

"Are you friend or foe?" he called. "With us, or with our enemies?"

"I am Captain of the Army of the Lord God," the man answered and Joshua fell on his face.

"God himself is speaking to me," he said, worshipping. "What are my Lord's commands to his servant?" he asked.

"Take off your sandals, you stand on holy ground." Joshua obeyed.

When he returned to the people, he was confident of victory.

"God has told me what to do," he shouted. "All you valiant warriors, come forward! Now let me

have seven priests to carry the Ark behind the soldiers. Fetch seven ram's horns for the priests to blow. We're going to march once right around the outside of the city. The priests are to blow their horns and no one else must make a sound. Not one sound! Just the priests' horns."

They marched once right round the city walls and came back to where they had started.

The next day everyone got up early.

"Round we go again, once round the city, just like yesterday," Joshua ordered.

Half-heartedly the warriors marched off, followed by the priests blowing their horns and the Ark and all the people. Right round the walls they went and back to Joshua.

The next day they marched round again.

"It's God's battle!" Joshua called after them. But by now some were protesting and some were longing for a real fight.

The fourth day, round they went again in silence except for the braying of the priests' horns. And the same happened on the fourth, fifth and sixth days.

"Can the trampling feet of many people knock down those mighty walls?" they queried, shaking their heads.

"When God gives us the city, your feet will be going into Jericho," promised Joshua. "Be ready early tomorrow, because we're going to march around that city not once but seven times!"

At dawn they were ready. In silence they lined up again. Again and again they circled the walls of Jericho. People on the walls laughed and jeered as they kept going round. They waved from the windows of their houses. The marchers set their teeth and carried on in silence.

Something about the sight of the silent army and the sound of the raucous horns that the priests kept blowing silenced the onlookers.

At the seventh time round the city Joshua shouted: "Raise the war cry! God has given us the city."

The people cheered and shouted. The horns blew a mighty ear-splitting blast. Yelling their wild war cry the people stormed forward, then stopped, shocked.

The outside wall was tottering. Great cracks scored the stonework. The houses and towers toppled forward and the wall came tumbling down.

"Go in now," Joshua shouted. "Didn't I tell you your feet would go into the city? God has given us Jericho. Burn it to the ground. But bring out all the silver, and gold, the things of bronze and iron for the treasury."

He searched out the two spies. "Remember your

promise. Bring Rahab and her family out safely."

Yelling and shouting the warriors surged forward, leaping over the rubble and the ruins that had been Jericho's mighty outer wall.

There were other cities to conquer, other tribes to win over by treaty, but the end seemed sure and the taste of victory was as sweet as the ripe grapes of Canaan. Joshua would lead them. God was on their side.

Gradually they gained ground in Canaan. Hebron and Shechem, the dwelling places of their fore-fathers Abraham, Isaac and Jacob, fell to the Hebrews.

Joshua called the people together at Shechem.

"I am old now, and I must go the way of all the earth. You have seen how all God's good promises have been fulfilled. Choose today. Are you going to worship the ancient gods our ancestors served long ago before they crossed the River Euphrates: the moon god and the sun? Are you going to worship the many gods of Canaan? Choose! But as for me and my family – we will serve the Lord our God!"

Then the people cried out together, "We will serve the Lord."

So they made a solemn promise not to bow down to the gods of their ancestors or the gods of Canaan. There at Shechem they buried the bones of Joseph, who so long ago had believed that God would bring the Hebrews back from Egypt and give them the land of Canaan.

Joshua 1–6; 23–24

"For the Lord and for Gideon"

"How can God help us now that we've settled in Canaan?" the doubters asked. "We've so much to learn. We've become farmers now."

"The gods of Canaan are farming gods. We must worship Baal, their god, when we sow our seed. Baal brings the cornfields to life, he makes the crops grow."

So, without too much thought, the Hebrews learned to worship the gods who, they believed, would bring them good grapes and full-eared grain.

They forgot about God until disaster struck. Then they prayed to him again and burnt all their idols.

There were very few people who refused to have anything to do with the gods of Canaan. One of these was a young man called Gideon.

All around him Gideon heard the Hebrews complain: "The Midianites, those wanderers from the desert cross our borders. They pitch their tents, and wherever they settle the ground is as black with them as if a swarm of locusts had landed."

"In fact, they are worse than locusts, for the locusts only eat up our crops, but the Midianites take everything we have. They leave us nothing, not a sheep or an ox or even a donkey!" someone added bitterly.

Gideon thought to himself, "these nomads from the desert plague us because you've all turned from God to Baal." But he was too frightened to say anything like that aloud.

Secretly one day, Gideon was threshing corn. He was hidden in the pit where, each September, the men trampled the grapes to press out the juice and make wine.

"How wonderful it would be if God would send someone to drive the Midianites away!" he thought. "Then we could thresh our corn openly as we used to do. We tossed the grain and the chaff together in the air and the wind carried the chaff away. It made the job so much easier," he sighed, but he dared not move away from the well-hidden winepress for fear of the Midianite invaders.

God spoke to him. "Valiant warrior! The Lord is with you!"

"If God is with us, why are the Midianites attacking us?" asked Gideon.

"Go in my strength and drive them out!"

"But, but . . . Lord," protested Gideon.

"I will be with you," God told him. "You shall crush the hosts of Midian."

That night, secretly, Gideon chose ten servants and smashed down the altar of Baal in his town. He tore down the sacred pillar and used the wood for a fire to offer a sacrifice to God. The next day when the furious townspeople found out what had happened, they wanted to kill Gideon, but his father protected him.

Then came the news that dismayed everyone.

"All the tribes of the East have joined the Midianites. They've crossed the Jordan and their tents are spread across our plains. We hear that they have more camels than anyone could possibly count."

"Lord God," prayed Gideon, "if you are really going to do what you said, and you are going to use me to drive out the Midianites, please, give me a sign. I'll spread a fleece out on the ground. If it is wet when all around it the earth is dry, I will know you want me to deliver Israel."

He spread a shorn fleece of a sheep across the threshing floor high on the hill top. Next morning

he ran and lifted the fleece. The long, curly wool was matted, sodden and heavy, drenched with dew, but the ground all around had remained dry. Gideon stood still, amazed. God had done what he had asked and given him a sign. His heart was pounding.

"Please, Lord, don't be angry with me," he prayed.

"I want another sign. Do it in reverse this time! The fleece will dry in the sun all day. Tomorrow let the ground be wet and the fleece remain dry."

God heard his prayer. The early morning sun sparkled on the dew drops as Gideon made his way to the threshing floor. His feet were soaking. He ran and felt the fleece. It was bone dry.

Gideon called the tribespeople to follow him, and a huge army, numbering about 36,000 men, came

to do battle against the enemy. Gideon was thrilled to see so many soldiers.

"How wonderful, Lord," he thought. "We'll certainly drive the Midianites away now!"

"No," said God. "It's Jericho all over again, Gideon. I want you to do it *my* way. No one will be able to say it was because you had such a huge army that you defeated the Midianites. Tell the soldiers just how mighty the Midianites are."

So Gideon told them about the power and strength of the Midianites. Men turned away in fear and Gideon couldn't help feeling dismayed as he counted the companies that remained. Ten thousand men!

"Oh, Lord," he thought, "it's not many against the enormous number of the Midianites, but you're on our side, I know."

"It's still too many, Gideon," God said.

Gideon led his army to the river nearby. They went quietly The Midianites were across the river, about two miles away down below them in the valley.

"Drink," Gideon ordered.

Most of the men knelt and let the running water trickle through their cupped hands.

"An enemy could come upon them unseen and unheard as they're bent over like that," thought Gideon. "They're not even looking! And the noise of the water drowns all other sound. One push, and the whole army would be swept away by the river!"

Three hundred man drank warily, raising their heads and looking about them, each man cupping one hand to hold the water, while the other hand was constantly fingering his sword.

"Those are your men," God told Gideon. "Send the rest home!"

Before he sent them away Gideon asked them to hand over their equipment to the three hundred who remained: water pitchers, rams' horn trumpets and torches.

The three hundred men spent the night beside the river, but Gideon couldn't sleep.

"I'm frightened, Lord," he prayed. "Just three hundred of us against the Midianites."

"There's no need to worry. I am with you, but get up, take Purah, your servant, and go close to the Midianite tents. I can tell you that you'll hear some-thing there that will encourage you!"

Gideon obeyed God.

"Look!" Purah whispered in dismay. "They stretch through the valley as far as we can see. Their tents cover the whole ground. And their camels! It's true, you just can't begin to count them!"

"Hush," Gideon warned him. "Listen!"

A man near to them was telling his fellow-soldier about a dream he'd just had.

"I saw a cake of barley bread come rolling through the camp. It reached our tent and knocked it flat!"

"That's terrible," his friend whispered, staring wide-eyed at the dying flames of the camp fire. "That loaf represents Gideon. He and his men will sweep through our camp and overcome us."

In the dark, beyond the firelight, Gideon fell on his knees and thanked God for what he had heard.

Then he went and woke his men.

"A surprise attack," he ordered. "It's God's way."

He divided the men into three groups. Each man held a horn, an empty pitcher and a lighted torch inside each pitcher.

Stealthily they crept down to the Midianite camp. They spaced themselves around the plain, encircling the camp. It was the middle watch of the night. New sentries were relieving the guards.

A harsh, ear-splitting blast resounded in the darkness. There was a deafening crash and a sudden blaze of light. Gideon had blown his horn, broken his pitcher, and raised the torch high, yelling:

"For the Lord and for Gideon!"

"For the Lord and for Gideon!" three hundred voices chanted over and over again. On all sides of the camp the horns brayed ceaselessly. Lights flared in the darkness.

"We're surrounded!" The alarm was given. "Gideon has come upon us with a vast army."

The sleepy Midianites groped for their weapons. Their camels snorted and stampeded. The donkeys broke free from their tethers and raced, rearing and kicking, through the camp, trampling the startled soldiers underfoot. Dark shapes rushed in all directions. The Midianites fled in confusion, fighting each other in the dark. Gideon and his army remained where they were, brandishing their torches, sounding their horns.

Never again did the Midianites trouble the Hebrew tribes in Canaan.

Judges 6–8

A strong man who couldn't keep a secret

The Sabbath lamp had been lit, the prayers had been said, the meal eaten.

"Tell us a story!" the four children demanded. "Tell us about Samson, Father," they begged.

"Samson, you know came from the tribe of Dan. When the Sea-people, the Philistines, settled round our coasts, they drove out the people of Dan from their homes. There they built their five strong cities . . ."

"Tell us their names!"

"Gaza, Ashkelon, Ashdod, all on the coast . . ." their father ticked off the names on his fingers. "Ekron and Gath. Five great cities where their kings rule, but they all join together when they go to war."

"I don't like them. Surely God will help us against them soon," said the smallest girl, in tears.

Her father took her on his knee. "Surely," he said. "Meantime, let's be encouraged as we hear about Samson.

"His parents were told by an angel that they

were going to have a son. God blessed him greatly and made him very strong. Samson had never drunk wine, never eaten anything our Law says is unclean, and had never cut his hair. It tumbled across his massive shoulders and fell down his back.

"But he was not wise. He would not listen to his parents, and he wanted to marry a Philistine girl.

"Get her for me! I like her!" he said, and would not listen when they tried to tell him not to have anything to do with our enemies.

"On his way to a meeting with the Philistine girl, Samson met a snarling young lion. He had no weapon, but he killed the lion . . ."

"Just with his two hands?" the boys asked, knowing the answer.

"Yes, for God had given him strength more than most men possess. He met the girl and enjoyed being with her. On his way home he went out of his way to find the carcass of the lion he had killed. A swarm of bees had settled there and Samson ate the honey. He gave some to his father and mother but he wouldn't tell them that he had taken it from the dead body of an animal.

"Off he went again and the girl's family held a wedding feast for him.

"'I'll get the better of these Philistines,' Samson thought. 'I have a riddle for you,' he said. 'Guess the answer in seven days and I'll give you sixty robes. But if you can't guess the answer, you must give them to me.'

"The young men agreed and Samson told them his riddle:

'Out of the eater came what is eaten
and out of the strong came what is sweet.'

"'They'll never think that means the honey I took out of the body of the lion,' he chuckled to himself. And it looked as if he were right, for the young men took four days to think over the answer and no one could supply one.

"'We'll all be beggars because of your bridegroom and his riddle,' they threatened Samson's bride. 'Get him to tell you the meaning, or we'll burn the house around your ears!' That's what the Philistines are like, you know," the father explained to his children.

"Well, the poor girl begged and begged Samson day after day for the next three days and in the end he gave away his secret. Of course she told the young men and they went up to Samson and told him his answer.

"Samson was furious. He went off to Ashkelon, entered its gates and killed thirty men. He stole their clothes and threw them at the feet of the

Philistines. Then he stormed home to his parents and the bride was hastily married off to the best man!"

The children laughed. "But he killed a lot more Philistines than that, didn't he?" one of the boys said.

"Oh yes. You see he had really stirred up trouble for himself in the five Philistine cities and they were out for his blood. A thousand men came after him, bearing shields, their bodies covered in armour and their long sharp swords drawn. Samson had no weapon and no armour. Nearby in the rocks lay the jawbone of an ass. Samson picked it up and killed every single one of the Philistines."

"Wonderful! I wish we had someone like him to fight them now!" the children sighed.

"Yes, God had given Samson wonderful strength, but his wisdom didn't match his muscles. Let me tell you the rest of the story, and you'll see what I mean," their father said.

"Samson fell in love with another Philistine girl."

"Delilah!" the children chorused.

"Yes. The Philistine chiefs soon got to know about it. They promised Delilah eleven hundred

silver pieces if she could discover for them the secret of Samson's strength.

"'Tell me, dearest,' Delilah cajoled him, 'How can I ever tame you?'

"Samson smiled. 'Bind me with seven bowstrings and I will lose my strength,' he lied.

"She believed him and hurried to the Philistine chiefs. They hid in her room and as Samson slept she bound him with the bowstrings.

"'Quick, Samson, the Philistines have got you!' she awakened him.

"He snapped the bowstrings at once, and Delilah, annoyed, begged him to tell her the truth this time.

"Twice more he lied to her about the source of his strength, and finally Delilah complained, 'Now I know you don't love me. You don't trust me . . .' Day after day she nagged him to tell her the secret of his strength, until he couldn't stand any more of it.

"'From birth I have belonged to God and no razor has touched my head. The secret of my strength is in my hair. Shave me and I'll lose my strength. I'll become like all other men. Now are you happy? Why do you ask me such questions?'

"'To see if you really love me,' she said. She lulled him to sleep. The chiefs came to her with eleven hundred silver pieces in their hands. Delilah called a man to shave seven locks from Samson's head. Then Delilah woke Samson. He was bound and couldn't free himself. The Philistines seized him . . ."

"I don't like it," the little girl cuddled closer

to her father, and put her hands over her ears.

"It's cruel, but listen to the very end . . ."

"Go on, it's the very best part," the other children urged their father.

"They gouged out his eyes and took him, blind, weak and enslaved to Gaza. They bound him with fetters of bronze, a double chain which bowed him down. Then they set him to work at the mill, plodding around and around making the millstone turn for hour after hour."

"Just like a beast of burden!" the boys protested.

"Yes, with the Philistines standing by, jeering at him! Poor Samson!

"But the hair that had been shorn began to grow again," the story-teller continued.

"Now, to celebrate the defeat of Samson, the Philistines all gathered together to hold a great feast to their god, Dagon. They heaped praises upon him.

"'Dagon has delivered our enemy into our hands,' they sang. 'Let's get Samson out. He can amuse us now!'

"A young boy led Samson by the hand. They scoffed at him.

"'Lead me to the pillars that support the building,' murmured Samson to the boy. 'You see how weak I am. Let me lean against them for a moment.'

"The building was crowded with a great throng. All the chiefs of the Philistines had gathered there and about 3,000 people were watching from the roof.

"Suddenly, above all the hubbub of thousands of voices, Samson's voice cried out to God.

"'Lord God!' he pleaded, 'remember me and just once, I pray you, give me back my strength!'

"The crowd watched in silence as Samson put his arms around the two centre pillars. He braced himself and threw all his weight against them.

"'Lord, God, let me die with the Philistines!' he cried. He pulled and heaved with all his might. The building rocked. Pieces of masonry went flying and then the whole thing toppled down, killing all the people there."

There was silence in the room when the story finished. The baby's head had long since drooped on to its mother's shoulder and she had laid it to sleep.

"God will send us a leader soon, wiser than Samson, one who believes, like Gideon, in the power of our God," their father finished. "Maybe you will live to see it happen."

Judges 13–16

The foreign girl in the barley field

"**T**his is the road back to Judah." The three women who had been walking along huddled closely together and, anxiously looking about them, stopped for a moment.

"Ten years ago four of us came this way," the older woman said, sadly. "My husband, our two young sons and myself fled from the famine that afflicted Judah our homeland. We came to your country, to Moab, where our boys grew up . . ."

She laid her hands on the girls' shoulders. "Go home now, my daughters. You were good wives to my sons while they lived, good to me and to my husband while he lived. Go back now, each one to her mother's house. You are still very young. You'll find other husbands among your own people. Go now!"

One of the girls kissed Naomi, her mother-in-law, and went away, back to Moab.

But the other girl stayed.

"Look, Ruth, my dear," said Naomi, "be wise and go home to your own people, your own god."

"Oh, Naomi," begged Ruth, "don't keep asking me to leave you. I will go with you wherever you go, live with you wherever you live. I will make your people mine; your God shall be my God. Nothing, not even death itself, shall part me from you."

"Then come," Naomi said.

On they went together until they reached the town of Bethlehem.

People flocked from their homes to greet them, but when they saw how Naomi walked along, bent and bowed with sorrow, their greetings died on their lips.

"Can this be Naomi?" they whispered to one another.

"Don't call me 'Naomi' any more," she said.

"Call me Mara, for my life has become bitter since my husband and sons died.

"But you're not quite alone," Ruth tried to comfort her. "Look, it's May and the barley fields all around us are ready to be harvested. I'll look after you, Naomi, and go into the fields as all the poor people do. You've told me that one of the laws your God gave your people was to be kind to the poor and to allow them to gather the scraps of corn that the reapers leave. Let me go then. I'll gather the ears of barley that fall around the edges of the field where the weeds and brambles grow. I'll beat it and grind it and we'll eat barley bread."

"Go then," Naomi said. "Perhaps you'll find the field of a good man who tells the reapers to leave plenty for the poor."

All day from morning till late in the afternoon, Ruth followed the reapers through the rustling barley. Her hands were blistered from tearing the long stalks. Her feet were cut by the sharp stubble. Her back ached. She was hungry and thirsty, but she worked without a break, gathering the corn.

Many people in the field that day stopped to look at the girl from the foreign country who toiled without rest.

One of them was the farmer himself, named Boaz.

"God be with you!" he greeted the reapers.

"God bless you!" they answered, straightening their backs, wearily, and rubbing away the sweat that trickled into their eyes.

"Who is the young foreign girl?" Boaz asked.

"Her name is Ruth. She came with Naomi, the widow who's just returned from Moab desolate because her husband and sons died there. The girl is her daughter-in-law."

"She works hard for her mother-in-law," Boaz mused.

He strolled over to her. She looked up in alarm, dismayed that the farmer himself should come and speak to her.

"My daughter," he began, and his kind voice made her feel less afraid. "My servants will look after you. Glean behind them. If you're thirsty – and you must be – you can drink water from those pitchers."

"Why are you so kind to me, a foreigner?" Ruth asked, bowing to the ground.

"Because I've heard how good you are to Naomi," Boaz answered. "God will reward you. You've left your country, your people and their gods and have come to our God who will shelter you beneath his wings, as a mother bird shelters her young."

Boaz invited her to eat, giving her bread dipped into wine and a pile of roasted ears of corn.

"Go into the middle of the field and glean among the sheaves themselves," he told her.

"Listen," he told his reapers, "make sure you pull a few ears from the bundles as you stack the sheaves and let them fall into Ruth's path."

In the evening Ruth beat out the barley and took it home to Naomi.

"Ruth, my dear!" Naomi exclaimed. "Someone has been very good to you. Where did you gather so much barley?"

"In the fields of such a kind man," said Ruth. "His name was Boaz."

Then Naomi cried out: "It is the Lord our God who is kind to you! That man is a close relative of my husband, and the one person who could help us."

Until the end of the barley harvest, Ruth gleaned in Boaz's fields. Each evening she took home a great amount to Naomi and they ground it and kneaded the dough and baked barley bread.

"Ruth," Naomi said one day. "You've been good to me, but I must see you happily married off and Boaz is the very man to help us. Tonight there'll be feasting on the threshing floor when they finish winnowing the grain. When it's over, go and make yourself known to him."

Ruth did what Naomi said. It was dark and Boaz did not recognise her at first.

"I gladly accept you into our family," he said when she had told him that he was their only relative. "Tomorrow I shall consult the only other close relative and, if he agrees, I shall make you my wife and provide for you and Naomi for the rest of your lives."

Boaz saw his relative at the city gates before a crowd of witnesses. They agreed that he should marry Ruth and he made her his wife that very day.

Early the next year, as the first buds were breaking through and the singing of birds announced the coming of spring, Ruth had a baby boy.

Naomi's heart was glad as she cuddled her grandson. "You've been so good to me, Ruth!" she said. "Now I am happy that I went to Moab, in spite of the terrible sorrow I suffered there. I came back empty and desolate. Now we share our little baby. It's as if I have my own boys over again." Tears rolled down her cheeks, but she was laughing too. "You have been more to me than seven sons."

They called the baby Obed. When he grew up he had a son called Jesse. Jesse had seven sons. One of them was a shepherd lad called David.

Ruth 1–4

The boy who looked after the lamps

Hannah was sitting with all the others at the festival, but she wasn't eating anything.

"Oh Hannah, please cheer up!" Elkanah, her husband, urged her. "It's the same every year when we come here to Shiloh to take part in the festival. I know what's wrong with you," he added, sympathetically. "You wish you had a baby!"

She nodded, her head bent, her sorrow choking her.

"Never mind," he tried to console her. "Don't I mean more to you than ten sons?"

Hannah slipped away from the table. She went back to the silent temple. Only Eli, the old priest, was still on duty where the sacred Ark was kept in the sanctuary.

"Please, Lord," Hannah sobbed, pouring out her grief to God, "give me a baby boy. I'll give him back to you as soon as he's old enough. He shall serve you all his life."

Her lips moved in prayer as she repeated the same words over and over again in her heart. She rocked back and forth, sobbing and praying, and was startled when Eli came and spoke quite roughly to her: "This is no place for drunks!"

"My lord!" Hannah was shocked. "Please don't think that of me! I've been pouring out all my sorrow to God."

Eli's face softened. He could see that Hannah really loved God. "Go in peace," he said. "And may God grant your prayer, whatever it was."

When Elkanah's family made the journey to Shiloh for the festival the following year, Hannah didn't go.

Elkanah looked lovingly at the little baby boy, Samuel, that Hannah was nursing at her breast. "Look after him well while we're away, Hannah. We'll be back soon."

"Remember to thank God especially for our little son!"

Three years later Hannah and Samuel travelled with the others to Shiloh. Hannah remembered her promise to let Samuel serve the Lord.

The little boy chattered non-stop, asking so

many questions that they were all weary long before they were anywhere near the little town that had become a sacred place to them.

Perhaps he cried a little when the old priest led him away from his mother and all his step-brothers and sisters into the dimly lit temple, that smelt so different from the goats-skin tent at home!

"I'll come again next year," Hannah called out after him.

"What a big boy you'll be then!" Eli comforted him. "Come, Samuel, my little son. Let me show you everything in the temple. Look, here is the place where you are going to sleep . . ." Samuel had already dried his eyes. There were so many new things to learn now. His job was to look after the lamps in the temple. He had to see that they were clean and kept well-filled with oil. He had to trim the wicks so that the flame would burn brightly, and he must never let them go out. He wore a linen cloth tied about his waist, and every year his mother came to visit him and brought him a little tunic that she had woven. How happy Samuel

God wanted him to be in the Temple instead of at home. He tried to do all his work as well as he could.

He kept his eyes and ears wide open and knew that when people came to offer sacrifices to God, they only came half-heartedly. It had become a habit, and in their saddle bags they had idols, statues of Baal and the other gods of Canaan. He knew that Eli's sons were bad men, who made a mockery of the worship of the Lord.

Samuel was still very young, but he recognised all this, and although he loved Eli dearly, it grieved him that the old man did nothing to stop his sons.

One evening old Eli lay dozing in the alcove that was his bedroom. It was late, but the lamp of God was still burning before the sacred Ark in the sanctuary where Samuel had his sleeping mat.

"Good little Samuel!" the old man thought. "How well he honours God! The lamps always shine brightly. The doors are always opened on time."

Just then Samuel came running up to him: "Here I am, Eli. I heard you call me."

"No, my boy, I didn't call you," said Eli, puzzled.

was when Hannah tried it on him, making sure it fitted perfectly.

Gradually he forgot what home was really like, and only knew it from the tales his parents told him. Hannah had always brought Samuel up to know that God had given him to her. "You are His special servant," she said. So Samuel knew that

"Go back now and sleep again."

"Perhaps I did call," he thought, sleepily. He closed his eyes again, only to wake abruptly.

"Do you want me this time, for I heard you call again. You said: 'Samuel, Samuel'."

"No, son, I didn't call you. Go back and sleep."

"God himself is calling Samuel," the old man thought, watching the boy slip away to lie down.

It was rare these days, he knew, for God to speak to people. He remembered how Samuel's mother had prayed in desperation and how she had brought her little boy to him. So he was not surprised when Samuel appeared at his side again.

"Here I am, Eli," the boy said, for the third time.

The old man was sure now. "It is God, and not myself, who is calling you, my son. If He calls again, say: 'Speak, Lord, your servant is listening'."

Obediently Samuel tiptoed away and lay down again. He watched the flame of the lamp burn steadily upward.

"Samuel, Samuel!"

"Speak, Lord, your servant is listening," the boy said clearly into the darkness.

God told him something that made him afraid. "Eli knows how sinful his sons are, yet he has not corrected them. They dishonour the Lord, their God, and I am going to dishonour them."

In the morning he ran to open the temple door. He lingered over the job longer than was necessary,

him. People from every tribe of Israel flocked to Shiloh to hear what Samuel had to say.

"We badly need a prophet now, for the Philistines have mustered an army and are coming to attack us once again," the tribesmen said.

"We'll take the Ark out with the soldiers of our armies," Eli's two sons suggested. "After all, in the days of Joshua they carried the Ark with them."

"Don't take the Ark," Eli begged, and Samuel agreed with him. "In Joshua's day they put away their idols and chose God! That's why they won the battle," he thought.

Eli and Samuel were right. The Philistines defeated the Israelite army and captured the Ark. Many people were killed, including Eli's sons.

Eli was sitting by the gates of Shiloh, anxious for the safety of the Ark, and longing for news. A soldier straight from the battle-field told the old priest that the Ark was in the hands of the enemy. Eli slumped down to the ground and died.

The Philistines only kept the Ark for seven months. They were too frightened by the power of the God of the Israelites, so they sent it back on a

dreading to hear the sound of Eli's voice.

"What did God tell you last night?" Eli was nearly blind, but he saw the look of fear cross Samuel's face.

"Tell me everything, for I am glad that God has spoken at last," the old man encouraged the boy.

When Samuel told him, Eli said simply: "He is God, let him do what he thinks is right."

As Samuel grew up, God continued to speak to

cart pulled by two cows. Everyone was pleased, but it took twenty years before Samuel was able to gather the people together and persuade them to burn their idols.

"Pray for us!" the people begged, so Samuel offered a sacrifice and prayed. While they were gathered there, the Philistines drew close. A tremendous thunderstorm broke out and the Israelites set off after the fleeing Philistines. They won the battle.

"God has helped us so far!" exclaimed Samuel.

In his heart he knew that the people needed a ruler, someone strong who loved God and honoured his Law.

Two dispirited travellers approached the girls at the well outside the town.

"Our donkeys strayed away and we've been looking for them for days," one of the travellers said.

"We know there's a man of God here," the other, obviously a servant, added.

"Samuel, the great prophet, lives here. Just walk straight on and you'll find him." The girls were all speaking at once, each trying to say something really helpful that would draw the attention of the tall, handsome stranger to her.

Saul, the traveller, thanked them and the two men continued up the slope.

"He's just like a king," they all sighed, looking after him.

Samuel, whom the two men met as soon as they entered the town, thought so too. He invited Saul to spend the night with him and in front of all his guests gave the young man the place of honour and the best food.

The next morning, Samuel accompanied Saul a little way down the road.

"Your donkeys have all been found," he reassured Saul. "Now, send your servant a little way ahead." Saul obeyed and was amazed to hear Samuel say: "Why worry about a few donkeys, when the whole of the wealth of Israel now belongs to you and your family?"

Samuel took oil from a ram's horn he had brought with him. He anointed Saul, pouring the oil on the young man's head. "God told me that you are to be prince over Israel. In his name I anoint you," he said, kissing Saul.

So Saul returned to his family and found the strayed donkeys, safe and sound.

"You actually saw Samuel, did you?" Saul's family gathered around, all of them talking at once, glad to see him home. "Yes, he told me not to worry, that the donkeys had arrived home safely," Saul said. He said no more, and no one knew that the great prophet had anointed Saul to be king.

1 Samuel 1–10

The disobedient king

T he war cry spread through Israel: "Let's march east with Saul!" The Ammonites had surrounded the town of Jabesh-Gilead, and the people there sent a plea for help to Saul.

He divided his army into three companies. They burst into the Ammonite camp just before dawn, when a surprise attack was least expected. The battle raged until noon. Very few Ammonites were left alive, and those who survived were scattered far and wide.

It was a tremendous victory! All the men of Israel flocked after Saul to a place called Gilgal, where Joshua had erected a stone circle.

"He is our king! He is our king!" they cried. They offered sacrifices to God.

Samuel thought highly of Saul. "He'll be a leader like Joshua, and the people will at last win our promised land."

But things didn't work out that way, and the story that started well ended in sorrow . . .

Saul was a good soldier and won some battles against the Philistines. He gathered an army of two thousand men. His brave son, Jonathan, smashed a Philistine fortress with an army half the size of his father's. But the Philistines gathered a great army around the Israelites.

"Sound the trumpet through the length and breadth of Israel!" ordered Saul. "Summon every man."

They came with their farming tools: axes and mattocks and sharpened ox goads. The Philistines had made sure that they kept the secret of iron smelting from the Hebrews. Men gathered at Gilgal, waiting for Saul to lead them into battle. Daily his frightened soldiers urged him to lose no time.

"But we must wait for Samuel," Saul said. "He's coming to offer sacrifices to God. We can't go to fight without praying first."

Daily large numbers deserted and slipped away to join their families, who had fled to the mountains and were hiding in every nook and cranny: caves, crevices and disused wells.

Saul waited seven days and still Samuel didn't come.

"Bring me the offering," Saul said at last. "We'll do it without Samuel."

They gathered round the altar and watched the sacrifice burn. Saul prayed but no one felt easy, because Samuel was missing.

"What have you done!" Samuel appeared just at that moment and stared in horror at the altar where the offering had been burned. "What have you done?" he repeated, ignoring Saul's greetings.

"The soldiers have deserted me. There's a huge Philistine army gathered at Michmash. We waited and waited and still you did not come."

"You fool!" stormed Samuel. "You're the commander, aren't you? You give orders and expect your soldiers to carry them out. Couldn't you do the same, and obey God when he gives you an order? I tell you, the Lord will find a man after his own heart and give your kingdom to him."

Samuel turned on his heels and left Saul.

Secretly, Jonathan also slipped away from the camp, followed by his armour-bearer.

"Listen," the young prince murmured, "nothing can stop the Lord our God if he wants us to win this battle."

"Go then against the Philistines," his armour-bearer replied. "I'm with you, heart and soul."

They climbed higher into the mountains. Between two jagged rocks a narrow path, a secret passageway, wound up to the Philistine camp. They crept along, scrambling over the rocks, using their hands to help them climb.

"Look!" a Philistine soldier shouted. "The Hebrew rats have come out of their holes. Come on up!" he called to Jonathan. "We've something to tell you."

Only one Philistine at a time could come along the path to fight them. Jonathan's first victim fell back on top of his companions, knocking them over the edge of the rocks. Panic spread through the army. They fled in confusion, attacking one another.

Saul's sentries saw the Philistines flee.

"After them! Find their weapons, and chase the Philistines back to their own country!" Saul shouted jubilantly. He led his six hundred men into the open. They won a great victory and the Philistines were scattered.

How popular Jonathan was with all the people!

Among the pomegranate trees of Gibeah, his own home town, Saul built a fortress, surrounded by two thick walls. The outer one was ten feet thick. There he recruited any strong man, or any man of valour who caught his eye, and so raised a strong army.

But always there was the threat of the hostile tribes around them: the Philistines, the Ammonites and the Amalekites in the south.

"Go," Samuel ordered. "Strike down the Amalekites. Kill and destroy everything and everybody: all the animals and all the people from the king on down. Go and fight in the name of the Lord, who will give you victory."

Saul gathered his force and marched off. He won a complete victory, as Samuel had said. He slaughtered all the people, but he spared the king, whom he made his prisoner. His soldiers killed only the poor, worthless, weak animals. They kept all the best ones: the fat sheep and cattle, the strong young herds and flocks.

They set off homeward and Samuel hurried to meet Saul. It was their last encounter. Samuel's face was dark with sorrow and anger.

"The Lord bless you!" called Saul. "I've carried out his orders, and we defeated the Amalekites."

"Then what is this noise of the bleating of sheep and the lowing of oxen that I hear?" asked Samuel.

"My people brought them from Amalek all the way here to offer the best of the flocks as a burnt offering to God," Saul lied uneasily.

"Burnt offerings! What do you think pleases God more: a burnt offering or an obedient heart?" Samuel said, and answered his own question. "Obedience is better than burning an animal as a sacrifice. You've rebelled against God. How can a man like you lead God's people?"

Saul was contrite. "Yes, I did disobey God. I was frightened of what the people would say if I didn't let them bring back any spoils of battle . . . you know what soldiers are like! But come back with me now, and let us worship God together."

Samuel turned his back on Saul. "Wait," pleaded Saul, on his knees. He caught at the hem of Samuel's robe. It tore in his grasp as Samuel walked away from him. "See," Samuel called back over his shoulder. "God has torn your kingdom from you just as you've torn my robe. A better man than you will be king."

"I have sinned," Saul admitted, "but I am still king. Some respect is still due to me in front of my soldiers. Come and offer worship with me." Samuel relented. He and Saul worshipped God together for the last time.

In front of all Saul's army, Samuel butchered the captive king of the Amalekites. Then he left for his home at Ramah and Saul took his men to the fortress at Gibeah.

Saul shut himself in his fortress and black moods of despair came over him. There were days and weeks of madness and terror. The sorrow had begun.

I Samuel 11–15

68

The shepherd boy of Bethlehem

"**T**he prophet Samuel is on his way here!" said the elders of Bethlehem anxiously.

"What does he want us for? Surely we've not done something wrong against God without even knowing?"

"Peace!" Samuel greeted them. "Don't look so worried! I've brought an animal for a sacrifice. We're going to worship God together."

The old man's heart was pounding. He had really come to find a king. He spotted a man called Jesse among the elders.

"Now, his grandmother was the foreign girl, Ruth, from Moab, wasn't she?" the old man thought to himself. "Do you want someone from his family, Lord," he prayed silently. "Surely not! They have foreign blood in them."

"Don't be misled by outward appearances," warned God. "Remember Saul. He was strong and handsome, but his heart was full of fear. He listened to his soldiers and fought the battle their way instead of having the courage to obey me."

So Samuel asked Jesse to send for all his sons.

Seven tall strong hillmen stood before him. "Oh yes, it must be one of them," Samuel thought.

"No," God said.

"Are these all your sons?" Samuel asked.

"I have another boy, but he's only a young boy. He's out in the hills with the sheep." Jesse sent a servant to fetch the boy.

"This is the one!" Samuel thought, watching David approach. "He's used to lonely dangerous places: the high hills where wild animals menace the sheep; and the steep rocks where the eagles perch. What fine eyes he has, fearless and honest. Look how respectfully he addresses his father and elder brothers. His bearing is pleasant, that's good in a boy," the old man thought.

He took his horn of oil and anointed David king in the name of the Lord.

David's head was bowed, but Samuel recognised the change in him immediately. When the boy looked up, his eyes were aflame. Samuel sensed that

songs were bubbling on his lips; that his legs were longing to dance.

"God's spirit has filled him," the old prophet thought. He saw envy in the sullen eyes of David's brothers, but knew that this boy had already chosen God long ago as his protector.

Rejoicing, Samuel went home to Ramah and David went back to his sheep.

1 Samuel 16

The sweet singer in the fortress

"The king is sick in his mind," King Saul's messengers told Jesse. "He looks for God and finds only despair. His spear is in his hand, but the enemy in his heart has defeated him already."

"Why come to me and tell me this?" Jesse wondered.

"We've heard all about your youngest son, David. We know how brave he is and that he plays skilfully upon the eight-stringed harp. Music alone can calm our king. He wants you to send David to him."

Jesse agreed and David set out to Saul's fortress at Gibeah with gifts for the king.

David stood before the king. He carried five freshly baked loaves, still warm in his hands, a skin of wine and a young bleating kid. Saul the soldier loved him at once.

"Fresh bread, how wonderful! And wine from your father's vines." He got up and stood beside David, fondling the young kid.

"Are you frightened in the gloomy cavern where a mad king dwells?" he murmured so low that David hardly heard.

"So you're our sweet singer?" Saul cried aloud, looking directly at David. The servants and prince Jonathan looked on amazed as Saul's haggard, unhealthy looking face was transformed by a radiant smile.

"My boy, I love you!" he cried. "I hardly need your music, for you have brought to me the peace and joy of the Lord our God! When I look at you, I remember how it is to sleep in the open. I hear the silence of the high places of Israel and the light laughter of our sweet-tasting, tumbling streams where the shepherd leads his flocks."

Then and there Saul took David into his service as his armour-bearer. Whenever the king was troubled and seized upon by madness, David took his harp and played and sang to Saul. Then Saul grew calm and recovered, and the dark clouds of despair left him for a while.

1 Samuel 16

A sling, a staff, and five stones

"It's too bad," David thought. "My three elder brothers are out with Saul's army, and I'm stuck at home here with the sheep."

"Come, David," Jesse called. "Take these loaves and cheese and go to your brothers to see how they're doing."

Early next morning, David set off and arrived at the battlefield in time to see a horrifying sight.

In the valley between the tents of the Israelites and the tents of the Philistines, a giant strutted. He was the Philistine champion. From top to bottom he was armed with bronze and iron.

"Send a man to fight with me!" he bellowed. "If he wins, we'll all be your servants."

"Well, why isn't anyone going out to fight him?" David's voice broke the petrified silence.

"Shsh! Get back to the sheep!" his brothers silenced him. "What do you know about fighting!"

David went straight for Saul's tent.

"You're too young!" Saul reasoned with him. "He's a champion, trained in the art of fighting from his earliest days."

"When I was keeping my father's flocks, whenever a lion got hold of a lamb, I snatched it from the lion's jaws, grabbed hold of the lion by its mane and killed it. I've killed both lions and bears, King Saul. I'll kill that Philistine giant, too. He's mocking the armies of the living God." Saul still hesitated.

"The God who rescued me from the lion and the bear will save me from Goliath!" David declared, confidently.

"Go then," Saul could withstand the boy no longer. "And God go with you. . . . But do be careful. Look, put on my armour."

Saul put his bronze helmet, metal coat and his own heavy sword on David, but when the boy tried to walk, he couldn't take a step.

"It's no good," he said, stripping it all off. "I'm just not used to them."

So, armed only with his shepherd's staff and his sling, David skipped lightly down the mountainside into the valley. He stopped by a brook and spent some time carefully choosing five smooth pebbles, which he put in his shepherd's wallet at his waist.

"Ho! Ho! Ho!" Goliath's laughter made the watching Israelites tremble. "What a joke! They've sent a boy to fight me! Am I a dog, boy, that you come out to chase me with your stick?" he growled threateningly. "Come to me! I'll give your corpse to the vultures to peck, and beasts shall gnaw your bones."

David's voice rang out fearlessly. "You come to me with a sword and a spear and a javelin. But I

come to you in the name of the Lord of all the armies; the God whom you are mocking. God will put you into my power. I'll cut off your head. The birds and beasts will feed well on Philistine corpses today. Then all over the world, everyone will know that our God is stronger than weapons of bronze or iron!"

Goliath let out a yell of fury and came thundering across the valley. David ran quickly towards him. As he ran he slipped a stone into his sling and with deadly skill took careful aim. Two armies watched in silence as the stone flew straight to its mark. Goliath roared with pain and staggered back, clutching his face. The stone had hit him in the middle of his forehead and he fell down dead. A groan went up from the Philistine army.

David raced on towards them. Triumphantly he jumped on Goliath's body and wrenched the heavy iron sword free from its scabbard. He lifted it high above his head and brought it flashing down. With one blow he cut off Goliath's head and held it high for both armies to see.

Then the Philistines fled in confusion, leaving their equipment in their tents. The Israelites chased them all the way into their own country right back to the gates of Ekron and Gath. Then the cheering Israelites came back and looted the deserted Philistine tents.

1 Samuel 17

How they cheered and praised David! Everyone's heart had gone out to him, especially prince Jonathan's.

"You can't go back to your sheep now!" Jonathan teased David. "My father won't let you out of his sight! How glad I am!" the prince added. "You are dearer to me than my own life."

He stripped off his robe and his armour and put them on David. Then Saul's son gave the shepherd boy his own sword, his bow and his heavy belt.

"God is with you," Jonathan said. "That is why we all love you so much."

All over Israel people said the same thing. David led Saul's armies into many battles and won them all. Soon they had made up a song about it. As the victorious soldiers returned, the women came dancing out to meet them, their quick fingers drumming

"...Dearer than my own life"

out a catchy rhythm on the timbrels, the flat drums they carried.

"See, the women meet us with songs of joy!" David told Saul.

But Saul's face darkened as he heard the words they sang:

"Saul has slain thousands of men," went the song, "but David has slain tens of thousands."

"What does this mean? They'll be making him

king next," thought Saul, and he rode on to his fortress at Gibeah in silence.

The very next day, Saul's madness returned and as David played and sang to him, Saul, raving and enraged, hurled his spear at David. Shocked, David managed to dodge away in time, but he knew that from then on his life was in danger.

Saul now sent David into desperate battles, hoping that the young commander would be killed. David always returned victorious.

"God is with him," thought Saul, gloomily. "How I loved him! But now I am twisted and knotted with hate."

"Think how David risked his life for you when he went out alone against Goliath," Jonathan tried to calm his father. Saul listened for a while, but he was being destroyed by his madness. Once again he hurled his spear at David. It stuck, quivering, in the thick stone wall and David fled.

"What can I do?" David sought Jonathan's help. "There's just a step between me and death."

"I'll do what I can," Jonathan said, but when he tried to speak up for David, Saul turned on him viciously. "You've chosen that shepherd boy to your shame," he fumed. "He's after our kingdom. You'll never be king as long as David is alive."

"He's done nothing wrong," Jonathan insisted, and Saul pointed his spear at his own son.

"I'm vexed for David," Jonathan said, fiercely. "You're my father and my king, but I can't sit at your table any more."

He ran out to meet David, who came out of his hiding place and bowed to the ground three times before the prince. Then they kissed each other, and because they knew that they would not meet again for a long time, indeed perhaps never again, they wept together.

"No matter what my father thinks, I shall never harm you," Jonathan said.

"Nor I you, or your family," promised David. "Saul has many enemies," he grieved, "but instead of going after them he pursues me, his truest friend."

So he fled beyond the boundaries of the mad king.

1 Samuel 18—20

75

Two kings in a cave

avid and his outlaws lay very still in the rocky recesses at the back of the cave. They were in the desert, amongst the sheepfolds of Engedi, in rocks known as "the rocks of the wild goats". Saul had persisted in chasing them throughout the land.

There was fear in the men's eyes. "Three thousand soldiers are marching outside looking for us," they whispered. "It won't be long before they spot this cave and come in to investigate."

They heard footsteps approaching, and desperately they pressed further back into the rocks. A man appeared at the mouth of the cave.

Someone tugged David's arm. "Now's your chance!" he murmured. "Look, it's Saul himself, and he's alone."

"God has given him to you!" the others whispered. "You can do what you like to him. One blow and he's dead."

Tense with excitement, the men watched David draw his sword and move slowly forward. But what was happening? Instead of killing Saul, David simply stooped down, and cut off the hem of Saul's cloak, completely unseen and unnoticed by the King. He crept back to the men with the frayed cloth in his hand.

"Why didn't you kill him?" they whispered urgently.

"Saul is our king," David said firmly. "I shall never lift my sword against him, and I forbid any one of you to attack him. Let him go unharmed."

Saul had stood up and was leaving the cave. David waited for a moment and then followed him.

"My lord king!" David's voice echoed in the overhanging rocks, and the three thousand men who were hunting high and low for him gasped. Saul turned in amazement.

David bowed down in the dust and did homage to Saul.

"Oh, Saul, why do you listen to people who tell you that David means to harm you?" David pleaded. "Look, I had you at my mercy in the cave and I could have killed you. I only cut off the hem of your cloak, yet you hunt me as if I was a wild animal. Oh, my father, you are Israel's anointed king and I shall never lay my hands on you."

Something stirred in Saul's tormented mind. "My son David, is that really your voice?" the king cried out. Tears poured down his haggard cheeks. "May God forgive me and reward you well for what you have done."

But Saul's madness would not let him rest. Still he hunted his loyal soldier while the Philistines raided the land.

"The king of Israel has gone out after my life as a man hunts a partridge in the mountains," said David bitterly. He made up his mind suddenly, in despair, "I'd do better among the Philistines. Then Saul will stop tracking me the length and breadth of Israel, and I shall be safe."

He took his 600 men and their families and left his homeland.

1 Samuel 24

"Where has David gone?"

The Philistine king, Achish, looked out of the watchtower of his palace in Gath. A Hebrew warrior with six hundred men behind him had come into the city. The sentries were alert . . . and astonished.

"It's David! It's the man who killed a hundred Philistines as a wedding gift when Saul made him his son-in-law."

"It's the shepherd boy who killed our champion, Goliath."

"David has gone over to the Philistines!" the news soon astounded Philistines and Hebrews alike.

"Welcome, David," said Achish. "Do you come in peace?"

"I come to escape from Saul."

"Good!" thought Achish. "I'll let him settle with me. David's a fine soldier – and he's got an army of six hundred men to feed. Soon they'll be fighting their own people and that will make trouble for Saul."

But David made sure that he went raiding among the peoples of the south who were also enemies of Saul. He brought back plunder for Achish: sheep and oxen, donkeys, camels and fine clothing, but never a captive. He left no one alive, so Achish never knew that David had let the Hebrews amongst the tribes go free.

"You can have the town of Ziklag for your own!" Achish promised David. "But when the Philistine armies go to fight against Saul, you'll join forces with me and my men, won't you?"

But when the Philistine leaders saw David arrive at the battlefield with Achish, they were horrified.

"Send the man back!" they told Achish. "You can't trust him. Remember the old song? 'Saul has slain thousands of men, but David has slain tens of thousands.' They were *Philistines* that David killed!"

"He's been with me for over a year and I've never had cause to doubt his loyalty," Achish protested.

"Maybe, but don't you think that he'll seize his chance of winning Saul's favour and will turn against us as soon as the fighting starts? Don't risk it, Achish."

So early next morning, David and his men went back to Ziklag only to find that the Amalekites from the south had burned down their town and carried off their wives and their children.

They chased after the raiders, and rescued their families. They camped among the ruins of the burnt-out city. It was two days later that a young Amalekite soldier came to the camp. His clothes were torn and the dust that mourners wore was on his head.

"I've come from the battlefield," he bowed to the ground before David.

"What happened? Is the battle over?" David asked.

"Many, many Hebrews are fallen. Jonathan was killed with his soldiers. Saul, his armour bearer and his three sons are dead, too."

David's face grew dark. "Saul and Jonathan are dead? How can it be? How do you know?" he questioned fiercely.

"I killed Saul," said the young soldier, watching David closely. He thought David would be pleased at the news. He was startled when he saw the look of horror that crossed David's face. "He was nearly captured by the Philistines," the young man quickly explained. "He'd been wounded by the bowmen and was leaning faint and reeling on his spear.

"'I don't want to be tortured like Samson,' he gasped. 'Kill me before the Philistines come and gloat over me.'

"So I killed Saul," the young man finished. "I took his crown and his bracelet. Here they are, my lord . . .'"

His voice trailed away as David gave a cry of sorrow and tore his clothes, and all the men about him did the same. Until evening they fasted, weeping for Saul and Jonathan and for the people of their God who had fallen on the battlefield of Mount Gilboa.

Then in the evening, David called the young Amalekite soldier to him.

"Now he'll give me my reward," the young soldier thought. "After all, I've killed his greatest enemy." But he was uneasy about the look on David's face.

"Weren't you afraid to kill the man whom Samuel anointed king in the name of God?" David asked. "God chose him from our people yet you have dared to kill him. I cannot show you mercy now." He gave a command, and one of his soldiers killed the young man with one blow.

Then David, who had sung so many songs to ease Saul's sorrow, poured out his grief into a dirge:

"High on your mountains, Oh Israel, Israel
Your beauty has fallen, your glory lies slain.
How did it happen that the heroes all fell?

Oh, hills of Gilboa, accursed battlefield,
Dew neither rain shall cleanse you; for no oil
But dying men's blood anoints Saul's disgraced
shield.

Lovely and pleasant, undivided in dying,
Swifter than eagles, far stronger than lions
Saul and his sons now together are lying.

Daughters of Israel weep for your lord. Your
king
Clothed you in scarlet; gave you brooches of
gold –
Blood of the battle is Saul's purple pall.

I am distressed, Jonathan, my dearest brother!
Wonderful love we shared: dearer and deeper
than
Love of a woman our love for each other.

How did it happen that your heroes all fell?
Why did your weapons fail you, Israel?"

1 Samuel 27–2 Samuel 1

David, the king

"**D**avid was anointed king long ago by Samuel. Of course he's our king, now that Saul is dead." The men of David's own tribe of Judah gathered at Hebron and gladly acknowledged him as their king.

Soon the news was spreading like wildfire through the Philistine cities and the worried leaders met in council.

"There's no need to worry. The Hebrew tribes are still hopelessly divided," they decided. "It's all to our good if David sets up a separate little kingdom in the south and Saul's surviving son, Ishbaal, rules the north. As long as Judah and Israel are divided, we have nothing to fear from them."

David ruled quietly in Hebron for seven years. He knew he would have to work slowly to win the trust of the northern tribes.

Commander Abner, who had fought many battles against David, took Saul's son, Ishbaal, and made him king over the ten tribes of Israel. There was fighting between David's men and Abner's men. The war dragged on and David's side grew stronger while Ishbaal's grew weaker.

Ishbaal was frightened of Abner, who took charge of everything.

"I want Rizbah, your royal princess," Abner said one day.

"No," Ishbaal tried to sound firm. "If you take one of my princesses, it's as good as saying that you're the king's son too."

Abner flew into a rage.

"So that's all you think of me, is it?" he stormed, and Ishbaal shrank back in fear. "Here I am, full of goodness towards you, protecting you against David's soldiers all this time and, instead of being grateful, you say 'no' to my very reasonable request. Well, listen, Ishbaal, it's not only David you're against now, it's me too. And stronger than both of us is the word of God. God has said David will be king of Israel, hasn't he? I'm going to be the man who brings it about. I'm going to join David, Ishbaal."

Abner spoke to all the elders of Israel. "You must take action now. David is the king God promised us," he said. Then he went to David to tell him that the tribes of Israel realised that David and not Saul's son was the rightful king.

But Abner was killed, murdered by David's commander, Joab, who hated him because Abner had killed Joab's brother. David publicly announced that this was a wicked deed and gave Abner a hero's funeral, which pleased the northern tribes.

Then one day two men from Israel came to David at Hebron with a present: the head of Ishbaal, Saul's son.

"You have been fighting against Ishbaal for

seven years, my lord. Look, here he is. He won't bother you now. We killed him as he lay asleep," they said, thinking to win David's approval and a great reward.

"You murderers!" David exclaimed in horror. "Haven't you heard how I rewarded the messenger who killed Saul on Gilboa? Saul's son is as sacred to me as Saul was." David gave an order. His soldiers surrounded the men and killed them.

"David, you are our king!" the northern tribes of Israel declared. "You're Saul's son-in-law after all, and you've always been loyal to his family. Look how you punished Ishbaal's murderers. And you've taken Jonathan's crippled son into your own home as if he were one of your children. We

promise to be loyal and true to you now."

As soon as the Philistines heard that Israel and Judah had united under David, they marched into a valley that cut David's army off from the northern tribes. David used his old base, the cave of Adullah, and completely destroyed the Philistines.

"They'll never invade us again!" the victorious Hebrews exulted. "So let's go on now and destroy every one of their strongholds in Judah."

As they marched, the armies of Judah and Israel agreed: "David's a great king. We'll go wherever he leads."

2 Samuel 2–5

Jerusalem

High on the ridge of hills that divided the tribes of Israel and Judah perched a strong-walled city. The people who held this ancient city were called Jebusites. They knew they were safe from attack! Their city was built on solid rock. On three sides sheer precipices dropped dizzily downward; on the fourth two strong walls guarded the inhabitants from any invader.

"Ho! Ho!" they jeered at David's army. "You'll never get in! Our city is so strong that even the blind and the lame could defend it against your army!"

"I'll give the command of my entire army to the man who gets up into the city," said David.

Commander Joab took up the challenge. A small spring bubbled on the east side of the city. Joab and his men climbed forty feet through the tunnel that carried the spring water into the city. It was dark and slimy; they were soaked, but elated when they finally saw a glimmer of light. Soon they were standing in the streets of the city. It was easy for the well-trained soldiers to surprise the sentries at the gate and open the gate for David's army to walk through.

They soon overcame the Jebusites and took over the city. They called it Jerusalem. Many people afterwards called it "the city of David", while others called it "Zion, the fortress" for David strengthened its foundations and repaired its walls. Still others called Jerusalem "the city of God" for David brought the holy Ark into his capital city.

That was a wonderful day! David the king stripped off his royal robes and headed the whole procession, whirling and leaping and dancing, singing the praises of God with all his people.

David lived in a palace of cedar, costly wood brought in ships rowed by many oarsmen. His kingdom and his wealth grew year after year, but David never forgot the hard times in the desert.

"I want to build a house for the Ark of God," he said. "I have a palace, but the Ark is in a tent. I'll build a great Temple, more beautiful than my palace."

"No, David," one of his prophets said. "God took you from the sheepfolds and anointed you as king. Your kingdom is great, your reign is glorious, but it will be one of your sons who will build the Temple of God."

"I am lord of Israel," said David, "but God is my King and I am subject to him."

He never forgot that during the forty years of his reign. He gave his people peace and happiness, but his own children fought together for his throne. Absalom, David's favourite son, rebelled against his father and was killed. Once again David lamented, shedding bitter tears.

When David was a very old man, trembling with cold, he named his son Solomon as king. "He shall reign after me, for I am dying," David said. "He shall build the Temple of our God who saves his king, and saves him again."

2 Samuel 5–7
parts of 2 Samuel 13–20
1 Kings 1

The king who asked to be wise

There was a new king in Israel. His name was Solomon, and he was one of David's sons. Solomon's half-brother, Prince Adonijah, was not at all pleased, because he wanted to become king himself. He held a party, trying to gather all the important people to his side. But Solomon was the consecrated king. Adonijah's party broke up and he had to run for his life.

"Please don't kill me," he begged.

"I will spare you as long as you do not try to steal the throne," promised Solomon. Adonijah broke his promise. He still tried to make himself as important as Solomon.

"I have been anointed in the name of God," thought Solomon. "Adonijah has broken his word. He must die." So Solomon had his step-brother killed.

But Solomon was young. He knew he had much to learn. So he went to ask God to help him. He climbed a lonely hilltop near Jerusalem, and there he offered a thousand sacrifices in one night.

"I love you, Lord God," he thought. "Yet I don't feel that I walk closely with you as my father David did. David seemed to walk hand in hand with you. Yet I will build you a glorious Temple, and I do want you to help me to be a good king."

There on the high place, beside the smouldering fire, God came to Solomon.

"What would you like me to give you?"

"Oh, God, I'm only a very young man. I've never led an army, and now you have made me king over all your people. Please give me wisdom, Lord God. Give me a discerning mind, God, the gift of judging between good and bad, so that I'll be able to govern wisely and justly."

"Because you have asked for this, and not for wealth or for the death of all your enemies," Solomon heard God say, "I shall give you what you ask for. You shall be wiser than any other king. But you must follow my laws, just as your father David did. I'll give you riches too, and honour, glory and a long life."

Solomon awoke.

"I believe everything God told me," he exclaimed. He went back to Jerusalem and offered sacrifices there, and held a party for all his servants.

Throughout the land, Solomon became famous for his wise dealings with people who came to him asking him to judge the right and the wrong for them. At his court, men wrote down all the clever things he said and made them into proverbs which everyone remembered because they were so witty.

Solomon grew richer and richer. David had never had an army, but Solomon raised armies and amassed numbers of chariots and horses. Men were kept busy building whole towns, not for people to live in but for Solomon's horses and chariots.

They worked hard for the king; as he grew richer, he built more and more beautiful buildings, but the people enjoyed peace and plenty, and were delighted when kings and queens of many nations began to visit Solomon and pay him their respects.

"I have built you a dwelling"

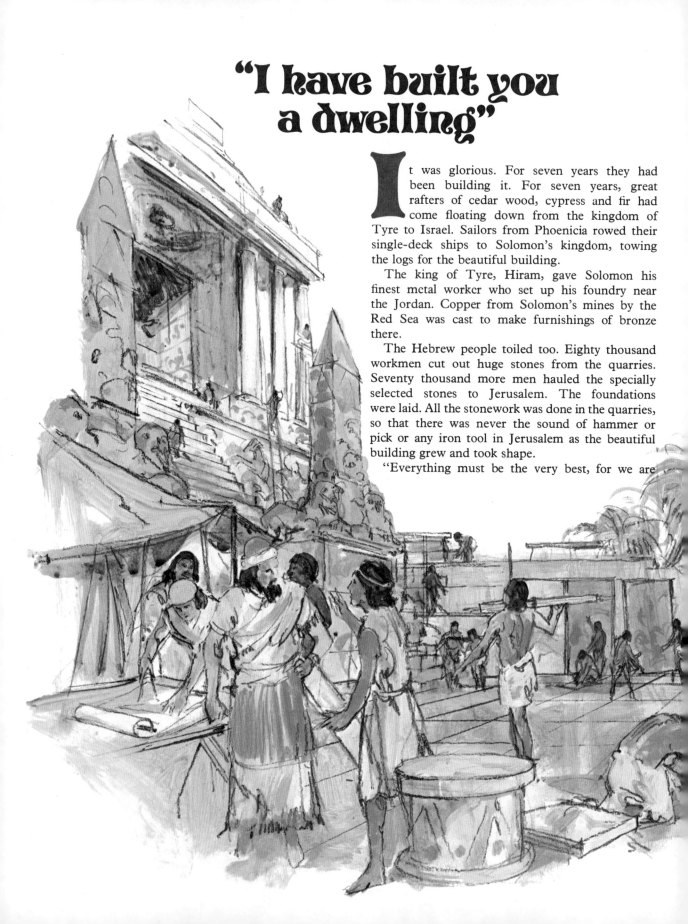

It was glorious. For seven years they had been building it. For seven years, great rafters of cedar wood, cypress and fir had come floating down from the kingdom of Tyre to Israel. Sailors from Phoenicia rowed their single-deck ships to Solomon's kingdom, towing the logs for the beautiful building.

The king of Tyre, Hiram, gave Solomon his finest metal worker who set up his foundry near the Jordan. Copper from Solomon's mines by the Red Sea was cast to make furnishings of bronze there.

The Hebrew people toiled too. Eighty thousand workmen cut out huge stones from the quarries. Seventy thousand more men hauled the specially selected stones to Jerusalem. The foundations were laid. All the stonework was done in the quarries, so that there was never the sound of hammer or pick or any iron tool in Jerusalem as the beautiful building grew and took shape.

"Everything must be the very best, for we are

building God's own Temple," said Solomon. He paid King Hiram well for all his help. He didn't give money, but paid in wheat and pure olive oil. In addition, he gave Hiram twenty towns in the part of Israel known as Galilee.

The Temple was long and narrow. Built beside it was a much bigger courtyard, where the people gathered for worship. In front of the Temple rose two enormous bronze pillars adorned with flowers and pomegranates, all worked in bronze. In the courtyard was an enormous circular container shaped like a fully-blown rose. It held water for the sacrifices and was made of solid bronze, weighing 300 tons.

"My walls are panelled with cedar; the floor is laid with juniper," thought Solomon. "There are carvings in the cedar wood: rosettes and palm trees and winged creatures. Now my Phoenician bronze-worker is plating it all with gold; entirely with gold," he thought with satisfaction. His eyes were closed. He could imagine the sun pouring in, lighting up the glory of gold.

"We'll bring the sacred Ark and let it rest in the Holy of Holies, the innermost shrine," Solomon ordered. "It's windowless and dark. Only one lamp will light up the holy place, and two great, golden-winged creatures will stand there. They are made of olive wood, and covered all with gold. Their wings are spread wide and we will place the Ark in the shelter of their great golden wings."

It was all finished at last. It *was* glorious. They waited till the time came to celebrate the Harvest Thanksgiving and then the priests carried the ark up to the Temple. Solomon and all the people sacrificed many, many oxen and sheep that day, but it was when the priests came out of the Holy of Holies that the real glory filled the whole Temple, brighter than sunlight on gold.

"It is the glory of the Lord," the people whispered. "Look! the priests can no longer perform their duties for the great brightness."

"Our Lord God has come to live in his Holy of Holies!" Solomon cried. "Oh, God, I have built you a dwelling where you can live for ever and ever."

He stretched out his hands toward heaven.

"Lord God of Israel, how good you are!" he exclaimed. "Yet will God really live with men on earth? Why, the heavens, the whole vastness of space are too small to contain you!"

For seven days they celebrated the feast. When they left to go back home to every part of Israel and Judah, they were thrilled. Now at last they dwelt in their promised land. Now they all belonged to one another, God's special people. They knew for sure where they could find God. They would come and worship him in the splendid Temple.

1 Kings 1–8

83

Sweet spices from Sheba

A richly dressed queen went by, riding on her haughty camel. Behind her came a whole procession of camels, each one carrying on his high humped back a precious load. There were boxes of spices, with a smell so wonderful that in the narrow crowded streets, the poor people who watched the queen go by, forgot their hunger for a moment; their senses were filled with the overpowering aroma of costly spices. There were boxes of gold and boxes of precious stones.

As the queen reached the palace, a fleet of ships sailed into the harbour Solomon had built on the shores of the Red Sea. They were laden with costly cargoes, for they carried rare and expensive timbers for his buildings and more precious stones. They were gifts from the queen who had come from Sheba in Arabia to visit Solomon.

"The Queen of Sheba has come to you, sire!" Solomon's courtiers bowed low as they made their announcement. "She has come from her land of spices to do you homage and hear your great wisdom."

"She is welcome," said Solomon gravely, rising from his throne.

They spoke for a long time together, for the queen was wise as well as wealthy, and she had many questions for Solomon, who listened seriously and answered every one, no matter how difficult they seemed to be.

Then he led her through his beautiful palace. It had taken thirteen years to build. The Queen of Sheba gasped in wonder as she saw the beautiful "Hall of the Forest of Lebanon" with its pillars and walls of cedar.

"Truly," she said, finding words at last, "the Hall is well named. I can imagine myself in the cedar woods of Lebanon."

Solomon nodded, well pleased.

"Men from all Israel work for me," he explained. "From the tribes of Israel I sent thirty thousand men in teams to Lebanon, ten thousand men each month. King Hiram of Tyre, who was in charge of the building, had his own men cut down the trees, for there is no one so skilled in all the world at felling trees as the men of Sidon."

The Queen nodded. She had heard that, too.

"My men hauled the logs to the sea. The Phoenician sailors rowed my ships to the ports I chose. Each ship towed the logs behind them across the sea."

"Now they stand, built by your art into a frozen forest," admired the Queen.

They went on together through the Hall of Pillars to the Hall of Justice where Solomon solved the problems of his people who came to him for judgement and justice.

"Wonderful," the Queen looked around the lofty pillars. "You are famed all over the world for your verdicts and the sentences you pronounce. The hearts

of your people surely go out in love and respect to you, O King."

Neither of them realised that Solomon was destroying his kingdom. All his buildings were put up for his own glory and, in order to build them, he had made slaves of the people and divided the ten tribes of Israel – though his own tribe Judah had been left in freedom.

"My father David was a simple man who lived in the wilderness and ate the food of ordinary people," he said as they went on through the Palace. "Here we drink only out of cups of gold."

"The food is prepared," Solomon said. "Daily we eat here ten fatted oxen, twenty free-grazing oxen, roebucks and fattened cuckoos."

"You make my mouth water!" smiled the Queen.

"But first, O Queen, we must offer a sacrifice to our Lord God," said Solomon leading his guest to the Temple, where she stared in amazement at its beauty and exclaimed at the great number of animals Solomon sacrificed daily. But Solomon knew that although he had honoured God by building the Temple, he did not walk with God, as his father had done.

As they went back to the palace to eat, the Queen said softly: "Now I know the source of all your wisdom and strength, King Solomon. God loves Israel so much that he set you on the throne, giving you great glory and making you a wise administrator of law and justice. I'd heard so much of you in my own country, and thought I knew what to expect here, but you've completely taken my breath away! How happy your wives and your servants are!"

She gave Solomon all the immense riches she had brought with her on her camels: the gold and spices and jewels.

After the Queen had gone, laden with many gifts from Solomon in return for hers, the king sat alone on his gold-plated ivory throne. His jewelled hands rested on the arms of the throne. Two carved lions stood at his side, and twelve more stood at his feet, two on each of the six steps that led up to his high throne. David the shepherd boy had killed a ravenous lion in the name of God. Solomon his son sat in splendour, visited by kings and queens, while seventy thousand men toiled for him in his quarries, bearing on their backs great stones, which eighty thousand men had hewn from the hills. In his copper mines by the Red Sea, more men worked underground. All of them had to leave their land, their crops and their sheep, their homes and their families while they worked one month out of every three for Solomon's buildings, for Solomon's glory.

1 Kings 10–11

A torn cloak and golden calves

"That's a fine young lad!" Solomon was strolling through his capital city, watching the builders at work.

"His name is Jeroboam," said one of the officials.

Solomon watched him at work for a few moments. "Jeroboam!" he called. Surprised, the young man put down his tools.

"You come from a noble family, I notice!" Solomon said as Jeroboam bowed before him. "I'm going to put you in charge of all the forced labour. We need officials to organise our work force."

Jeroboam nodded. He knew how bitter everyone felt when Solomon divided up the tribes and forced everyone in Israel to work unpaid for the king. Perhaps it would have not been so bad if Judah had been included, but the tribes of Judah were not forced to work for the king. Jeroboam knew he was being given an important job and he worked hard for the king. He also heard the discontented workmen grumbling as they toiled.

"The tribes are divided," he heard them grumble. "And Solomon is making us work like slaves in our own land."

"And he doesn't keep God's laws, as David used to," grunted one man. "The laws about marrying foreign women and worshipping other gods. Solomon's wives have come from tribes God told us not to choose wives from. Oh, they're all princesses and brought wealth to Solomon from their fathers, but still. . . ."

"He's allowed each wife to build a temple to her god. So, imagine it, there are seven hundred temples to foreign gods right here in Jerusalem!" exclaimed another.

Jeroboam took note of all that was said.

One day he met a holy man, a prophet as Samuel had been. He came from Shiloh, the town where the Ark had been kept before Eli's sons took it into battle with the Philistines.

The holy man wore a fine new cloak. He pulled it off and tore it into twelve long strips.

"Take ten strips for yourself, Jeroboam," he said. "God is going to make you king of the ten tribes of Israel, when Solomon is dead. God is

angry with Solomon but David's family will still reign over Judah. You will be king of Israel, but you must obey all the laws of God."

Jeroboam took the strips of cloth. Could God really be telling him, a widow's son, to become king of Israel? He knew that many people in the ten tribes of Israel would follow him. Carefully he

86

made his plans, but when news reached Solomon that Jeroboam was planning a revolt against him in the name of God, he sent his army which quickly crushed the revolt. They didn't kill Jeroboam, who escaped to Egypt where he stayed until he heard the news of Solomon's death.

At Shechem the tribes of Israel gathered round Solomon's son, Rehoboam. "We will serve you if you will ease the heavy burdens your father gave us to bear," they offered.

Rehoboam hadn't expected this.

"What shall I tell them?" he asked the elders.

"Rehoboam," advised the elders, "a good king knows when to give in to his subjects. Treat these northern tribes fairly and they will be good subjects to you."

But Rehoboam listened to the young men who had grown up with him in the luxury and grandeur of Solomon's palace.

"You're the king, aren't you?" they said. "Prove it to them then! Tell them that Solomon gave them heavy burdens but you will give them a heavier one still!"

"That's right!" Rehoboam agreed. "They'll think I have none of the power and authority of my father, if I give in to them right at the start of my reign."

So he told the people: "My father gave you heavy burdens, I'll make the load even heavier. He beat your backs with whips; I shall use scourges with leaden tips!"

The leaders of Israel answered immediately: "Then we'll have no share in David's kingdom. From now on, look after your own tribe, grandson of David! We're going back to our tents and our flocks!"

So the tribes of Israel streamed away from the labour camps of Judah and returned to their tents. Rehoboam sent an official to them, but they stoned him to death, and Rehoboam had to flee to safety behind the strong walls of Jerusalem.

There he gathered a large army, but a prophet told him:

"You are all brothers. Don't fight against Israel. It is God who has divided your father's kingdom."

Rehoboam obeyed and from then on there were two separate kingdoms: Israel and Judah.

Jeroboam ruled over Israel as the prophet had said. He built a Temple there, so that the people would not have to go to Jerusalem any more. Just as the Ark had winged creatures before it in the Holy of Holies, Jeroboam set up two golden calves, one at Dan and one at Bethel, both of which had been holy places. He chose priests who would be loyal to him.

"It's still the worship of God," thought Jeroboam, but calves were also the symbols of Baal, the pagan god worshipped by the tribes in the area.

The Ark remained in Judah and the small, hilly infertile country remained faithful to God. But in Israel five kings ruled in fifty years.

1 Kings 11–13

The man the ravens fed

What a wedding it was! Ahab, the son of Omri, king of Israel, was marrying the daughter of Ethbaal, the king of Phoenicia, who was also a priest. It was the Phoenicians who were the accomplished sailors of the day. They ventured all over the known world, bringing back merchandise from the most distant corners of the world. They were also skilled builders and craftsmen.

But they were pagans. Their Baal was called Melcart, and because her father had been a priest, a sacred king, Jezebel was a priestess of Baal. How surprised she was to find that the king of Israel, like all the people, was supposed to obey the laws of God.

"Everywhere else the king has the power of a god," she thought. "Of course, we'll worship Baal from now on at the royal palace."

"Ahab, my dear," she told her husband, "I've brought a few priests with me from Tyre. We'll build a little temple to Baal here, won't we?"

"Of course," Ahab said, charmed by her elegance and poise, her gorgeous robes and lovely jewellery.

"Now we must stamp out the worship of this Israelite God," Jezebel told her priests. "The first king of Israel set up golden calves, and of course that's one of the symbols of Baal. Most of the people will happily worship Baal and this God of theirs together. The few who stand against us we will kill."

So Jezebel killed the people who refused to worship Baal and soon it seemed as though Israel would become just another pagan people.

"But never as long as I live and God is still with me," thought Elijah, as he strode, a lonely, gaunt figure, westward over the Jordan from the highlands of Gilead, his home, to Ahab's luxurious palace in Samaria.

"The Lord of Israel is my God," thought Elijah. "That's what my name means."

He lived alone, thinking of God. He wore rough clothing, a coat made of the coarse hair from a goat, fastened with a leather belt.

"God's champion has come to defy Queen Jezebel and her priests," the people told one another. They came flocking to the royal palace to see what would happen.

As Elijah stood before Ahab, his voice rang out

to the farthest corner of the ivory palace: "As the Lord lives, the God of Israel whom *I* serve, I tell you truly, King Ahab, that because of your wickedness there shall be no rain nor even any dew for years until I give the order."

He turned and left the king without a backward look. In the silence they could hear the hardened soles of his bare feet padding across the richly inlaid floor.

"He's like a wolf from the hills," Jezebel shuddered. She and Ahab plotted to kill Elijah, but they couldn't find him throughout the length and breadth of the land.

Led by God, Elijah crossed the Jordan and hid in a little valley beside a small stream. He drank the water of the stream, and in the mornings the ravens, his companions on the lonely hillsides, brought him bread. In the evening they fed him with meat.

One day the stream dried up. "What shall I do now, Lord God?" prayed Elijah.

"Go to the coast to a town called Zarephath in Sidon," he heard God's words in his heart. "A poor widow there will give you food."

Zarephath was nearly a hundred miles away. Elijah felt tired, hungry and thirsty. He saw a poor widow out gathering sticks. "Please could you give me some water to drink?" Elijah asked her. She looked at him. He saw from her face that she was hungry.

"Please, when you bring me water, could you give me as well just a little bread."

"You are the man who follows God," she said. "I believe your God, although I'm a foreigner and I tell you truly that I've not a scrap of bread at home. All that I have is a handful of flour at the bottom of my jar and a drop of oil in my jug. I'm out here gathering sticks so that I can make a fire. I shall knead the oil into the flour, and my son and I will eat our last small loaf. Then we shall die, for we have no more food, and no husband to provide us with any."

"God will help you," Elijah knew it for sure. "Don't be afraid. Go home; do just what you planned, but bring me just a small scone first, then

make another for yourself and your child."

When the widow came back, he hardly knew her. Her face was alight with happiness.

"I took the flour and the oil and made your scone," she said, giving it to him. "But when I went to the jar again, I found still more flour in the jar and oil in the jug. I baked another scone, and there was still flour in the jar and still oil left in the jug.

"God will care for you and your little boy," said Elijah. "Until the drought ends and the rains come, you will always have flour in your jar and oil in your jug."

The famine grew worse everywhere, until even King Ahab became desperate. Led by God Elijah went back to Samaria. He demanded that the people be gathered at Baal's sacred mountain, Mount Carmel. There they would decide, finally, who was God in Israel.

1 Kings 16–18

"Who will send fire?"

A great crowd gathered on the mountain where Baal had been worshipped long before the Hebrew people had come to their promised land. Ahab was there; all the prophets of Baal were there; all the leaders of Israel were there. Elijah was there, fearless because he walked with God in the high barren hills.

"How long are you going to hobble around like this?" he asked the people. "You hop first on one leg, then on another. If the Lord is God, follow him! If Baal is god, why, then, follow him!"

He looked around him, but no one answered a word. They had never thought of this. It had been so easy to call on the name of the God of Israel at his feasts and to follow Baal when they wanted their crops to grow.

"I, I alone am left in Israel as a servant of our God," called Elijah. "There are 400 prophets of Baal. Well then, get two bulls for us. They can prepare one for sacrifice and lay it on an unlit fire. I'll do the same. Then you must call on the name of your god and I shall pray to mine; let's see who will send fire, for the God who does is the one Israel will serve."

"Agreed!" shouted the people.

So from morning to noon, the prophets of Baal danced with hobbling, shuffling steps around their fire, begging Baal to send down fire.

"Baal, O Baal, answer us!" they shouted, but there was no voice and no answer.

At noon Elijah mocked them. "Call a little louder!" he suggested. "He's a god after all. Perhaps he's busy or off on a journey. Perhaps he's asleep. He'll wake up if you shout loudly enough!"

So they shouted louder and, as their religion demanded, they gashed themselves with swords and spears as they danced, and the blood poured down them; but still there was no answer from their god.

Then Elijah said to all the people: "Come closer to me." As the people gathered around, he repaired an altar which some believers in the God of Israel had built not so very long ago, but which had been neglected. All around the altar in the hard dry soil he dug a trench. Then he arranged the wood and laid the bull on top.

"Now fill four jars with water," ordered Elijah. They did as he said and poured the water over the bull and over the wood. They did it three times until the wood and the altar were soaking and water flowed all around the altar into the trench. The thirsty ground soaked up the water but, as they kept filling the enormous water jars, and pouring out the water, the trench around the altar filled with water too.

Then Elijah stepped forward. Simply, without cutting his body with swords, without any ranting or raving, Elijah prayed. "O God of Abraham, Isaac and Jacob, let all the people know that you are God in Israel. Answer me, Lord, so that the people will see that you, their God, are winning back their hearts."

The people looked up into the sky, still and cloudless above them: "Look, look, fire!"

"The fire of the Lord is falling." Like grass before the wind they bowed to the ground, as the fire fell and burnt the sodden wood. Flames leapt around the bull's body, burning it.

"The Lord is God! The Lord is God!" chanted the people, and as a sign that there was no such god as Baal they killed all the priests of Baal.

"Go back to your palace, Ahab," Elijah turned to the King. "Eat and drink your fill for the drought is ended. I hear the sound of rain."

Ahab glanced upwards. There wasn't a cloud to be seen. But he wasn't going to disobey Elijah now in front of all the people. He went back to Samaria to eat and drink, but Elijah with a servant climbed Mount Carmel. At the summit Elijah prayed, his face bowed down to the ground.

"Now go and look out to sea," he told the servant.

"There is nothing to be seen," said the servant, "not a single cloud."

"Go again," said Elijah. "Go seven times." The seventh time the servant called excitedly. "I see a small cloud, no bigger than a man's hand rising from the sea."

"Go and tell Ahab," said Elijah. "Tell him to hurry up before the rain stops him."

Already the sky was swollen and dark with clouds. When the rain came it fell in torrents. Ahab and his chariots fled for shelter in the town of Jezreel but Elijah, his cloak tucked up, outran them and was there before them.

1 Kings 18

90

The storm, the earthquake and the fire

"I'll kill this man. By all the gods I worship, I'll kill this man." In her ivory palace, Queen Jezebel stamped her feet in fury, and Ahab looked on helplessly. "Did Elijah really kill all the priests of Baal? I'll kill him!"

She sent Elijah a messenger. "By this time tomorrow you'll be a dead man!" the queen's message ran. Elijah realised she meant what she said. He fled into Judah and then on into the wilderness. There despair overtook the man who had stood

alone for God in the front of the king, 400 priests of Baal and all the people. He crouched in the shelter of a juniper tree.

"Oh God," he cried out into the loneliness. "I've worked for you, and now I've had enough. I can't go on any more, let me die." Then exhaustion overcame him and he fell asleep. An angel came to him. "God knows you need help," the angel said, touching him. "Look, he has sent you food and drink." Elijah looked up, startled. Freshly-baked bread, smelling so good, lay on hot stones on a fire close by. He ate the bread and felt warm. There was a jug of water near by and he drank it. He lay down to sleep again, comforted, but the angel awoke him again.

"Come, you have a long journey to take. God knows what you need. Eat and drink again." So Elijah ate and drank again and on the strength of the food he travelled right on to the sacred mountain, sometimes called Mount Sinai, sometimes Mount Horeb, where God had met Moses and given him the Law.

God met him there.

"What are you doing here, Elijah?" he heard God's voice.

"I am grieved because the people of Israel have deserted you, Lord. I'm the only one left who is faithful to you and they want to kill me."

"Go!" he heard God say. "Leave the shelter of the rocks. Stand out on the face of the mountain."

"God himself is going to pass this way before my eyes," Elijah thought, trembling, but he obeyed.

The wind swirled around him. It tore at his hair, his rough cloak. It whistled through his ears. He braced himself against it. It tore the mountain and shattered the rocks. Elijah watched and listened for God, but he was not in the storm or the wind.

Then there came an earthquake. The ground beneath him shuddered and rumbled, and Elijah watched and listened for God amid the destruction, but God was not in the earthquake.

After the earthquake came a fire. Flames leapt high among the bracken and scorched the hardy windswept trees. Elijah saw the brightness of the firelight and heard the crackle and the roar, but God was not in the fire.

Elijah understood. "These are the signs God gave to Moses and our ancestors long ago when he gave the Law," he thought. "But now they are just heralds of the coming of God. How will God speak to me now?" he wondered.

Everything on the mountain was very still. Hardly a breath of wind blew, just enough to set the singed leaves sighing. God's voice came to Elijah in the quiet. It came as softly as the gentle puffs of wind; hushed as the voices of friends when they tell their secrets, and when Elijah heard it he went forward to meet God.

"What are you doing here, Elijah?" Elijah, the lonely man, proud and fearless, a man with many enemies and few friends, could have wept. "God understands my loneliness," he thought.

"I'm alone, Lord God," he said again. "No one in Israel except me loves you."

"Go Elijah. Am I not the King of kings? I will use the kings of Damascus and Israel to work out my plans. So go and anoint Jehu as king of Israel. Anoint Hazael as the king of Syria, and I shall use them to work for me. Between them they will kill all those who worship Baal. Find Elisha. Anoint him as prophet to succeed you. He will be your friend. Besides him there are seven thousand men in Israel, the real people of Israel, who have remained true to me and never worshipped Baal."

Comforted, Elijah left Horeb and found Elisha who was ploughing, guiding two oxen who were kept together by a wooden yoke. Elisha broke up the plough and made a fire, cooked the oxen and gave the meat to the men who were ploughing with him. Then he turned away and followed Elijah. God had given his lonely spokesman a servant and a friend, who would carry out the tasks God had given him.

1 Kings 19

The fallen cloak

"How the people honour you, my father!" Elisha was walking towards Jericho with Elijah. They were silent, for they both felt God was speaking to them, warning them that soon Elijah would die.

"You must leave me at Jericho, please," Elijah said. "Wait in the town for me. God is telling me to go on to the Jordan alone."

"I won't leave you!" declared Elisha. "You know how much you mean to us all. Do you know, they even have a saying: 'Elijah is more to Israel than the king's chariots and war horses.'"

In Jericho, Elijah found that God had been right and that there were others in Israel who had remained true to God. He found a whole group of disciples there who formed a kind of brotherhood. Many of them followed as Elijah and Elisha went on to the Jordan. They all felt that Elijah was about to die. They knew he had lived alone far from cities and the haunts of men. They knew that God had spoken to him on the high hills.

"He is the hope of Israel. He has kept our people true to God," they said.

"What will we do when he is dead?"

"I don't believe he will die," one young man said suddenly. "I'm sure God will just take him away from our eyes, and that one day he'll return suddenly, straight from God."

"Oh, oh, look," another shouted. "I see Elijah and Elisha walking over the Jordan. Elijah is barefoot as usual, but Elisha's sandals and long robe aren't even wet."

"The water has divided, as it did for Joshua!" Meanwhile Elisha and Elijah travelled on into the desert.

They said little, but finally Elijah asked if he could do anything more for Elisha before they were parted.

Elisha responded quickly. "Let me inherit the full share of your spiritual power," he pleaded.

"That is a hard thing for me to grant," said Elijah gravely, "but if you see me as I am taken away from you, then you shall have it."

And as they walked on, suddenly Elijah was taken away. To Elisha it seemed like horses and a chariot of fire which swept the prophet heavenwards in a great whirl of wind.

Elisha clutched at Elijah's fallen cloak and then ripped his own clothes as a sign of grief.

Then he turned back toward the Jordan. The group that had followed Elisha and Elijah to the river saw him coming.

"Here comes Elisha with Elijah's cloak. Look, he's touched the water with his master's cloak, and the water has parted again."

"God is telling us that he is going to be with Elisha too, just as he was with Elijah."

They ran to meet him and bowed to the ground.

"You are the servant of God!" they cried. "We are your servants, Elisha."

2 Kings 2

Followers of God

Elisha was loved by all the ordinary people. He helped make their hard lives easier. During a famine, Elisha came to one of the many poor bands of people known as the disciples of the prophets. Debt and poverty had driven many of them away from the villages and small towns to band together. Some of them were outlaws, men who sought shelter in the sanctuaries which God's Law had provided for such people. Once, when they gathered eagerly around a pot of soup, someone shouted: "Don't eat it! There are poisonous herbs in the pot." But Elisha threw a handful of meal into the pot and they all ate their fill without coming to harm.

Another time he fed a hundred hungry men with twenty barley loaves, and on yet another occasion he helped a man find his lost axe head. It was made of iron and the man was upset because he had borrowed it and must give such a precious tool back to its owner.

So Elisha, who was respected in the royal courts, was welcomed by rich and poor alike up and down the country. With God's help he revived a little boy who had died of sunstroke and whose mother, a wealthy woman, furnished a room in her house with a bed, a table, a stool and a candlestick – real luxuries when most people sat on the floor or slept on sleeping mats. She gave this room to Elisha to use as his own whenever he came to her town.

In far away Syria a little Hebrew slave girl found her mistress sitting crying one day. "What is the matter?" the little girl asked.

"My husband is ill," sobbed the woman. "He has leprosy. Oh! Just think of it! He's the commander of the king's army. He'll lose his job and everything."

"If he could only go to Elisha the prophet in my homeland," said the little girl. "He would be cured immediately."

"Oh do you think so? I'll tell him right away. He's such a good man and a fine soldier. I'm sure the King will let him go."

"Of course you can go," said the king to his commander, Naaman. "Well, we must do it properly. Now the person to go to is the king. He's always the one who knows everything – things of state and things from the gods." He gave Naaman a letter, "Please heal this man of leprosy."

"What does this mean?" the king of Israel wondered. "Does he think I'm a god? He's trying to pick a quarrel with me, that's what it is. If I don't heal his commander, he's sure to come and fight us."

Elisha sent a message to the king. "Let him come to me. He will find that God has his prophet in Israel."

Naaman was surprised, but he went off to Elisha's house with his large procession of servants and followers. He was even more surprised when Elisha didn't come to the door himself but sent a servant.

"Go and wash in the Jordan seven times."

"What's this? I was thinking he'd come out with all his magic powers, and pray and chant and heal me. We've got two beautiful rivers in Damascus. Think of our lovely Abanah river, crystal clear, and its tributary the Pharpar is just as lovely. Couldn't I have gone and bathed in them?" He went stamping off in a rage.

"Oh, please do what the prophet tells you," his

servants begged him. "You would have obeyed him without hesitation if he had asked you to do some difficult thing, wouldn't you?"

Naaman calmed down. He went and washed seven times and returned to Elisha cured of his disease, humble and openly thanking God. Elisha refused to accept any of the presents Naaman offered. "Well, allow me to take something back with me then," asked Naaman. "I want to worship your God. I'll be his servant from now on. Only he's the God of Israel. This is his country. So please let me take back as much earth as two of my mules can carry. Then I'll stand on ground that has come from Israel and I'm sure the God of Israel will hear me. Only, and may the Lord God forgive me, please, it's part of my job to go with my master the king to the temple. He leans on my arm and when he bows in worship to Rimmon, the god of storms, please will God forgive me if I bow down when my master does?"

Elisha smiled at Naaman. "Go in peace," he said. "I impose no strict rules upon you. You have given yourself to God. He speaks to the hearts of his servants. He will guide you to the right path."

So Naaman went back to his wife and a happy little slave girl, glad to find that not only had her master been healed but that he had become a worshipper of her God.

When Elisha died, he left behind him many people who had come to love God. They treasured all the old stories of the heroes of God. They were the real people of Israel who remained true to the ways of God.

Finally Elisha carried out the two tasks that Elijah had been unable to finish before he died.

Sadly, knowing the danger to Israel, Elisha anointed Hazael to be king of Syria. Before long Hazael and his army swept through Israel, killing without mercy, carrying off many captives.

"So the people who followed Baal now cry out to God," Elisha thought, turning to the task that lay before him in Israel.

There he sent one of his followers to anoint Jehu, the commander of the Army to be king of Israel. Elisha was aware of the great changes this would bring in Israel. Part of Jehu's commission was to kill all those who remained of Ahab's family. Jezebel was one.

But though Jehu was thorough about the slaughter, he was less thorough in his observance of God's Law. And he failed to destroy the two golden calves set up by Jeroboam so long before.

2 Kings 3–9

The roar of a lion

The stars were bright above the lonely hills of Judah. Amos the shepherd, wrapped in his rough garments, couldn't sleep that night. He kept looking up at the swirling glory above him.

"God made the stars, the Pleiades and Orion. He brings the dark and he makes the dawn. Our God walks with the rushing wind on the heights of the world. He is mightier than the sea, for he made the waters and poured them out over the land. He is stronger than the forts men build."

Dawn came. Amos watched it wearily and welcomed it gladly. At night the wild beasts, lions and

bears drew closer to the sheep. Once a lion had come roaring upon his flock. The frightened sheep had scattered in all directions. When the sun rose next morning, their pasture was empty except for remains of the sheep.

"Is God a lion?" Amos thought suddenly. "Might he roar? Might he destroy his flock?"

The thought weighed him down as he made his way northwards to sell wool in the markets of Israel.

"Israel is rich now. For forty years there has been no danger of foreign soldiers or invaders, and the king has extended his kingdom. It's nearly as big as David's kingdom, but what a difference!" Amos thought as he strode past great stone houses, surrounded by vineyards. Poor people toiled there. A few years ago this land had been theirs; they each owned a little plot of it and were neighbourly to one another, helping one another out when times were bad.

Amos stopped to watch. He saw a young boy trudge over in the direction of the cattle shed.

"The family that own this estate keep young calves in there and fatten them for their meat," the boy replied in answer to Amos' questions.

"Do you ever eat meat?" Amos asked, looking at the boy's thin cheeks and bony shoulders. "I thought not. Have you always worked here?"

"Yes, well, that is for almost as long as I can remember. But there was a time a long, long time ago – I sometimes think it was all a dream, when my father was alive and we children just played at home. Oh, we had a goat to look after and there were plenty

of jobs to do, but it wasn't the same. We weren't slaves."

"Father died," he went on. "Mother borrowed money from the rich man who owns that fine house. But she couldn't pay back. He made her pay much more than she's borrowed . . ."

"I know," Amos said bitterly. "It's called interest."

"Yes, so we became his slaves and they took our little plot of land."

"And now *you* never have meat, for the rich like to eat meat and they can afford to buy it and so the price goes higher and higher. And there's never any oil for the lamps or for cooking in the homes of the peasants who aren't yet slaves," Amos went on. "For these rich folk, men and women, lavishly anoint themselves with perfumes made of oil. They lie in beds of ivory. They build summer houses and winter houses, all the work of the poor."

He could hardly bear to say good-bye to the little boy. "God's ways aren't like this!" he thought. "Yet these people keep all the religious feasts. Who will speak to them? Who will speak for God?"

It was the same in the market. There he saw how the merchants cheated, using false weights and measures. They even sneaked the dust and bits of straw from the barn floors into the grain the poorest housewives bought for bread.

At the city gates where the law courts were held, Amos saw how the needy were turned away because they couldn't pay the wealthy judges. He watched the judge strip a young man's clothing off his back as payment for a pledge. He saw judges take bribes from anyone who could afford to pay – even a pair of sandals could make a judge change his decision.

"Who will speak to them?" Amos wondered, remembering that when the lion roars, the shepherd must rush to save his flock as best he can.

"But, Lord God," he was tense now, afraid, puzzled. "I'm from a peasant family. I'm not a member of a group of prophets." The storm raged inside his heart as he went back to his sheep in the hills. There, in the silence God's voice came again

and again, until it was like the roaring of a lion among the rocks and Amos knew the time had come for him to go back to Israel.

People mocked him as he stood in the bustling market-place of Bethel and shouted out: "God cares for the needy you neglect. God will punish you for your evil ways. Listen, Israel, God has chosen you above all the families of the earth. You think this means that you can wait for him to destroy your enemies for you. God has roared from Zion and you who lie about half-drunk on couches of ivory shall be snatched away like sheep."

"Listen to this nonsense," they jeered.

"Your religion is empty. It's all a show," Amos shouted. "It won't help you, nor will the strong walls of Samaria."

But Bethel was a royal city where the sacred shrine with its golden calf stood. The priests sent a message to the king. "You've got a traitor here!" Then they jeered at Amos. "Go on, prophet. Get back to Judah, you lunatic, and earn your food there with your wild words."

Amos told them, "I'm no prophet. I'm a simple shepherd, but God took me from my flock and said, 'Go and speak for me to my people Israel'." But they threw him out of their city. They refused to listen to what he had to say.

Amos went back to his own hills in Judah. He had failed after all, it seemed.

"I have not failed, for love does not fail," God's voice in his heart comforted the lonely shepherd. "They will listen one day."

He knew that what God said was true and if the people refused to listen to him, God would still go on speaking to them about his love for them. Other prophets would come, each one with a timeless message from God to the people of his day.

Amos 1–9

The song in the market-place

It was market day. But today all the people who had come along to buy and to sell had a surprise. One of the leading statesmen of Judah, almost as well-known as the king himself, was standing in the market.

"Look, it's Isaiah himself."

"Yes, he's the only person who wasn't afraid when the kings of Israel and Syria marched against us in the days of King Ahaz, the older people reminisced. "Ahaz went nearly mad with fear. Isaiah alone kept calm. Do you know what he said? 'Don't worry, King Ahaz! The kings of Syria and Israel are just like damp firecrackers. They'll hiss and spit for a bit, and then they'll go right out'."

The people laughed.

"But what a pity the king didn't listen to Isaiah," someone said seriously. "Ahaz sent a desperate message of help to the mighty Assyrians. Isaiah was right. Soon Israel and Samaria were completely conquered."

They shuddered. It was a terrible thing to fall to the ruthless conquering armies of Assyria.

"They became our friends, but look what it's done for us." They dropped their voices. For now in their own Temple was a copy of the altar of the gods of Assyria, and each year enormous supplies of grain and wine and gold went to the Emperor as payment for his help.

"But listen! Isaiah's standing there singing."

"A song I'll sing about my friend
Who dug a field from end to end;
He cleared the stones and dug the soil –
For love he thought it little toil.
The choicest vines hour after hour
He planted, then he built his tower.
His vines were dug; his winepress, too,
But at harvest time the grapes were few.
The poor man cried: 'My grapes are sour
Although I worked here hour by hour'."

"Poor man," the people sympathized, applauding. "That's a good song, Isaiah. Go on."

Isaiah smiled. He was trying to teach the people something about God.

"Yes, it's a good song and bad luck for my friend. But now I ask you what more my poor friend could do for the vineyard he chose so carefully."

"Nothing," they all agreed. "Once the grapes have gone sour, there's nothing to be done."

"Yes," said Isaiah, "and so my friend is going to tear down the fences, and let the vineyard return to pastureland. It will be trampled on by cattle and sheep. He won't prune it, or hoe it any more – it will become all overgrown."

The people looked upset. Did the vineyard really deserve this treatment? What was Isaiah trying to teach them? He spoke again, "Let me finish the song for you:

"Israel is the vineyard's name,
Judah's the vine from which there came
No justice, only lawlessness;
Bloodshed; a long cry of distress."

This time the people glanced uneasily at each other in silence. They hadn't expected this!

"God is holy!" cried Isaiah. "For in the year when our good King Uzziah died, a lonely man with leprosy, I saw the Lord God."

They were hanging on to his words now, hushed.

"Yes," the nobleman went on. "I was in the Temple and I saw him seated on a high throne. Winged seraphs hovered above him crying to one another: 'Holy, Holy Holy!'

"'That is the word they used," Isaiah told the people. "Holy, set apart and pure is the Lord God of heaven and earth. His glory fills the whole earth.

"I fell down wretched and unworthy to look on God. But one of the seraphs touched my lips with a live coal he had taken glowing from the altar fire. 'Now you are clean,' he said, and it was then I heard the voice of God."

"What did he say?" they wondered.

"'Whom shall I send? Who will be my messenger?'" Isaiah told them. "And I said: 'Here am I, Lord, send me'."

"Then God told me that the invading armies will drive all our people away from our land. The countryside will be stripped bare. Yet a few, a very few will remain, and they will be the fruitful vine; their grapes will be sweet, for they will delight in the Lord God and obey him."

Mighty God, prince of peace

All the people of Jerusalem, from the king in his palace to the poorest family in the city's close crowded buildings were frightened.

For two kings had marched with their armies right up to their city and tried to lay siege to it. The king of Israel and the king of Syria had joined together against Judah.

"The King and all his people are shaking with fear." Isaiah heard God's voice. "Go and tell the king not to be afraid but to trust in me."

So Isaiah took his little boy with him and went to meet the king.

"Pay attention to me, King Ahaz," he said. "For there's no need to be afraid. Listen, the kings of Syria and Israel are like two damp firecrackers. They'll splutter and hiss and then they'll go out without even a bang. God has told me this but if you do not stand by our Lord God, you will not stand at all."

Ahaz, who had already sacrificed one of his sons to the pagan god Molech did not have Isaiah's faith in God. "I am the king," he thought, when Isaiah had gone. "It's *my* capital city that two powerful kings are besieging. Oh! If only they'd go away! I must have help. Some other king more powerful than these two must come and help me."

He paced up and down his palace. "I wish my heart would stop trembling inside me," he clutched his side. "It's throbbing like the boughs of the trees when the wind roars through the woods."

He sat down, his knees were weak. God spoke to him.

"Ahaz, won't you trust your God? Ask me for a sign. I am with you."

Ahaz was more frightened than ever.

"Oh, no!" he exclaimed, starting up again. "No," he argued with himself, "I mustn't ask God for a sign. I mustn't put him to such a test."

But Isaiah the prophet knew how false King Ahaz really was, and he had a word from God for him.

"Listen, now, Ahaz, ruler on David's throne, listen to God.

You, with your many fears, sorely my patience you try:

But now you are trying the patience of God. Therefore hear:

For the Lord himself will give you a sign: a child will come;

A child borne by a young girl: Immanuel is his name:

Immanuel, God is with us, that is his name."

Ahaz would not listen to Isaiah's words. He sent a frantic message to the king of Assyria whose armies were soon to conquer the world of that day. "Oh King," fawned Ahaz, "I, Ahaz of Judah am your servant. I place myself under your protection. Come and rescue me from the kings of Syria and Israel."

The powerful king of Assyria drove away the two invading armies, but Ahaz had to pay dearly. The Assyrians demanded tribute money from the countries who, out of fear, signed alliances with them. Ahaz took all the silver and gold from the glorious Temple of the Lord and sent it to the Assyrians. Then, when his enemies were defeated, he bowed down to the false gods of Assyria and made an exact model of the altar in the Assyrian Temple of Damascus. This pagan altar stood in the Temple of God.

Then Isaiah wrote down on a scroll which he passed on to his followers the words that God gave him:

"Against you, O Judah, the Lord will pour out a deep fast flowing flood. The waters will spread All over your land. An army will conquer:
Assyria's might engulfs all your land. Yet
It is God you must fear: the Lord you must dread.
He is your sanctuary; your stumbling stone too.

Blackness spreads over you: there's nothing but night.

Look now! Rejoice!
The people of darkness have seen a great light!
Deep lurked the shadow, now God shines a light.
For now a child is born for ever for us;
Our God has given a son to us;
On his shoulder dominion's laid for us
From this time onwards for ever he'll reign.
Prince of Peace, Mighty God is His Name.

The Kings of Judah had disappointed their people time and time again. For there were still many, who, like Isaiah wanted to follow God's ways. When they saw one after another of their kings fail them they started to hope for a King who would come from God. He would be greater than David. He would bring them peace and his kingdom would never end.

The hope grew and spread, the hope of Israel in their Promised King.

Isaiah 7–9, 11

Sennacherib, the king of the universe

Isaiah sat writing on a long parchment scroll: "In the fourteenth year of King Hezekiah," his pen scratched out the words. "Sennacherib, the King of Assyria, attacked all the fortified cities of Judah and captured them one by one . . ."

What a proud man the Assyrian king was! Isaiah remembered. What boastful words he had used to describe himself! "I am the favourite of the great gods . . . the perfect hero . . . the first among all the princes." Isaiah smiled to himself, remembering the empty boasts.

He recalled how Hezekiah had taken fright when Sennacherib captured the fort at Lachish only thirty miles away from Jerusalem. What a cringing message Hezekiah had sent to the ruler of the ruthless Assyrian armies! "I submit myself to whatever you impose on me." The tax was so heavy that Hezekiah had to turn over all the silver in the Temple and in his palace.

"Don't send such a message," Isaiah had advised the king. "Trust God, instead of entering into alliances with foreign powers."

As usual Hezekiah hadn't listened, but he realised Isaiah had been right when the cupbearer of the invading king came and taunted the frightened citizens of Jerusalem in their own language: "Don't trust King Hezekiah! He's powerless! Don't let him persuade you to rely on your God either! Has any god of any nation saved his country from the armies of Assyria? Do you think that your God will be able to save Jerusalem? Listen to mighty King Sennacherib who says, 'Make peace with me and everyone of you will eat and drink your food safely in your own homes until I come and deport you. . . . It will be to a country very like your own, a land with corn and wine in plenty'."

The people trembled, but said nothing, for King Hezekiah had ordered them all to keep quiet. The cupbearer went away: "Sennacherib is nearly at your gates," he warned.

Only Isaiah remained calm. "God won't let the Assyrian king enter his holy city," he reassured anxious King Hezekiah. "Sennacherib will return the way he came. God will protect his own city."

That night the Assyrians prepared to march against Jerusalem. Then they lay down to sleep. Plague swept through the camp. In the early morning, when it was time to get up, 185,000 corpses lay in their tents. The survivors tossed the bodies of the dead hurriedly into a grave outside Lachish and fled before an enemy that even their mighty king could not conquer.

The people at Jerusalem went wild with joy and relief. They crowded around Hezekiah, rejoicing. They ran up to the tops of their houses and danced on the flat roofs.

One man turned away from the jubilant, boisterous crowds. Isaiah was shattered. For years he had longed for Hezekiah to see that his enemies were overcome because he trusted in God.

"They still haven't learnt to believe in you, Lord," he thought. For three years Isaiah the statesman had laid aside his soft garments and had walked naked and barefoot through the streets of Jerusalem, acting out what would happen to the people if they entered into alliances with the other nations instead of trusting God to win their battles for them.

"One day Jerusalem will be destroyed," thought Isaiah bitterly.

People stared curiously at their prophet as he walked away weeping.

Isaiah 36–39

Scarecrows in a melon patch

Isaiah was dead – cruelly murdered, people whispered. A few people remembered his words, but they seemed an impossible dream. For in Jerusalem terrible things were being done. The Assyrian gods were worshipped. Witchcraft and magic darkened peoples' lives and filled them with fear. Worst of all, in the valley called Ge-Hinnom just outside the city walls, the king had set up the statue of a god called Molech. In order to worship Molech, people had to sacrifice not animals but their own children. Little babies were burnt alive before the statue of the god whose arms were held open before him, but not in love. He was greedily reaching out for more and more cruel sacrifices.

The king killed his own son there before the statue of Molech. Finally his little grandson who became king.

King Josiah was only eight years old, but he was a very good king. He longed to rebuild the Temple and rid it of all the idols. When he was twenty-one he heard a prophet shouting in Jerusalem:

"These false gods the other nations make are nothing but scarecrows in a melon patch, and they're just as dumb! They have to be carried along; they cannot walk by themselves. Don't be frightened of them. They can do no harm – nor any good either!"

The prophet was a shy young man from the country. Josiah liked his words. "Rebuild the Temple!" he ordered.

Carpenters, builders and masons got busy at once. They mended, rebuilt and shifted the rubble.

"Look, what's this?" One of them lifted up a musty old parchment scroll. He blew off some of the dust and took the scroll to the high priest who read it. He took it at once to the king's secretary who in turn took it to the king.

"Read it aloud," King Josiah said.

"Hear O Israel! The Lord our God is one God.

You shall love the Lord with all your heart, with all your soul and with all your might."

King Josiah sat bolt upright now, listening hard. "God does not think one person better than another," the secretary read on. "He cares for the little children who have no father. He loves the foreigners who come to live in your country. You must love the foreigners, too, for you were foreigners in Egypt. You must not think one person better than another. You must never take a bribe. Your weights and measures must be perfectly accurate, and when you gather in your harvest be sure to leave some corn in the field, some olives on the bough and some grapes on the vine for the poor to eat."

King Josiah leapt down from his throne. He took off his crown and tore his royal garments.

"God must be furious and his anger must be blazing against us, because no one in Jerusalem, in Judah or in Israel obeys what he commands in this book."

.Josiah set to work at once. He made the new Law, so long forgotten, part of his country's laws. He drove away all the heathen altars and smashed the statue of Molech to pieces. The valley of Ge-Hinnom became the rubbish dump of Jerusalem. Josiah even sent out orders that all the altars to God in every other part of the countryside except for Jerusalem were to be destroyed. He did this to make sure that people would come to Jerusalem and worship God properly there. A great Passover Feast was held in Jerusalem to celebrate the finding of the new law and to promise before God that it would be kept.

At first, carried along by the King's enthusiasm, everyone obeyed. But soon the people slid back to their old ways. Jeremiah watched these events. At first he rejoiced, but later he realized that his work was not over, that the people still had to learn to love God and obey his laws.

2 Chronicles 33

A prophet to the nations

A shy young man lived happily in the country in a little village called Anaboth, four miles from Jerusalem. His name was Jeremiah. Jeremiah's father was a priest at the local shrine. The family worked in the rocky, barren patch of land in the village and the priest led the people in worship. Ever since he was a small child, Jeremiah had felt that he belonged to God in a special way, but some years ago God had spoken directly to him. It had been early spring. The trees were still bare; the brown buds were tightly shut, but the first small flowers had blossomed on the almond tree.

"I have appointed you to be a prophet to the nations."

"Oh, Lord, no!" Jeremiah had cried. "Look, I don't know how to speak. And I'm so young. No one will listen to me."

"Don't be afraid. I will go with you and I'll care for you," God told him.

Then Jeremiah felt his lips throb.

"God has touched my mouth," he knew and he felt more confident at once.

"Jeremiah!" God said. "Look, what do you see here?"

Jeremiah looked up. "Lord, I see a branch of almond, 'the watchful tree' we call it because it's alert and watchful for the earliest signs of spring."

"I am like the watchful tree," said God. "I watch over my word to see it fulfilled."

So Jeremiah left his little village and went to great bustling Jerusalem. It was there that King Josiah had heard him crying out against the false gods.

For five years Jeremiah stood in the crowded market place and told the people things they did not like. . . .

"Do you know what you're like?" he shouted. "You're like a camel gone mad, charging in all directions at once. Look up: the storks are flying northward. They know the right moment to leave their homes for the cooler lands of the north. The cooing turtle-dove, the fork-tailed swallow and the long-legged crane all know when to fly – but you don't know the words that God has given us to guide us."

Then Josiah found the Law. Jeremiah was happy. He hoped that everything would be better. Perhaps his task was finished and he could go home.

"No, Jeremiah," God warned him. "For Josiah's men have pulled down the altar at Anathoth. Instead of being glad, the people are furious. Your own family are trying to kill you. It's not safe for you to go home now; besides you are my prophet."

Jeremiah was heart-broken. Not go home? He loved his village and the quiet land around. How he had longed for it as he stood shouting for God in the crowded streets of Jerusalem, where no grass grew, no little birds sang.

"My tent is destroyed," he wept. "All my ropes are snapped and no one is left to put up my tent again."

"My Temple was broken," God told him. "My people turned away from me."

"Yes, Lord. I know, and I know that you are with me even though my own family have turned against me."

"You are my prophet, Jeremiah. I said I would go with you."

Jeremiah 1–2

"A fire burning within me"

The mighty empire of the Assyrians had disappeared. New kings held power, especially the king of Babylon. When the Assyrians were losing ground everywhere, the Egyptians went over to help them. King Josiah bravely set out to attack the Egyptians and cut them off from the Assyrian army. He was killed, and a weak king ruled instead of him. His name was Jehoiakim and he quickly gave way to the Egyptians and to Nebuchadnezzar, the king of Babylon.

"We want to be free from the yoke of Babylon!" people said.

Jeremiah took a big heavy earthenware jug. In front of the people he smashed it into pieces on the ground.

"Who can mend it now?" he asked, but no one answered. It was broken beyond repair. "Judah is going to be broken like that earthenware pot!" The priests in the Temple were furious.

"Beat that man!" So Jeremiah was beaten, and then had to sit all day and all through the night in the stocks like a criminal. Everyone who went past stopped to jeer at him.

Next morning, stiff, cold and wretched, he stumbled away.

"Oh God, you are stronger than I am!" he groaned. "I'm the laughing stock of the city. You keep telling me to prophesy violence and ruin, but it never comes. Being your prophet means insults and scorn for me day after day. Yet whenever I rebel in my heart, and say I won't think about God any more, then there seems to be a fire burning inside me and I have to speak." He walked on slowly. "O God, I know you will look after me," he said, and suddenly found himself with a song coming to his lips.

"Sing, oh sing to the Lord. Praise the Lord.

He looks after the needy and saves the poor from evil people."

Jeremiah 19–20

The words the fire could not put out

The weak King Jehoiakim sat in his winter house, warming his hands at a fire that burned in a metal bucket with holes in its sides.

"What's this you're telling me?"

"Jeremiah's scribe Baruch has been reading aloud from a scroll he's written. Jeremiah can't go to the Temple any more – we've banned him. But he's got round our ruling by sending his scribe to read out his messages."

"Yes, sire," one official added. "The scroll contained every word of prophecy that Jeremiah has spoken from the days of King Josiah until now, and Baruch read it in the upper court where every single person could hear him."

"Read me this scroll!" the king ordered. "What a trouble-maker Jeremiah is!" he added.

To the alarm of all the officials, every time a few lines were read to him, King Jehoiakim took a knife that scribes used and slashed off long ribbons of the scroll. Then he burnt them in his fire.

"Don't burn the scroll," the officials begged the king in horror. "God might be angry . . ." their voices trailed away.

"Now find me Jeremiah and Baruch!" thundered the King when the scroll had been burnt.

But they were nowhere to be found. Some of the more sympathetic officials had advised them to hide. And God had kept his spokesman safe.

Safe in hiding Baruch again took his reed pen, dipped it into ink and wrote down all the words that God had spoken to Jeremiah. This scroll was not burnt. The words lived on and were read and treasured as the centuries went by. From them people learnt many of the wonderful things about God that Jeremiah had found out in his suffering.

"Moses made a covenant between God and the Israelite people," Jeremiah told Baruch and others who would listen. "But I tell you something far more wonderful. God has revealed to me that the days are coming when God will make a new covenant with Israel and Judah. They broke the old covenant, but this covenant will be planted deep within the heart of every single person. God says: 'I will plant my law in every person's heart and everyone from the youngest to the oldest, the humblest to the mightiest will know the Lord'."

"Oh, Jeremiah," Baruch sighed. "And will God forgive all our sins too?"

"It is God who speaks," repeated Jeremiah. "'I will forgive their sins and never think about them any more'."

Those words could not be burnt. Like seed hidden in the soil, they took root deeply and when the time was ready they grew and flowered and bore fruit.

Jeremiah 36
Jeremiah 31

The ruined city

The throne of Judah belonged to one weak descendant of Josiah after another. Finally a man named Zedekiah became king. He was a puppet king in the hands of the mighty Nebuchadnezzar of Babylon. Zedekiah didn't listen to Jeremiah either. He pinned his hopes not on God but on Pharaoh's army, which had come marching from Egypt.

"They're coming to help me against Nebuchadnezzar," thought Zedekiah.

"No!" said Jeremiah. "Pharaoh's army will withdraw to their own land. The Babylonians will attack Jerusalem and capture it and burn it down. Oh, Zedekiah, give in to them before it's too late. Surrender to them and save the city."

Zedekiah refused to listen. "Surrender! That's the coward's way," he said. But really he was afraid – afraid of all the officials Nebuchadnezzar had planted in his court and of the Jews who had already been taken to Babylon.

The armies of Nebuchadnezzar besieged Jerusalem. During a pause in the siege Jeremiah tried to leave the city.

"Halt," cried the sentry on duty at Benjamin Gate.

"I'm going to Anathoth where they've given me some land." Jeremiah stopped in his tracks. "I want to look over my inheritance."

"You're deserting us! You're going over to the Babylonian armies."

"That's a lie!"

But no one would listen. Jeremiah was beaten and put in an underground cell in a house which had been turned into a prison. He stayed there for a

long time, forgotten and hungry, for the rations were low.

One day Zedekiah sent for him in secret.

"Oh, how long can this siege go on?" the King wondered. "Is there any word from God?"

"God is always ready to speak to us. Only you will never listen or obey him," said Jeremiah. "God says that you are going to be handed over to the Babylonians, King Zedekiah."

They looked at each other. "Oh, Zedekiah," pleaded Jeremiah. "What harm have I ever done to you or our people that you put me in prison? I'll die if I go back to the underground cell."

Zedekiah was frightened that God, whom he never obeyed, might punish him if he killed God's prophet. "All right," he said, and Jeremiah was put in a better room and fed a loaf a day until there was no more bread left in the city.

But he still spoke out the words that God had given him: "Surrender to the Babylonians and all will be well with you. If you remain in the city, God says, you will all die by the sword or famine or plague."

"What nonsense!" the leaders complained to King Zedekiah. "It's too much. Kill that gloomy prophet. He's disheartening our soldiers."

Poor, helpless Zedekiah said weakly, "He's in your hands as you know. I can't do anything against you."

They took Jeremiah and tied a rope round his shoulders. Then they let him down into the well in the courtyard. There was no water in the well, only mud, and deep down into the mud Jeremiah sank. They left him there to die of starvation.

But one of the servants of the court, a man from far away Ethiopia, heard that Jeremiah had been treated so cruelly.

"My lord King," protested the African, whose name was Ebed-melech, "that's an evil, cruel thing they've done to Jeremiah. He'll die in that well."

So the king said, "All right, pull him out of the well."

Ebed-melech went into the storehouse wardrobe and fetched some rags. He lowered the rags and some cords to tie over them.

"These rags are for you to put under your arms. Tie them there with the cords, then when we pull you up the rope won't cut into you," he called.

Gratefully Jeremiah tied the rags in place. Then they hauled him out of the well.

Once again Zedekiah came secretly to him. He still wanted to know what God was saying.

"This city will be burned down, unless you surrender," Jeremiah repeated. "You will be led away a prisoner."

Zedekiah clutched his head. "But suppose I surrender and the Babylonian soldiers hand me over to the Jews who have been taken away in captivity? They'll certainly be cruel to me."

So he would not listen to Jeremiah.

It was the last conversation they ever had. Nebuchadnezzar's great battering rams finally made a breach in the city wall and all the high-ranking officers of Babylon marched into Jerusalem.

Zedekiah tried to escape. He was captured. Before his eyes the Babylonians killed his sons. Then they blinded him and led him away in chains.

Jerusalem became a smoking, ruined city. The palace was burnt down, the high walls demolished and all the treasures of gold and silver and ivory were carried away to Babylon. Jeremiah's prophecies had come true. Doom had come to Judah.

The Babylonians had heard of Jeremiah. They gave him a choice. He could stay in Jerusalem with the few who remained or go to Babylon where he would be treated with honour. He chose to stay, encouraging the people to believe in God and follow his law. But the people would not listen. They rebelled again and when the Babylonians attacked were forced to flee to Egypt, taking a protesting Jeremiah with them.

Jeremiah died in Egypt, in exile. To the very end he spoke for God. He told the Jews in Egypt not to worship false gods and goddesses. He died alone and friendless, but his words did not die. Six hundred years later Jesus lived out the words of Jeremiah and God made his new covenant with every single person. As Jeremiah foretold, now everybody could know God.

Jeremiah 37–40; 42–43; 52

A valley full of bones

ar away in Babylon, the exiles settled down. They became involved in trade, in business, in farming and in craft work. Some of the Jewish exiles had to do forced labour but some became rich and important.

They longed only for the day when they would go home. They did not want to listen to the words of a young prophet called Ezekiel.

"My father was a priest in the glorious Temple I miss it as much as you, the glory and worship of our holy God," he cried. "But God has told me that he is punishing you for your wrong-doing. He has told me that Jerusalem will be destroyed."

"But we've done nothing wrong. We don't think you're right, Ezekiel. Jerusalem will never be destroyed. It's God's own city," they protested.

Their hopes were shattered when Jerusalem fell and more and more captives streamed, broken-hearted, through the lofty, ornate gates of Babylon.

Desolate, they huddled together.

"As we came into Babylon our captives asked us to entertain them with songs," some of the new-comers told their own countrymen.

"But we couldn't sing," another said. "Instead we sat down by the broad rivers of Babylon and wept. We left our wooden four-stringed harps hanging on the poplar trees. For how could we sing the Lord's song in a strange land."

Sadly they turned for comfort to Ezekiel.

"God lived in Jerusalem. Where is he now?"

"God is good to us. He will lead us home." Ezekiel comforted them. "You shall be his people. He will be your God. Instead of stubborn hearts of stone, God will give you hearts that will know him and love him. God has shown me this in a strange way. I'll tell you."

"It seemed to me," Ezekiel said, "that I stood in a far away valley, a valley full of bones."

His hearers nodded. Mounds of corpses or dried

skeletons were only too common a sight during those days of war and plague.

"From one end to another the valley was covered with bones."

"'Can these bones live?' God asked me. He told me to prophesy over those bones. So I said: 'Dry bones, hear the word of the Lord. God is going to make you live.'

"Then there was such a noise, a rattling and a clattering and the bones all joined up together, legs and feet; arms and hands; back bone and ribs; skull and neck. They all fitted and as I looked skin and flesh and muscles grew, but they were still lifeless. There was no breath in them.

"'Prophesy, prophesy,' God said. 'Say, come from the four winds, breath, breathe on these dead. Let them live.'

"So I prophesied as the Lord told me, and they came to life and stood upright on their feet, a great silent army."

"'Now,' God said to me, 'tell my poor, hopeless, despairing people who say "we're as good as dead" that they still belong to me'."

Ezekiel looked hard at them. "Do you believe this? Then God will lead us home one day. He will dwell among us for ever and we will belong to him."

So Ezekiel comforted the people and kept them from following the pagan worship of Babylon in a city with 1,380 shrines to different gods. He died in Babylon with Jerusalem still in ruins. But now the people knew that in God's time their city would be rebuilt.

Ezekiel 37
Psalm 137

A ten day trial

The family kept the Sabbath as usual, lighting the Sabbath lights and saying the prayers. But they were watchful and alert for the sound of tramping feet in the street outside, for the Greek emperor punished by death anyone who kept the Holy Sabbath.

When the Sabbath meal was over, the adults started talking again in low voices about the bad times their people were suffering, now that Antiochus wanted to stamp out the Jewish religion which could not accept Antiochus as God. They sighed for the times they had heard of when Judea had been free to worship God. All that had ended when the land had been conquered once again by a foreign power, two hundred years before Jesus was born.

"But I have a story for you," said Uncle Nathaniel. "A fine story that took place long, long ago when Nebuchadnezzar the king of Babylon captured our holy city."

"Oh, please tell us," the children crowded around now.

"It's about a boy called Daniel, and about his three friends."

Uncle Nathaniel cleared his throat and began:

"The king, Nebuchadnezzar, ordered one of his officials called Ashpenaz . . ." The children smiled at the funny sounding name.

"Ashpenaz was to choose boys from all over Babylon. They had to be from royal or noble families – handsome and healthy and quick to learn.

"Ashpenaz had no difficulty in choosing Daniel and his three friends: Hananiah, Mishael and Azariah. They were all from Judah. He took them off at once to the king's palace where they were to receive a special kind of schooling that lasted three years."

"Did they learn addition?" five-year-old Benjamin asked.

"No, they learnt how to behave in the king's presence, how to address all the members of the court . . . oh, there was so much to learn.

"They had specially prepared food to eat. It came from the king's own dishes. But this is the very thing Daniel and his friends didn't want to do. 'We must obey God's laws,' they told Ashpenaz, who had become a real friend. 'We can't eat this food.'

"Ashpenaz listened to them, but then he said, 'But I'm worried about what the king will say. This food is the very best. It's given to you to keep you well, and if he sees you looking thinner in the face than the other boys of your age, he'll be very angry.'

"'Please, then, give us a ten days' trial. May we eat only vegetables and drink only water and if we are looking thinner and paler than the other boys, well you'll have to deal with us as you think fit. But we must obey our God even more than the King'."

The family all looked at one another. They were disobeying the Emperor, for they kept the Sabbath which he had forbidden, and they had refused to eat all the pagan foods, especially pork.

"What happened?" the mother asked.

"At the end of the ten days, Daniel and his friends looked healthier than any of the other boys," Uncle Nathaniel said. "They had been faithful to God and so he had looked after them. He helped them in their studies too, so that they soon knew all the poetry, history and proverbs of Babylon, and Daniel had the special gift, like Joseph long before, of explaining the meaning of dreams.

"Then at the end of three years Ashpenaz brought the boys before King Nebuchadnezzar. He was so pleased with them he made them members of his court.

"But it was difficult and dangerous for them to remain true to God at the court of the Emperor who thought he was a god," Uncle Nathaniel finished. "I'll tell you next time I see you more stories of Daniel and his three friends."

"Yes, please," the children begged.

The fiery furnace

When Uncle Nathaniel came again, he had frightening but exciting news to tell. He was going to join the revolt that the Jews had started. They could no longer sit by and watch whole families being killed because they would not worship the Emperor. They were going to fight for their beliefs.

"But first I'm going to finish the story of Daniel and his three friends," he said.

"Oh, yes, please," the children begged him.

"Well, the first part of the story is about the three friends. Do any of you remember their names?"

"Mish . . . Mish something," said little Benjamin.

"I know!" Daniel said. "Mishael and Hananiah and Azariah."

"Well done! But King Nebuchadnezzar gave them Babylonian names. He called Hananiah Shadrach; Mishael was Meshach, and Azariah was Abednego.

"The king set up a great golden statue of himself, and one fine day it was dedicated in front of a great company of people from all over the vast Empire.

"'The moment you hear the sound of the horn,

pipe, harp, lyre, bagpipe or any other instrument you must fall down and worship the statue of the king,' ordered the herald. 'Those who do not fall down will be thrown into a burning fiery furnace.'

"And so the moment the musicians blew their instruments with a noise that echoed all over the

palace, everyone fell down flat on their faces before the great golden idol. Everyone that is except for . . .'"

"Hananiah, Mishael and Azariah!" the children chorussed.

"That's right. The king sent for them immediately."

"'What's this?' he asked. 'You'll be thrown into the furnace if you don't worship my statue.'

"'We don't mind,' they said. 'For if our God wants to save us from the furnace, he'll save us. But even if he doesn't, we're still not going to worship your statue, O King, for our God is the One we serve.'

"The king was furious.

"'Make the furnace seven times hotter!' he ordered. 'Bind Shadrach, Meshach and Abednego and throw them into the furnace.'

"So, fully clothed, they were tied with ropes and thrown in the furnace. They fell forward into the flames . . .'"

"Oh, no!" exclaimed Daniel.

"Were they all burned to death?" asked Benjamin, not quite sure whether he liked this part of the story.

"They sang praises to God and blessed his name and they were not burned, while the king in fury ordered the furnace to be made still hotter. They even threw oil, pitch and more and more wood into the flames, but the fire did not hurt them at all, and they sang songs of praise to God.

"The king looked on amazed.

"'Didn't we throw three men into the fire?'

"'Indeed we did, O King,'' said his councillors.

"'But I see four men walking about unharmed in the heart of the fire and the fourth one looks like one of the gods.' Then the king went as close as he dared to the burning fiery furnace and shouted, 'Shadrach, Meshach and Abednego, servants of the most high God, come out from the fire.'

"From the heart of the fire they came, and everyone gathered around in amazement.

"'There is no God like the God of heaven, who sent his angel to his servants in the furnace,' called Nebuchadnezzar. And all the people who had gathered to worship the golden idol blessed the name of the Lord our God, whose servants had remained faithful to him.'"

Uncle Nathaniel stopped. He was very tired now.

"Your food put new heart in me," he told the children's mother. "But now I must sleep. I've got one more story for you, children," he said as he got ready for sleep. "I'll tell it to you in the morning before I leave to join our people in the hills."

The lions' den

ncle Nathaniel was ready for his journey. The children's mother had been up before dawn, grinding corn, kneading dough and baking bread which she packed away for him to take into the hills.

"I wish I were going too," said Daniel, but Benjamin chewed the corner of the little leather wallet he was holding and said nothing.

"When you are big you can join us and fight as bravely for God as the Daniel who let himself be thrown into a den of lions . . ."

"Tell us, tell us," they begged.

"It happened in the days of Emperor Darius.

Daniel was quite old now, an honoured member of the king's court, and respected for his wisdom. In fact, the king thought so highly of him that he wanted to appoint him ruler of the entire empire. You can guess that this didn't please the king's governors, ministers and other officials. They tried hard to find some way of finding fault with Daniel, but they couldn't discover any plan. He was blameless in everything.

"'The only way we can remove him is to do something about the Law of his God whom he so faithfully worships,' someone said.

"'You know he goes into his room and prays to

115

his God three times a day.'

"'That's it, then.' So they hurried to the King.

"'O King, live forever,' they said. 'We know how great you are and we've all agreed that you should issue an edict forbidding your people to worship any other god than yourself, for a whole month, O King. If anyone does he should be thrown at once into the lions' den. So sign the edict, King Darius, and then it is law unalterable for ever according to the decrees of the Medes and Persians.'

"Foolishly, the king signed the law. 'I'm as good as a god to my subjects,' he thought. 'Well, let them worship me.'

"But there is only one God, the God of heaven," went on Uncle Nathaniel. "And Daniel knew this too. So he went home to his own house. The open windows of his room faced broken, ruined Jerusalem. Quietly Daniel, knowing the edict and the punishment, prayed to God as he always did.

"The men who were so jealous of him burst into his room and saw him at prayer.

"'O King,' they said, rushing eagerly to him. 'One of the exiles from Judah prays three times a day to his God and doesn't worship you.'

"'Which man?' Darius asked, and when he heard it was Daniel he was deeply grieved, but he could not change his law for he had signed it and it could never be altered.

"Until sunset he racked his brain to find a way of saving Daniel. Then he had to see him led away to the lions' den.

"'Oh, Daniel,' said the king. 'I'm so sorry. I see I was tricked, but I can't change my law. I can do nothing to save you. The God whom you serve so faithfully will have to save you now.'

"A stone was brought and laid over the entrance to the cave where the lions were. The unhappy king sealed it with his own signet and then went home where he refused any supper and tossed and turned in bed all night, unable to sleep.

"At the first sight of dawn he hurried off to the lions' cave.

"'Daniel, oh, Daniel,' he cried in great grief. 'Has your God been able to save you?'

"Imagine his happiness when he heard Daniel's voice from behind the rock.

"'God has sealed the lions' jaws,' he said, 'since in his sight and yours, O King, I am blameless.'

"Overjoyed, the king ordered Daniel to be released, unhurt, from the lions' den. Then Darius signed a new decree and sent it to all the nations of his empire. 'Daniel's God is the living God whose kingdom will never end. He saves his people who trust in him'."

Uncle Nathaniel finished his story. He laid his hands on his little nephews' heads and blessed them in the name of God. Then he gratefully took the pack of fresh, warm bread and went out to join the rebels in the hills.

The family never saw him again.

Daniel 1–3 and 6

116

A prayer to God and a request to the king

Nehemiah

Babylonia had fallen to the kings of Persia. Some of the Jewish exiles made the long difficult journey home to a ruined city and a land torn apart by enemies. But it was Jews far away from Jerusalem who were the ones that remained true to all the laws of God, especially the laws on keeping the Sabbath, and on keeping themselves apart, a holy people serving a holy God. They met week by week to read the Law of God in their meeting places, called synagogues.

During the reign of King Artaxerxes of Persia, one Jew had the important job of serving the king his wine at meals.

His name was Nehemiah.

"Visitors for you, Nehemiah," an official announced. "Visitors from Jerusalem."

"From Jerusalem!" Nehemiah was overjoyed. He hurried to find his own brother Hanani at the head of a special delegation.

"Oh, how good to see you! Oh, Hanani, this is better than a present of gold."

"I'm afraid I bring bad news, my brother." Hanani's face was sad. "The Jews who were not carried away captive into exile are in great trouble

now. Their rulers in Samaria and the nearby kingdoms are tormenting them terribly. The people have been trying to build up the ruined walls of Jerusalem. But hardly had they started, when the leaders in Samaria sent lying, malicious letters to the king – something about a rebellion, and the king ordered the work to stop. Immediately the Samaritans burnt down the gates and destroyed the walls again."

"Oh, Hanani, that's bad news indeed." Nehemiah was born and brought up in Babylon, but he was faithful to God and devoted to distant, ruined Jerusalem.

He took action immediately. For several days Nehemiah went without food, praying to God.

"Lord God," he said. "My people and myself have done wrong. We have not kept your commandments. In your Law you promised to bring us back again to our homeland. We come to ask your forgiveness. Oh God, I'm sorry. In the name of all Israel, I weep before you and say I'm sorry."

Four months later Nehemiah's chance came.

Nehemiah tasted the king's wine as usual and offered it to him. "Nehemiah! How depressed you look today," said the king, sipping his wine. "You're usually so cheerful! Surely you're not ill, are you? This must be some sadness of heart."

Nehemiah knew that this was his chance to speak. "Oh king Artaxerxes, no wonder I'm sad when my native city is in ruins; its gates have been destroyed."

"What is your request then?" asked the king.

Nehemiah's heart beat wildly. The king exercised absolute control. Would he give Nehemiah permission?

Briefly, silently, Nehemiah prayed before he spoke: "Please let me go to Judah and rebuild Jerusalem."

To Nehemiah's delight the king granted his request readily and also made Nehemiah governor of Judah. Now Judah became a separate province of the Persian crown, free from the leaders of Samaria who had created so much trouble ever since Jerusalem had been burnt down.

Nehemiah 1–2

Builders with drawn swords

In the dark a little donkey stumbled among the ruins. Nehemiah, the new governor, was making a secret survey of the walls. He had only a few trusted men with him. None of the officials in Jerusalem knew what was afoot.

"We'll patch the walls up first," Nehemiah decided at the end of his survey. "We can strengthen the defences later – that will take much longer."

Nehemiah gathered all the priests and the leaders of Jerusalem. "Look at the trouble we're in! Our walls are broken and our gates burnt. Why should we let our enemies humiliate us? God is with us. His good hand has guided me all the way here with permission from King Artaxerxes to build. So come on, let's start building."

So the work started. All around the walls, groups of men set to work, carrying away the rubble, building up the walls and fixing the gates.

"Ho! Ho! Ho!" jeered Sanballat, the governor of nearby Samaria. "Just look at these pathetic Jews." Tobiah, always at his master's side, piped up, "Never mind, let them build. A jackal has only to jump on to the charred rotten stones and they'll come tumbling down again."

But the people worked with such a good heart that the walls grew each day. Then the rulers of the kingdoms around Judah: Samaria, Arabia, Ammon and Ashdod plotted together to come and attack the builders.

Nehemiah knew exactly what to do. First he called all the people together and they prayed to God. Then, day and night they set sentries around the city walls. So the building went on, but this time the builders worked with their drawn swords in their hands. The men who carted away the rubble were also armed, and other men stood guard over the wives and families of Jerusalem.

Nehemiah was everywhere. He spoke to the officials: he chatted with the ordinary folk. All through the fifty-two days neither he, nor his family, nor their servants, nor any members of his personal guard ever took their clothes off to lie and rest in bed. They snatched an odd hour's sleep whenever they could, and worked on, doing sentry duty, and encouraging the builders and even working on the wall themselves.

Nehemiah 2–6

The governor at work

"**D**addy, don't let them take us away."

"Mother, Mother!" the little girl's screams were stifled by an angry blow and the child started to sob hopelessly.

"My little ones," the mother was standing helplessly watching the servants of the rich man drag her children away as slaves.

"Stop it," a voice thundered. "What does this mean?"

The servants started to retort angrily, but their words died on their lips as they recognised the speaker. Governor Nehemiah was coming toward them. His face was pale and his eyes sunken, but there was no trace of fatigue in his voice.

"Do you know that in Babylon we all collect money to buy back our brother Jews who are sold as slaves to foreigners. Yet here in Jerusalem you barter with children for debts of corn and wine. I'm going to call a meeting at once of all the leaders of Jerusalem to stop this shameful business."

Nehemiah called the meeting. "God speaks out against this in his Law," he said severely. "Cancel all your debts at once. Give back to the poor people all the things you've taken from them."

"All right, we promise!" The rich people gave way. In front of the priests they swore in the name of God to carry out their promise.

"From the day that King Artaxerxes made me governor, have I ever taken a single silver piece from you?" Nehemiah asked the people. They were silent. Other governors had made everyone pay them forty silver coins a day. Nehemiah had not done this, nor had any of his servants exacted money from the people. "Every day I feed 150 of you leaders and officials, not to mention all the ambassadors and deputies who come from the neighbouring countries. I buy numbers of skin bottles of wine. You drink it, don't you, you leaders, and I never ask you for a single coin. And why not? Because I respect and honour the Law of God."

Nehemiah went storming back to his work on the walls. On the way he saw the rich man's servants hand back the girl and boy to their parents. That day the poor of Jerusalem were glad.

Nehemiah 5

Joy that could be heard

Although Sanballat, Geshem and Tobiah kept trying to sabotage the work, the wall was repaired in fifty-two days.

"Now all our enemies and the people around know that God is still with his people in Jerusalem," said Nehemiah with satisfaction.

Then all the people gathered together and Ezra the scribe from Babylon read out the Law of God. He unrolled the scroll and all the people stood up. Then he praised the name of God and all the people lifted their hands high above their heads and praised God; then like a forest of trees falling before the woodman's axe, they fell to the ground before God. Ezra read the Law and the Levites explained the meaning. The people listened with tears streaming down their faces.

"We have not kept this Law," they wept.

But Nehemiah and Ezra reassured them: "Don't cry. You're keeping this day as a holy day to our God."

"Go now," Nehemiah said. "Eat well, drink sweet wine and give away some of your meal to the poor people who have nothing. Don't be sad. The joy of the Lord our God is your strength."

So the people went away happily to eat and drink and give some of their food away.

Then they obeyed the Law of God and kept the feast of Tabernacles, the seven-day feast, an age-old Harvest Festival. But this time they followed out all the instructions exactly, and to the delight of the children they went into the hills and brought back branches of olive, pine, myrtle and palm to build little shelters.

"This reminds us of the wandering of our fore-fathers and of God's covenant with them," said Ezra. "This feast has been neglected for so long but now we keep it because we are still God's own special people. Only we must obey his laws. We mustn't marry the pagan people around us. We must keep our holy sabbath day as a complete day of rest and worship to God. And of course we must never worship other gods. These are the things that make us the special people of God, whether we live in Babylon, or in Egypt, in Jerusalem or in any other part of the world."

Then the Levites who had come from every corner of the land took up their instruments. The music of the cymbals, lutes and lyres resounded across the rebuilt walls.

Everyone rejoiced. They danced, clapping their hands, and they sang praises to God.

"Today," said Nehemiah to Ezra as they went home, weary but happy, "the joy of Jerusalem could be heard from far away."

Nehemiah 8–13

The prophet who ran away

The walls of Jerusalem had been rebuilt. Ezra the scribe had given the law, and taught the people how they were to live lives that marked them as God's people.

"God loves and cares for everyone," a scribe stood on the steps of the Temple, teaching the people. "So if the pagan people will come to God and worship here, he will make peace with them," said the scribe. "Listen then, let me tell you a story.

"Many years ago when the cruel Assyrians had gone out conquering and looting across the entire world, the word of the Lord came to Jonah. 'Go to Nineveh, that great city. Tell them that I know all about their terrible deeds.'

"'I can't possibly do that,' thought Jonah, and he decided to run away from God.

"'I'll go to Tarshish,' Jonah decided. 'That's far away in Spain. It's right on the edge of the world. But they say the Phoenicians venture that far, even further.' So he went to Joppa, found a ship that was bound for Tarshish, paid his fare and went aboard."

"Wasn't he frightened?" asked one of the listeners, for the Jews were terrified of the sea and all the monsters they thought inhabited the deep.

"Of course he was, but he was more afraid to do what God told him! They set sail, and soon there was such a violent storm that they thought the ship would break in pieces.

"The sailors were terrified. They each prayed to their own pagan gods and to lighten the ship they threw the cargo overboard. Jonah was asleep.

They shook him roughly awake. 'Come on, you pray to your God too. Maybe he will save us.'

"'Someone on board has made his god angry,' said the sailors. 'That's why the storm has come.'

"Well, of course it was Jonah. He realised now how foolish he had been. He told them: 'I am a Hebrew. I worship the Lord God of heaven who made the sea and the dry land. But I'm running away from God.'

"'No wonder the storm's so bad!' they exclaimed. 'But what can we do to you to make the sea calm again? It's getting worse every moment.'

"'Take me up and throw me into the sea,' said Jonah. 'For I see it's all my fault.'

"The sailors were pagans. They didn't know God, but they didn't want to do this to a fellow human-being. So they all rowed as hard as they could – the sails were torn in pieces and in any case they usually rolled them up when there was a storm. But the sea grew rougher than ever.

"Then they called on the Lord our God. 'Don't blame us, Lord!' they said, and they threw Jonah overboard."

"Ah!" the listeners sighed. "Poor Jonah."

"It was the right thing. Immediately the sea grew calm and the ship sailed away with all the sailors praising our Lord God."

"What happened to Jonah?"

"A great big fish swallowed him up!"

A shudder ran through the group of listeners which was growing bigger every minute as more people crowded round to hear the story.

"But God still looked after him there. In fact, he had sent the fish so that Jonah wouldn't drown. Inside the guts and innards of the fish Jonah nearly suffocated, but he prayed to God and praised his name, and the fish swam to dry land and was sick. It vomited Jonah on to the shore."

"What happened next?"

"Once again God asked Jonah to go to Nineveh – and this time Jonah went!

"What an enormous city Nineveh was! Jonah preached amid its vast buildings. 'This city is going to be destroyed because the God of heaven and earth knows all the wicked, terrible deeds you do without showing any mercy'."

"I'm sure they never listened!" someone said.

"Oh, but they did. They all repented, from the

123

king to the smallest child. They all asked God to forgive them. They ate no food, they put on the coarsest clothing and prayed all day long.

"And God saved the city of Nineveh. It was not destroyed at that time.

"But Jonah was very angry. In fact he was furious with God. He fell into a rage. 'This is exactly what I knew would happen when I was still at home. I knew you were a kind, loving God, gracious and merciful. So now you've saved Nineveh and all those people who have done so much wrong! I can't bear it, Lord. I want to die.'

"'Poor Jonah, but are you right to be angry like this?' God said. 'Look, I'll make this castor-oil plant grow right here where you're sitting. It will shade you from the sun and soothe your ill-humour.'

"Jonah was delighted with the castor-oil plant.

"'It's beautiful, Lord. Thank you,' he said.

"But at dawn the next day the plant withered and died. A worm had started to gnaw at it and had killed it.

"Jonah was furious! 'That beautiful plant!' he stormed. 'Why did that worm have to eat it and make it die?'

"'Jonah, Jonah!' God told him. 'You're upset about a plant that you neither planted, nor watered, nor tended. It sprouted in a moment and perished in a moment. Well, then. Surely it's right for me to care what happens to Nineveh, a big city with many people living in it – people who go in terror of their gods and know nothing of a God of love. All those people, Jonah, not to mention the animals! Didn't I do right to spare them?'

"So that is my story," finished the scribe. The people loved it. They read it out in their synagogues year after year at the services at which they all asked God to forgive their wrongdoing. But they did not understand its lesson. Like Jonah, they couldn't believe that God loves and cares for everyone all over the world. They went on holding fast to their Law and kept utterly separate from all other people.

Jonah 1–4

124

The sun with healing rays

The Temple had been rebuilt, but people only offered lip-service to God.

"What is this?" A man nicknamed Malachi watched the men who came to present their offerings. "You're not giving that calf to the Lord, are you? Look, it's lame and sickly."

"Oh, it doesn't matter: it's all a boring ritual anyway," the man replied. "We go through with it, but it doesn't mean very much does it?"

"It certainly doesn't mean much to the priests. They just don't bother to teach us or to worship God. So we don't bother to pay them."

"The Levites have to work on the Sabbath day to bring in their corn from the fields because we don't bother with them."

"What does it matter after all? The rich are the only ones who prosper. Look how they trample on us humble folk! We have to give up our lands to pay our debts."

"Well, it does matter," thundered Malachi. "I am God's messenger. That's what my name means. Listen to what I tell you: stop cheating God. Worship him with your whole heart and he will shower down on you a mighty flood of blessings. The locusts will not destroy your crops, and all nations shall call you blessed.

"That's what God says," Malachi told the people. "So, you see, it does matter! For the day of the Lord will come. You have been longing for the Deliverer the prophets of old told you about. He is coming. Yes, he is coming like the fire the goldsmith uses to purify his gold; like the alkali the dyer uses to bleach his cloth. He will make the priests holy again and he will help the oppressed.

"Have you seen the sun rise? Of course you have. Well, the Deliverer will come like the sun breaking through the dawn sky. As the sun chasing away the night, spreading its rays far across the sky, so the Deliverer will bring healing to the people of God. He is the sun with healing rays, and you will leap like the young calves as they go out to their pasture, hopping, then gambolling, butting each other with joy and impatience to eat the sweet grass.

"But before that day comes, God tells me he will send his messenger. He will be like Elijah the prophet. He will bring love and peace between parents and children. The Lord you are seeking, the Promised One, the Deliverer, will suddenly be seen in the Temple, but before he comes I will send my messenger to prepare his way.

"So wait patiently," said Malachi. "For the messenger will come and then the Lord himself will be seen in his Temple."

Malachi 1–4

New Testament

A messenger in Nazareth

A young girl called Mary was busy sweeping out the one-roomed house where she lived with her father and mother and brothers and sisters in the little town of Nazareth. The house was small. It had a floor made of beaten earth with hand-woven rugs spread across it. Mary picked them up and shook

the dust out of them. She shooed away a hen that had come clucking in.

When autumn came and the grape harvest had been gathered in, Mary was going to be married to a man called Joseph, the carpenter, builder and woodworker. His house was in a nearby street.

"It will seem strange to be someone's wife,"

Mary thought. "I'll have a baby too. Oh, that will be lovely. It's terrible to be married and not have any children. I'm so glad my cousin Elizabeth is going to have her baby soon. She's waited for so many years and now it won't be long before her baby is born."

Mary laid down the rugs neatly, but a bit dreamily. There was so much to think about these days, with her wedding not far away.

"Rejoice!" the voice rang in her ears like the golden trumpets she'd heard in the Temple.

Mary jumped, startled, and looked up.

"Oh-oh," she exclaimed. A stranger stood in the doorway of her little home; light streamed around him. It seemed that he was aglow with joy.

"Rejoice, Mary. The Lord is with you."

"What does he mean?" thought Mary. She felt her legs grow weak as she stood there, still clutching one of the hand-woven rugs, grown shabby with age.

"God is going to give you a baby, Mary."

"But I'm not married yet," Mary said. "I'm marrying Joseph in the autumn. Will God give me a baby then?"

"God's baby will start to grow inside your body now," said the angel. "His Holy Spirit that moved in the dark at the dawn of the world will begin in you the little life that will be your baby. The power of God the most High will cover you. The baby will be a boy. You must call him Jesus."

"Jesus," repeated Mary, and in her language it was "Yeshua". "That means God saves."

"Yes, your child will be God's Promised One. He is the Saviour your people have been waiting for."

"Oh," Mary buried her face in her hands.

"Nothing is impossible with God," the messenger's beautiful voice was like music.

"If I have a child, Joseph won't want to marry me," Mary thought. "Who will believe that a poor peasant girl like me should carry the Son of God? What will my parents say?"

"Think of Elizabeth your cousin. God has given her a baby when she thought such joy would never come. In three months her child will be born."

Mary loved God. She believed this bright radiant stranger. "I am the handmaiden of the Lord," she said simply. "Let it all happen to me just as you have said."

Then he left her. She stood alone.

"What will they all say?" she thought. "Oh, whatever will they say?"

The clucking hen came back in again. This time Mary did not shoo it away. She stood rooted to the spot.

"I'll go and visit Elizabeth, if my parents agree," she said aloud.

Luke 1

129

"He has filled the hungry with good things"

Mary's parents did agree. It was a long journey to Elizabeth's village. Perhaps someone else from Nazareth was going that way. It certainly wouldn't have been safe for Mary to travel alone.

When she arrived at Zechariah's house, she called out. "Elizabeth! It's Mary. I've come to see you."

Elizabeth looked up. Suddenly she pressed her hand to her side.

"Why, what is it?" Mary asked. "You look strange, Elizabeth. Is it your baby? Is it time for you to give birth?"

"It *is* my baby," said Elizabeth and now her face was happy again. "No, it's not time for the child to be born. As soon as you came in, I felt my baby jump for joy inside me." She gave a cry of happiness. "Oh, Mary, Mary, does the mother of my Lord honour me with a visit?" In an instant they were in each other's arms.

"How wonderful it is that you knew," Mary said, and she started to sing a song of praise.

"My spirit exults in God my Saviour. He has come to his lowly handmaid and now until the end of time I will be called blessed. How good God is! He looks after everyone who loves him. He is strong and powerful. He pulls down the princes from their thrones and exalts the poor and needy. He has filled the hungry with good things, but the rich he has sent empty away."

Mary stayed with Elizabeth for three months, up until the time when Elizabeth's baby was born.

Luke 1

God's dawn

The news spread quickly around. "Elizabeth has had her baby."

"Well, that's wonderful," said her friends. "Let's go and see her at once."

All the women gathered in the little house of Elizabeth and her husband Zechariah to see the baby.

"Elizabeth is almost old enough to be a grandmother and now she has her own baby," said one.

"The strange thing is that her husband has been dumb. He's not been able to speak for nearly a year," replied her friend. "He was in the Temple one day and when he came out he could only make signs to us. He couldn't say a word. We're sure God told him something in the Temple that day."

"Perhaps it was something about his baby," someone remarked. "I wonder what they'll call the baby. I expect they'll call him Zechariah after his father."

When the little baby boy was eight days old, they took him into the Temple as the custom was. There he was circumcised and given his name.

"What is his name?" asked the priest.

"Zechariah," the relations and friends chorused, but Elizabeth spoke up: "No, his name is John."

"Whatever do you mean?" they all asked her. "No one in your family is called John."

"Let's ask his father."

Zechariah wrote down on a writing tablet: "His name is John."

"Why?" they all asked amazed, but they were even more astonished the next moment, for Zechariah who had been dumb for a year suddenly began to speak. He praised God. "Oh God, thank you for giving us both a little boy. You came and told me about it, Lord, when I was in the Temple nearly a year ago. But I didn't believe you and that's why I've been dumb."

He took the baby in his arms. "Our Deliverer is coming," he sang, "and you, my little son, shall be called the Prophet of the Most High. You are to be his messenger. You will prepare the way for the Lord. God who loves us is bringing us His dawn. There will come someone like a rising sun with healing rays, lighting up those who dwell in darkness."

All the friends and neighbours were filled with amazement.

"Little baby John is to be God's messenger. Our Deliverer is coming," they said, and the news spread around all over the hill country of Judaea.

Luke 1

"Take Mary as your wife"

The happy time with Elizabeth helped Mary when she went back home. Her baby was making her body big. All over Nazareth people were gossiping unkindly about her, and poor Joseph decided that the best thing to do would be to break off their engagement.

"I can hardly believe it," he thought, tossing and turning as he slept. "Dear Mary! She's so loving and good. I can't believe that she's having a baby before our marriage."

"Don't be afraid," an angel said to him in a dream. "Take Mary as your wife. The baby that is growing inside her is the Son of God. You must call him Jesus, for he is the Saviour, the Promised One of whom the prophets spoke. Don't be astonished or afraid."

So Joseph married Mary and she went into his house as his wife and the unkind gossiping soon stopped. Besides, people had something else to think about – a census.

"Our Roman rulers want us all to go and be counted. It's just so that they can make us pay more taxes," grumbled one.

"We've to leave our homes and our livelihood and go all the way back to the place our ancestors came from," another said indignantly.

They hated the pagan Roman soldiers who had conquered their land. The taxes they had to pay burdened them heavily for they already had to pay so much to the Temple.

In their little home Mary and Joseph looked at each other.

"We'll have to go and enrol in Bethlehem," Joseph said. "I am descended from the family of David, and Bethlehem was his home town."

"But it's miles away and . . ." Mary had no need to finish her sentence. It was nearly time for her baby to be born. They would have to travel eighty-five miles along rough roads, sleeping wherever they could find shelter. Mary would ride on the donkey.

"Can you manage, Mary?" asked Joseph doubtfully.

"God will look after me, Joseph," she said.

Matthew 1

The baby in the manger

In the hills five miles south of Jerusalem lay the ancient walled town of Bethlehem. When Mary and Joseph arrived, the little town was crowded out with people who, like themselves, had come to be enrolled.

"There's nowhere for us to shelter," Joseph said. "The inn is quite crowded. Look, the courtyard is packed with people who have unrolled their mattresses and are getting ready to sleep. Oh, Mary," he turned to her. "Are you all right?"

"Your poor young wife," one sympathetic traveller stopped. Everyone else was too busy with their own concerns to bother about them. "Have you come far?"

"From Nazareth," said Joseph.

The man whistled. "That's a good distance. Come for the census like the rest of us, I suppose?"

Joseph nodded. "Well, I'll show you a place where you can shelter. There are caves under the inn. They use them for stables. Gently now, we'll have you there in no time."

In the cave Mary's baby was born.

There was no nurse nearby, but she knew exactly what to do. She had watched her mother care for new-born babies. Joseph fetched warm water. Gently and tenderly they washed the tiny, new-born baby. Then they rubbed salt into his little body as the custom was. Mary laid him naked on her lap and wrapped a linen cloth round him tightly. Around this cloth she bound strips of cloth called swaddling bands. Then she laid him in his manger bed on fresh, clean straw so that he would be safe from the animals in the cave.

"He's just perfect," Mary whispered, as she and Joseph sat beside him, watching him.

"Someone's coming, Joseph," Mary said, suddenly alert.

The cloak Joseph had fastened at the entrance to the cave was pushed back.

"Is there a baby here?" someone asked.

"Why, yes," Joseph said in surprise. "My wife has just given birth to her firstborn child. How did you know?"

The shepherds crowded close as they told their story.

"We were out in the hills, guarding our flocks from jackals and wolves. . . . When suddenly it grew bright, like day time."

"It was the glory of the Lord," one of them said simply.

"God sent his messengers to us. We were terrified, but he told us: 'Don't be afraid. I'm bringing you joyful news for everyone. Today a baby has been born in Bethlehem. He is the Anointed One of God, the Deliverer. You'll find him wrapped in swaddling bands and lying in a manger.'

"Then the light grew so bright we could scarcely stand it, and a whole multitude of the heavenly host appeared. . . ."

"Like stars circling around in the sky," burst in one shepherd. "How they sang! 'Glory to God on High, and peace on earth'."

"Then they left us and we hurried here and we've found it's all just as the angels said. Please, could we see the baby," they finished quietly.

"Of course," Mary and Joseph said. The shepherds crowded round the manger and then they hurried off to tell all the townsfolk.

"A child has been born who is God's Chosen One."

When baby Jesus was eight days old, they took him to the Temple and they did everything that the Law demanded. Because they were both poor people, they offered God two turtle doves as a thanks offering. Together they gave the baby his name: Jesus. Thankfully they offered him to God.

An old man called Simeon, who loved God, hurried forward.

"Oh!" he exclaimed. "How wonderful God is. He has let me see his Special Child." He held the baby lovingly in his arms. "My eyes now see the salvation promised by God to all peoples. This little one shall be a light, showing the pagan people the way to God. He is the glory of God's people Israel."

Mary and Joseph stood there, wondering about Simeon's words, and the old man blessed them. Then he spoke to Mary in strange and difficult

words. She did not understand them then, but afterwards, very often afterwards, she remembered them.

"Your child," said Simeon, "has been sent from God, but many people in Israel will refuse to accept him. The secret thoughts of many people will be laid bare and a sword shall pierce your heart."

"Praise God! Praise God!" A very old lady called Anna came forward. She was eighty-four and never left the Temple. "God's Deliverer is here. This child is the Holy One of Israel."

So they went back to Nazareth, where the baby brought joy to their little home.

Luke 2

The three gifts

Herod the King came from the desert lands in the South. He built the Jews a glorious Temple at Jerusalem. He married a Jewish princess and accepted the Jewish religion. But the Jews hated him. It was at the end of the reign of cruel King Herod that Jesus was born.

Guided by a star, wise men appeared at Herod's palace.

"We have seen a bright, beautiful star," said one. "We followed it for many miles, for we knew it meant a new king had been born."

"A new king?" Herod was suspicious and afraid. "There's no child here."

"The star led us westwards. We have come with gifts for the infant king."

Herod was very upset. He called for his wise men and asked them where the Scriptures had foretold the Deliverer should be born.

"O King, in Bethlehem in the land of Judah, the prophets foretell the birth of God's Chosen One."

"Go on to Bethlehem," Herod told the wise men. "It's only five miles away. When you find the child, come back and tell me all about him. I want very much to worship him, too." His smile deceived the three sages.

As they left he flew into one of his mad rages.

"A new king? There'll be no new king! We'll have him killed before he tries to take my throne."

The wise men travelled wearily on.

"Look, there's our star again!" they were filled with delight. "God is still leading us. But it's such a mean, pitiful lodging for the newborn king."

"So God's son lies on straw," they murmured to each other and they laid aside their jewelled turbans and bowed low in the dust before the child and his mother Mary.

"We bring gifts for your child," they said, opening their treasures. "Here is gold. That is for the king," said one.

"I bring frankincense. The little one here is holy. I worship him," said the second sage, bowing again before the baby.

Mary looked alarmed. "We can't take such precious gifts," she said.

The lamplight shone on the gold. The costly fragrance of incense mingled with the smell of straw, of animals and of dung.

A third seer stepped forward, bowing low. "Mother of the Messiah who will die for the life of the world, I bring myrrh."

Mary's eyes grew wide. "Do you anoint a corpse?" she cried. "I thought you came to see a child!"

"The child who will save mankind," they said, and went away to find lodging for the night before returning to Herod as they promised.

But God warned them in a dream not to go back to evil Herod, and they left for their own country a different way.

Matthew 2

"My father's house"

collectors who were sitting in the customs-seat.

But as the group of pilgrims from Nazareth came into their holy city, they had one thing in mind – the Temple.

In its courts they worshipped God. They kept their Passover feast, remembering the day so many centuries ago when God had set his people free from Egypt.

"Maybe soon he'll send his Messiah, his Promised One and deliver us from Rome," people murmured. "And from the cruel rule of Herod's three sons."

Then it was all over. It was time to go home.

"Has anyone seen Jesus?" Mary asked some of her friends.

"Oh, I expect he's gone ahead with all the other boys," was the reply.

School days were over. Jesus was twelve years old. Now he was ready to join Mary and Joseph when they went to Jerusalem for the Feast of the Passover.

"You're all going this year," the teacher at school told the twelve-year old boys. "Now you are sons of the Law and you must keep it in every way. When you go to Jerusalem with your parents, the wise men in the Temple will examine you to see how well you know the Law. Don't be frightened. Answer them well, remembering all that you have learnt."

The journey took three days. On the road they saw the beggars, crying out for money, pitiful, bent figures shuffling along; blind men being led along by friends. They saw Pharisees praying at the street corners, making a great show of being pious and holy. Some of the pilgrims jeered at the tax-

They travelled for a day. Then at nightfall they got busy putting up their tents.

"Jesus must come along now," Mary said, "Joseph, have you seen him anywhere?"

They searched among all the families who were gathering for the evening meal.

"He's missing!" she cried out in dismay. "Oh, Joseph, what can have happened?"

They looked at one another. Fear was in their eyes, but all Joseph said was: "We must go back to Jerusalem at once and find him."

Tired, hungry and worried, they set off, retracing their steps.

After they had hunted everywhere, Mary said "Let's go to the Temple."

The courts that had been thronged all during the feast were almost empty now.

"Look, over there. There's Jesus. He's sitting with the learned teachers of the Law. Just look at him. He's asking them questions, and see how thoughtfully they answer him!"

But although she felt proud of Jesus sitting there with all the wise men of Jerusalem, all her worry and weariness made her rush up to him, crying, "Son, why have you done this to us? Your father and I have been terribly worried. We didn't know what had happened to you."

"This is my Father's house," Jesus said. "Here I am at home. So why did you come searching for me?"

Mary and Joseph looked at each other, not understanding.

"Come home with us now," Joseph said. Obediently Jesus followed them out of the Temple.

He went with them to Nazareth and worked with Joseph until the carpenter of Nazareth died. Then Jesus took all the responsibility of the family on to his shoulders. He stayed at home with them until he was thirty years old and the younger brothers and sisters were old enough to look after Mary.

Luke 2

"Someone is shouting in the desert"

"Make the Lord's road ready for Him. God's salvation is here."

Instead of becoming a priest like his father Zechariah, John had gone into the lonely desert places. Like Elijah of old, he wore a rough cloak made of woven camel hair, tied around him with a leather belt. He lived on locusts and wild honey. Crowds of people flocked from all over the country to hear him.

John stood beside the Jordan at the main ford.

"Elijah has come back again!" people said.

"I am like the slave who runs ahead of the king telling all the people, 'The Lord is coming. Clear the road for him'," said John.

He baptized the people in the Jordan, wading waist deep into the river with them and dipping them in. This was a sign that they were sorry for their sins.

All sorts of people came. Religious folk from Jerusalem, the strict Pharisees and the rich-living scribes came to see whether John was likely to be a trouble-maker or not.

"You snakes!" John shouted when he saw them in their fine robes. "You say 'We're religious!' but I tell you God is angry with you because you make a show of religion but you don't really love God."

"Oh, what are we to do?" the people asked.

"Share your clothes and your food with all the poor people," he told them.

Tax collectors came, to the amazement of the crowd.

"Oh, teacher," the richly-dressed officials spoke to the fiery-eyed preacher, "What are we to do?" John saw the loneliness in their eyes. He spoke more gently.

"Don't tell the poor people to pay high taxes, half of which you put into your own pockets," he said.

Even soldiers came; laying aside their armour, they too went into the water to be baptized.

"What about us?" they asked. "What must we do?"

"Don't rob the poor. You take money from them by force or else you bring all sorts of false charges against them." John's voice was stern, but then he added with a smile. "Don't grumble when you get your wages. Be content with your pay."

"Are you the Messiah?" people asked. "Are you the Deliverer God is going to send us?"

"No," John said. "Your Deliverer is coming, and I'm not good enough to do even a slave's job for him and bend down and undo his sandals."

"Look, here he comes!" he suddenly called out. "Here is the Lamb of God who will offer himself as a sacrifice to take away the sins of the world."

Eagerly people craned their necks. They saw a humble workman in a patched linen tunic which he had tucked up into his belt because he had walked a long way.

"Is this the Messiah? This plain, humble man!" people said, disappointed. One or two recognised him.

"It's John's cousin. It's Jesus the carpenter from Nazareth. He's been looking after his widowed mother all these years."

But John insisted, "This is the man I was talking about when I said: 'I'm not worthy to do a slave's job and unfasten his sandals'."

"Will you baptize me?" Jesus asked, pulling off his tunic.

"Oh, no!" John said. "Surely I should be baptized by you."

"Please do as I say!" Jesus begged his cousin. "I want to do everything that God requires."

So they went together into the Jordan, and there, as soon as he had been baptized, Jesus looked up, his face shining.

All the people were very still. "Surely God is speaking to him," they whispered to each other.

"God opened up the heavens to me and showed me himself," Jesus said. "I saw his Holy Spirit, like a dove, gently nestle on my shoulder and I heard the voice of God."

"What did he say? What did he say?"

Jesus spoke softly. There were many who did not like the words. "God said: 'This is my own dear son. I am pleased with him'."

Matthew 3
Luke 3

Strength in a parched place

Far from the crowds, Jesus climbed the lonely hills of the desert.

"I must be alone with God, my Father."

It was not easy to turn his back on the people. Some of them were already listening eagerly to his words.

"Lord, they are like sheep. How they need a shepherd!" he thought. "Someone to lead them gently and heal their hurts."

The scorching wind from the barren rocks blew full in his face. It was so quiet here, far from the hubbub of Nazareth. He thought again of the crowd. How many hungry people he'd seen there! All his life he had seen poor families like his own toil from dawn till twilight and still have hardly enough to eat.

"How shall they be fed?" he cried, looking at the wilderness around him. He was beginning to feel hungry now. The bare hills around had no food for him, but words of Scripture strengthened him.

Jesus stayed alone in the wilderness without eating for a very long time.

At the end of the time he felt hungry. That was when the devil tempted him.

"If you are God's Son, his Chosen One, just turn all these stones into bread."

Bread! The smell of dough baking. The warmth of the flat loaves in your hands, in your mouth, inside your body. Jesus was hungry. He knew that if he performed a magical trick like that, people would come flocking after him without question. All the hungry, all the poor from all over the world would follow him.

Jesus heard God's voice. He answered the devil simply: "The Scriptures say: 'Man cannot exist on bread alone. He needs the words of God to satisfy his soul'."

He leant against the rocks. Hunger made him weak. The devil took him to the highest point of the Temple in Jerusalem. Dizzily high, 130 feet above the city, he stood and heard the devil say:

"Son of God. Throw yourself down from here. God will look after you. The Scripture says so, doesn't it?"

"Yes," Jesus thought. "And the people would know for sure that God had sent his Chosen One. They expected their Messiah to come through the clouds, in the charge of all the heavenly beings. They would proclaim him as a great and glorious king."

"Scripture says: 'God will send his holy angels who will hold you up. You won't even hurt your feet on the stones'." The devil's voice rang in his ears.

"Scripture says: 'You must not put God to the test'," Jesus said finally. "It's not as a miracle worker that I've been sent."

The devil had one last temptation for him. "Bow down and worship me. I am the evil one. I have great power. I'll give it all to you. See, there are all the kingdoms of the world: Rome, Greece, the kingdoms in the East, the kingdoms far in the West. Worship me, Son of God. I'll make you king of the world."

But Isaiah had said that the Son of God would bring God's kingdom in a different way:
"Bind up the broken hearts and set the captives free:
This is the task the Lord has laid on me
I'll gladden and comfort the mourners in the dust;

I'll be the light of God in whom I trust.
My eyes are lifted up, and from afar I see
Children long lost returning home to me.
Dusk covers all the earth; folk stumble in the night,
But kings and their people flock to my dawning light."

So Jesus said, "Get away, Satan. The Scripture says: 'Worship the Lord your God.' Him only will I serve."

Defeated, the devil left him, and instead angels came. They looked after Jesus, weak, hungry, wearied with fasting.

Matthew 4

"I'll teach you how to catch men"

Two fishermen were getting their nets ready. They had been out in their boat fishing all night, and now they were mending their nets before they went home for some sleep.

They were brothers. Big, brawny Simon was married but his younger brother Andrew still lived with him.

"John has been put in prison," Andrew said. Simon spat in disgust. "That sly old king Herod is as bad as his father," he said. "Well, that is bad news."

They were silent and remembering. Andrew had been a follower of John. But the day after Jesus had been baptized in the Jordan, Andrew had left John and followed Jesus. He had addressed Jesus respectfully as a teacher: "Rabbi, where are you living now?"

"Come and see," Jesus had said.

Andrew spent all afternoon with Jesus. Then he fetched Simon. "I've found the Messiah, the Deliverer we've all been waiting for."

But Jesus had gone away. They hadn't heard anything of him for a long time. And now John had been put in prison.

Had it all ended as quickly as it had begun?

A man's shadow fell across their nets. They looked up, blinking against the brightness of the early morning sun.

"It's Jesus!" Simon nudged Andrew.

Once they would have shouted a greeting. "Shalom. Peace. How's business?" He would have come over and looked at the boat he had made in Nazareth to see if any repairs needed to be done.

But it was all different now.

"Come with me," Jesus said. "I'm going to teach you to catch men for God's kingdom!"

They looked at each other for a long moment. Then Simon laughed, his teeth very white in his weather-beaten face.

"They'll be harder to catch, but we won't need our nets."

They jumped up, left their nets on the floor and followed Jesus joyfully.

Farther along Jesus saw his cousins James and John. Their mother, Salome, was Mary's sister. They, too, were mending their nets on the shore

while their father was out in the boat with his employees.

"Come on!" Jesus called. "It's time to go out after a different kind of fish."

"Men," shouted Simon. "We're off to haul men into the kingdom of God."

"Good-bye, Father!" shouted John. "We're going to follow Jesus."

Zebedee looked up. "So, the time has come at last, has it?" he thought. "Well, well, I never thought God would choose Galilee, or a humble home like Mary's." He remembered something and tugged his beard thoughtfully. "Ah, but Mary married into the clan of David, didn't she, and Jesus her first-born, now, he was born in Bethlehem, just as the Scripture says. Well, well. God go with you," he called after his sons.

John 1
Matthew 4

The tax collector at his desk

Jesus spent the night at Simon's house. Till late in the evening he healed many sick people, but long before dawn he got up, went into a quiet, lonely place and prayed there.

But Simon and the others followed him. "We've been looking for you everywhere and so has everybody else," they said.

So they travelled on to all the neighbouring villages, telling everyone that God's kingdom of love had come.

On their way they saw a man called Matthew Levi collecting taxes. Simon and the others hissed their hatred, but Jesus said: "Follow me."

Eagerly Matthew left his seat, and followed Jesus.

"Rabbi, Rabbi, come and have a meal in my house," he pleaded.

Simon, Andrew and James and John looked doubtfully at one another. They were good Jews. They knew that all the outcasts whom no one wanted would be the only friends a tax collector would have. They wouldn't be too particular about obeying all the rules about food.

But Jesus didn't seem to mind about this. He went to Matthew's house and they held a great party.

"See how they long for the kingdom of God!" Jesus said to his fishermen friends.

Many of them followed him and became his disciples, to the horror of the pious Pharisees who scrupulously obeyed every small item of the Law, but who closed their hearts to its real message of God's love.

Mark 2

The simple and the shrewd

Jesus also went to a man called Philip from Galilee; "Come with me," Jesus invited Philip, who ran to his friend Nathanael.

"Come quickly, Nathanael, we've found the Messiah that all the prophets have told us about. He is Jesus, the son of Joseph from Nazareth."

Nathanael came from Cana in Galilee. "Nazareth!" he echoed in surprise, and he quoted the proverb that had been made up about Nazareth: "Nothing good can come out of Nazareth!" he said.

"Well, here's something that has! Come and see," said Philip.

"Greetings, Nathanael," said Jesus with a smile that broadened to a laugh. "You're a true Jew, I know! There's nothing false in you."

"How do you know me?" gasped Nathanael, surprised.

"I saw you sitting under the fig tree, before Philip called you."

"Oh, teacher," declared Nathanael fervently. "You are the Son of God, the King of Israel.",

"Does such a little thing as my knowing who you were make you believe?" said Jesus. "You'll see greater things than these, Nathanael."

The time came when Jesus had to choose from the crowd who had already gathered about him a small number to be his closest friends. After a night of prayer, Jesus chose twelve men. Eleven were from Galilee: Simon, Andrew, James and John, who were all fishermen; Matthew the tax collector from the town of Capernaum; Nathanael from Cana and his friend Philip from Bethsaida and four others: Thomas the twin, Jude and James the younger, and Simon the Zealot.

There was one other man. He came from Judaea, from a village called Kerioth. He was a fierce man who hated the Romans and had fought against them. He was clever and shrewd and looked after the money.

His name was Judas.

John 1
Mark 3

The dungeon

"Kill John the Baptist," the Queen stormed. "Kill him! Kill him!"

"I can't," Herod's son, Herod Antipas, said weakly.

"What do you mean? You can't? You're the King, aren't you?"

"Yes, well, it's the people I'm concerned about, my dear. They just flock after John. They think he's a prophet sent from God."

Herodias laughed aloud. "That . . . that lunatic from the desert. He's quite mad!" She looked at her husband and said slowly, "You know, I think you believe in him too."

"What me? Well, I, no, of course not," said Herod crossly. But he was superstitious and even though he didn't love God, he feared him.

"Well, he'll turn all the people against you and push you off your throne," threatened Herodias.

"Besides, the man insults me dreadfully. He calls me . . . well, you know very well what he says about me, and about you for marrying me!"

"Yes, because you were my brother's wife. Well, my dear, if you feel so strongly about it, we'll have John arrested, shall we?"

So Herod chained John, the man who since his boyhood had slept alone under the stars, and shut him in a dungeon cut deep in the rock on which Herod's fortress Machaerus was built.

There John suffered terribly. It was torture for him to be shut away, caged like a mountain lion. He began to have doubts. Some of his disciples went to Jesus, who was surrounded by a great crowd of sick, needy people.

"Are you really the Messiah?" they said. "Or should we look for another?"

"Tell John what you've just seen," Jesus said. "The lame walk, the blind see, the good news goes out to the poor. Tell him not to doubt."

He turned to the people and said, "John has been shut away in a dungeon, but he's the greatest man in the world, because he is the messenger who proclaimed the coming of the Messiah."

Mark 6
Luke 7

The dance

How beautifully she danced! The little girl moved among the drunken, vomiting guests at Herod's birthday party. All the top government officials of Galilee, the military chiefs and leading citizens of Galilee, had been stuffing more and more highly spiced food into their overloaded stomachs and drinking goblet after goblet of wine.

Yet something about the little girl's dance made them sit straight and watch, entranced even in the midst of their drunkenness.

When she finished, loud applause burst out on every side.

"Salome, my dear," drunk King Herod took his little stepdaughter on his knee. "Whatever you ask for I'll give you as a reward for that wonderful dance."

"Oh thank you," lisped Salome, while she searched the crowded lamp-lit room for her mother. She lip-read the frantic message Herodias mouthed to her.

"Give me John the Baptist's head on a plate!" she said, loudly and clearly.

Herod grew pale. She'd tricked him after all! He put the child off his knee, but he didn't dare refuse. Not in front of all those guests.

So he sent a guard, and into the richly furnished banqueting hall came John's head, dripping blood. Herod turned green and beckoned to the guard to give it to the little girl, who took it to her mother.

Secretly, John's disciples came and laid his body in a grave.

Mark 6

Lost...and found

A crowd gathered about Jesus as he began to tell another of his stories about God's kingdom.

"A farmer in the country had two sons," he said. Everyone listened eagerly. Some of them had come from the country too, and they longed to be back among the fields and the hills.

"The farmer had a small farm. One day most of the property would go to the elder son. The younger brother would get the second son's share: one third of the property. But as he grew up, he longed to have plenty of money to spend as he wished."

People in the crowd nodded. They knew just what the boy was feeling. Many of them were second sons, forced to make their own way in the world while the elder brother got the little farm and the land around it.

"'Father,' he demanded one day, 'let me have my share of the property now.'

"The father felt very sad. He knew he was about to lose his son. The boy went off to market and bought himself fine clothing; he packed his things and left home.

"It didn't take him long to find a crowd of friends in the big city. People are always ready to gather around a person with plenty of money. They showed him all the exciting things in the city: he went to the theatre, watched the best athletes compete in the vast stadium, and then entertained his friends lavishly in the evenings at banquets and parties."

Again people round Jesus nodded, remembering . . . At these parties you didn't worry whether the food was the special sort the Law required you to eat. Gradually you broke one law after another until there was no more hope for you.

"Soon he'd squandered away all his money and you can guess that none of his fine friends stuck by him then. He was left alone. And then that part of the country was hit hard by a severe famine. The young boy was in such a bad way he went away from the city and wandered around the countryside searching for food. In the end he hired himself to one of the local farmers. He had to feed the pigs . . ."

Pharisees had joined the crowd. They drew back in disgust at the very mention of the unclean pig.

"Poor boy!" one woman exclaimed.

"Yes," Jesus agreed. "He was starving now, so famished that he would gladly have joined the pigs at their feeding troughs and eaten the pods they were guzzling, only it revolted him just a little too much.

"Nobody offered him any food, not even pig food, and nobody wanted him.

"'What a fool I've been!' he thought. 'Why

ever did I grab my share of my father's property and leave home where I was loved and wanted. Here I am dying of hunger and all my father's servants have more than enough to eat.'

"And so he came to his senses. 'I know,' he told himself. 'I'll go back to my father. Of course I can't ask him to take me back as his son. I know God tells us to respect our parents and love them. I've really sinned. I've broken the Law, and I've hurt my father. I'll go back and tell him so. I'll say, "Father, I know I've done wrong, both against God and against you and I don't deserve to be your son any more. Please take me back as one of your workers".'

"So he left the place, ragged and barefoot and started on his way home.

"While he was still a long way off his father spotted him, hobbling along the road, weak with hunger. His father had never forgotten him, not for a single moment. As soon as he saw his son, he cast the dignity of his years to the winds and raced like an errand boy down the road toward him."

People smiled, picturing the elderly father running so joyfully to his long-lost son. But some were sobbing, for they understood now the secret meaning of the story: God is like this father. For those who understood, it was too good to be true.

"Before the young man could utter a word," Jesus went on, "the father had clasped his boy into his arms and kissed him over and over again.

"'Father,' the boy finally stammered, 'I have done wrong. I've sinned against God and against you. I don't deserve to be your son any more.'

"But his father cut him short. Lovingly he led him homeward.

"'Quick!' he called to his servants. 'Don't you see what has happened? My lost son is found again. Go and get the best robe, the one we keep for our most honoured guest. Get my ring,' he ordered another servant, 'and put it on his finger. Oh yes, and get fine slippers for his feet – we can't have you barefoot as if you were one of the slaves,' he told

his son. 'We'll kill the calf we've been fattening. We'll have a party, a real feast!'

"What a hustle and a bustle there was as they made all the preparations! How good the meal smelled to the son who'd come home! When it was ready, they all ate their fill, and then the musicians got out their flutes. The menfolk danced, stamping their feet. Everyone was clapping. The noise carried outside the house to the fields, and the elder brother heard it."

The crowd glanced over to the group of Pharisees. They knew Jesus meant the elder brother to be a picture of the law-abiding religious leaders.

"'What's all this noise?' he called out to a servant. 'Is there a party going on?'

"'Yes,' said the servant. 'Your brother's come home.'

"The elder brother was furious.

"His father came out and pleaded with him. 'You are my elder son. Do come in and take the place of honour which is yours at our feast.'

"The elder brother brushed his father aside.

'I've toiled and slaved for you all these years!' he shouted at the old man. 'I've done everything you've wanted. Yet you've never once offered me even a lamb to kill to have a party with *my* friends. But when this no good son of yours turns up after squandering your property, you go and kill the calf we've been fattening and have a party! It's nonsense,' he grumbled. 'I'd have disowned him completely!'

"'All that I have belongs to you,' the old man reminded him. 'But we must celebrate because we're so happy.'"

Jesus finished his story. He looked across at the Pharisees. They met his gaze with black looks, but they didn't dare say anything because of the crowd who pressed around him, laughing and crying together. Muttering together, the Pharisees went on their way, but Jesus' friends knew they were planning to kill him.

Luke 15

The sower, the seed and the soil

The little bay on the side of Lake Galilee was packed with people. Jesus turned to his disciples. "Look," he said, "the people at the back of the crowd can neither hear nor see. I will get into the boat. Can you push it out from the shore a little way? Then I can see everyone and they will all be able to hear what I am trying to tell them."

They cheered and smiled when they saw what Jesus was doing. "What a good idea," they said, "now we can all see."

Jesus looked up above the people. He saw the rocky path and the thorns and brambles that grew round the edge of the field just above the little bay.

"Listen," he told the people. "Imagine a sower going out to plant his crops." They nodded, picturing the sower up before the sun carrying his flat basket on one arm going out to scatter grain into the field.

"What kind of soil does he use to plant his seed?" Jesus asked.

"Why, good soil, of course!" they all called back to him.

"Of course," Jesus agreed. "But as he goes along, scattering seed, some of it falls in other places, doesn't it? Some falls on the pathway as he walks along. Then the birds come and enjoy a fine feast!

Nothing will ever grow from that seed. It is carried away immediately.

"Some of the seed falls on rocky soil, where there is only a small layer of earth. It springs up straightaway, but when the sun gets up, the little plants are scorched. And because they have no real roots they wither away at once.

"Then some of the seed gets scattered among the thorns and brambles round the edge of the field. When the thorns grow up they choke the little plants. No crops come from them!

"But, of course, a lot of the seed falls just where the sower wants it to," Jesus finished his story.

"When the harvest time comes, the sower finds that the grain has grown up tall and strong and produced a crop. Some seed yields thirty ears of wheat, some sixty, and some even a hundred – a really good crop!"

Jesus looked round them all. "Do you understand what that story means?" he asked. "It is a kind of puzzle, but anyone who has really listened should be able to understand the meaning."

Later on, when all the people had gone, the disciples asked Jesus what the story really meant.

"Don't you understand this story?" Jesus asked them. "Then how will you possibly understand any of the other things I tell you about God?

"Well, this is the meaning. The seed that the sower is planting is the word of God. The earth at the edge of the field is a picture of the people who hear the message, but as soon as they have heard it, Satan carries away the word sown in their hearts.

"In the same way, the rocky ground also stands for people. This time the people do listen with great joy to the things God tells them but don't let his word take real root in their lives, and as soon as any trial or trouble comes, like the seed out in the hot sun, they are scorched and fade away at once.

"Then there are the thorns. You see, some people receive the word but all the worries and wealth of this world choke their minds. So God's word in them produces no real result in their daily lives.

"Last of all, there are those who receive the word in their hearts. They are like the good soil. They hold on to the word, and let it grow in their lives so it produces fruit, some thirty times as much, some sixty, and some a hundred times over.

"That is the meaning of my story about the sower, the seed and the soil," Jesus explained.

Mark 4

The greatest treasure of all

"Ouch! That hurt my toe." The man working in the field stopped and hopped around, clasping his bruised toenail. "I wonder what it was that cut me like that. Well, just look at that bit of iron sticking up! Let's heave that out of the way before someone else gets hurt!"

Jesus looked round his listeners. "The man heaved and tugged and couldn't pull it out. So he scratched around until he'd dug quite a big hole and there it was! Buried treasure! He couldn't believe his luck.

"'Finders keepers, that's our law,' he said, delighted. Then he looked all around him anxiously.

"'Good, no one in sight!' he thought. He shovelled the earth back to hide the treasure. He ran back to town to find out the price of the field.

"'I'll sell everything I've got to pay for it,' he said. 'It'll be well worth it. Let's hope no one gets to the field before I do and makes off with the treasure.'

"So he bought the field and became the owner of a great treasure that had cost him everything he possessed.

"That's the way it is with the kingdom of God," Jesus finished his story. "You might stumble across it by chance, but as soon as you realise its full value, you gladly give up everything and just seek God's will above all else. You know it's the greatest treasure of all."

Matthew 13

The loveliest pearl

A rich merchant who collected pearls was hunting for the loveliest pearl of all. One day he found it.

"Ah!" he gloated. "Peerless perfection! Oh, but I must *own this* pearl."

He couldn't rest until he possessed it. He sold his other pearls, his house, his lands – everything. Then he bought the lovely pearl.

"That, too, is like the kingdom of God," Jesus explained. "Some people find it by accident. Others search hard and long for it. When they find it they count it their dearest treasure, and gladly give up everything else to gain it."

Matthew 13

"Please open the door"

"**D**o you know what else the kingdom of God is like?" Jesus asked. People shook their heads. "Well, listen to the story of the five bridesmaids who let their lamps burn low."

"They always need a spare flask of oil with them," the women spoke up. "You never know when the bridegroom will come."

"Well, this bridegroom had been delayed and it was midnight before he reached the bride's house," Jesus said. "His friends hammered at the door.

"All the bridesmaids and the bride jumped up at once.

"The girls had their lamps ready lit, but the bridegroom was so late that the lamps had burnt very low. Quickly five of the girls filled their lamps from their spare flasks of oil and trimmed the wicks so that the flames burnt brightly again.

"'Oh, hurry,' cried the nervous bride, pulling her veil straight, but five of her friends exclaimed in dismay: 'Oh dear, we've forgotten to bring spare flasks of oil. Oh, our lamps are nearly out! Please give us some of your spare oil.'

"'But we've used it all up. We must have bright lamps for the procession. It would be a terrible shame for our poor friend if she didn't have any lamps about her when she arrives at her bridegroom's home.

"'It wouldn't be a proper wedding procession at all. Look, we must go now. You'd better rush off and see if you can buy some. Hurry, you might still catch up with us at the bridegroom's house!'

"But they didn't. When the five girls arrived out of breath at the bridegroom's house, they found that the door was bolted and of course, once the feast has started, no one else can get in.

"The girls banged at the door, calling to the bridegroom, 'Sir, open the door! We're the other bridesmaids! Let us in.'

"'It's too late!' he called. 'All the guests have arrived. We've begun our celebrations. Go away!'"

Jesus finished the story he had been telling. "You have seen all the things I've done in the power of God. You have listened to my stories about the love of God. Be wise! Open your hearts to God, say you are sorry for your sins and you'll be ready for the kingdom to come."

Matthew 25

"Go, and do the same yourself"

"Master," the man asked respectfully, "What must I do to earn eternal life?"

The questioner was a scribe, a teacher of God's Law. People saw the smirk on the man's face. They knew he was trying to trick Jesus with a question like that!

Jesus replied by asking another question.

"What is written in the Law? What do you read about your problem there?"

One or two faces around him relaxed into smiles. That was the right sort of answer to give the teacher of the Law! The scribe answered, "The Law tells us: 'You must love the Lord your God with all your heart, and with all your soul, with all your strength and with all your mind, and your neighbour as yourself'."

It was a good answer. Jesus was pleased. "You have answered well," he approved. "Do this and eternal life belongs to you."

Once again people round about smiled as they saw how annoyed the scribe looked.

The scribe was on the defensive now.

"Well, then, who is my neighbour?" he asked.

"Once upon a time a traveller set off by himself to go from Jerusalem to Jericho . . ." Jesus began his story. And the people guessed that this was going to be an adventure story, for no one went off on a journey alone if he could help it, and especially not along the twenty-mile road from Jerusalem to Jericho. So many people were attacked there it was called "the red road". The disciples had just come along that road with Jesus. They remembered the steep cliffs all around; the steady climb, up, up, up, always up, mile after mile – and the breath-taking glimpses below them of deep gorges where robbers lurked.

"Robbers jumped out on him as he travelled along," Jesus continued. "They attacked him, stripped him of everything he had, beat him up and then ran off. He was left lying more dead than alive at the roadside.

"Now a priest chanced along the same road."

"Of course he won't help," a man interrupted. "Why the man might really have been dead! No priest in our Jewish faith touches a corpse. If he

does, he becomes unclean and has to go through a ceremony to make him clean again."

"Shsh," another person said. "Let's listen to the tale. After all, he's a holy man, isn't he, on his way to worship God in the Temple here in Jerusalem; maybe he'll have pity on a poor fellow Jew."

"When the priest noticed the man," Jesus said, "he crossed the road and passed on his way."

"Frightened for his own skin," a big burly man shouted out, raising quite a laugh.

"So on he went," Jesus continued, "and the poor man lay there in a very bad condition, but a little later someone else passed. It was a Levite . . ."

"The priest wouldn't help. I wonder if the holy man, the Levite, will?"

"He won't!" several voices shouted together.

"Well, he might. After all the Law says, as we've just heard, that we're to love our neighbour . . ." protested one woman.

"He'd just think God was punishing the poor man for some bad thing or other that he's done. The Law doesn't say anything about helping wounded people."

"But love means that," the same woman insisted.

"Go on, Jesus," people pleaded. "Did the Levite help the man?"

"No," said Jesus. "He came up to the place where the man was lying and he too passed by on

158

the other side of the road. So the poor man lay helpless and wounded for a long time until another traveller came along. He was a Samaritan . . ."

"Our poor wounded man's dead already then," laughed one man.

"Yes," responded another. "We Jews have nothing to do with the Samaritans."

Jesus knew all the hatred that existed between the Jews and the Samaritans. He waited till the hubbub died down.

"The Samaritan was filled with pity when he saw the poor wounded man," Jesus went on with the story, quietly, heedless of the hisses and angry faces around him. "He got off his donkey and opened his travel bags. With olive oil from his own supplies he bathed the wounded man's cuts. He tore strips of cloth from his own clothes and soaked them in wine. He laid them gently on the wounds to stanch the flow of blood. Then he bandaged all the wounds and lifted the unconscious man on to his donkey. He supported the lurching body of the wounded traveller with one arm, and with the other he guided the donkey very slowly and carefully all the way back to the inn.

"There he spread out a bed for them both and all night he looked after the wounded man. The next day he had to go on with his journey. He found the innkeeper.

"'I've got to go on now,' he said. 'Here's some cash for you.' He drew out from his bag two silver Roman denarii, two whole days pay. 'Look after him well for me. I'll be stopping on my way back, so I'll pay you any extra expenses then.'"

Jesus looked around the crowd. They were quiet now, thinking hard. He looked across at the scribe who had asked the question.

"Which of these three men, do you think was neighbour to the traveller who was beaten up by the robbers?" Jesus asked the scribe.

The scribe swallowed hard. Of course he knew the answer. He couldn't bring himself to say "the Samaritan," so he answered, grudgingly:

"The man who took pity on him and helped him."

"Then go away now," Jesus said to him, "and do the same yourself."

Luke 10

Grapes to be gathered

"**H**ere's another story about the kingdom of God," Jesus began. One September, a man who had a vineyard got very anxious when he saw there were still a lot of grapes to be gathered.

So early in the morning at six o'clock, as soon as the sun rose, he hurried into the market-place.

Quite a few men were there already, hoping for a day's work. They were good, eager workmen, and the owner of the vineyard was pleased to hire them.

"I'll give you a Roman denarius for a day's work in my vineyard!"

So off they went and they worked hard in the vineyard.

Before many hours had passed, the owner could see that more workmen were needed if he was going to get his grapes gathered in before the rains.

Out he went again to the market-place. It was nine o'clock and by now, of course, quite a crowd of unemployed men had gathered.

"I'll give you a fair wage," the man who owned the vineyard promised them.

The other workers were glad to see more people arrive to help. On they worked, hard and steadily, gathering the grapes.

By noon, the owner saw that he would need still more men to help him. Out to the market he went again.

At three o'clock the owner decided to go to the market-place again. There was quite a crowd of men who had no work to go to. They were glad even to have a three-hour job.

Two hours later the owner thought: "It will soon be sunset and still my grapes are on the vines. Late as it is, I might find some men who would come and work for an hour for me."

160

So off he went again to the market-place.

"Hurry up, and go into my vineyard. There's still an hour of the day left. Get to work before the sun goes down."

So off they went and worked really hard for the last hour of the day.

Imagine their surprise when the foreman not only gave them their pay first, but, at his master's orders, gave them a Roman denarius.

How happy they were as they went off home to their families! Their children would get a good supper that night!

Of course, when the other workers saw what the man was paying for just one hour's work, they began to wonder what they would get. "Surely he'll give us at least double that!" they thought.

But he gave them all the same pay: a silver denarius.

"It's not fair," grumbled some as they took their pay. "We worked a full twelve hours under the hot sun. Those others only worked for an hour or two yet you paid them the same as us. It's not fair!"

"Listen, friends," the owner replied, quite unruffled. "Why do you think I've cheated you? Didn't we agree that you should work in my vineyard for a silver denarius?"

"Yes," they nodded their heads sullenly.

"Then why are you jealous because I'm generous? I want to give the men who were hired last the same pay as you. It's not their fault that they've had to wait around the market place, hoping that someone would hire them. Now take your pay and go off home."

Jesus finished his story. "God is like that. He gives his children the things they need. Just think how generous and just he is to everyone. There's no need to bargain with God!"

Matthew 20

The trusted servants

The crowd which had gathered excitedly around Jesus grew solemn. They knew Jesus had something to teach them about God's kingdom.

"You see," Jesus explained, clasping his strong hands round his knees, "it's like a very wealthy man who had to go on a journey.

"'Where can I put my money?' he thought. 'There isn't a bank for miles, and I can't possibly travel with all my money on me. It just wouldn't be safe.'

"So he decided to trust three of his slaves with his money. He chose them carefully, knowing who could be trusted with the most.

"He gave 5 talents to one slave, 2 talents to another slave and 1 talent to a third slave. Then he went off on his journey.

"The first slave was delighted at being trusted by his master. He got busy trading. He bought a supply of corn, gold and silver with his money and then sold it all again and bought more and sold it. So he doubled the amount of money. The second slave did the same. But the third slave looked at the money carefully. He let the coins run through his fingers. He studied them closely. He put them in piles and counted them. Then he tied them all up tightly in a cloth and buried it deep in the ground.

"When the master came back, he called for his three slaves.

"He was delighted when the first slave laid ten money bags on the table.

"'Sir,' he said, 'I've worked hard and I've doubled the amount of money for you. Here you are.'

"'Oh, well done!' praised the master. 'You've been faithful and honest. I'm going to entrust you with really important things. But now – come and sit down at my table with me. Share my feast as a free man.'

"He said the same thing to the second slave, and they both went off happily to the banqueting hall, friends, not slaves, of the rich man.

"The third slave sheepishly laid his cloth on the table. It was muddy and mouldy from the soil.

"'Sir,' he stammered. 'Here's your money. It's all there, sir. I looked after it very carefully for you.' His master was furious.

"'You lazy, good for nothing,' he scolded him. 'You could at least have travelled to the bank and put the money there for it to gather interest till I got back. Throw him out!' he ordered. 'Give his money to my friend who had the most money.'

"Does that seem hard?" Jesus finished. "Well, be warned then, because God is like that."

Those who followed him understood a little of what he meant. Everyone of them had gifts which could be put to good effect to serve God, or they could be squandered. They realised it was a serious warning that they would lose gifts they did not use.

But what did the story mean – was Jesus really going away? And when would he come back? They shook their heads. Sometimes his teaching was hard to understand.

Matthew 25

The wheat and the weeds grow together until harvest

"One year at sowing time a farmer planted good seed in his field," Jesus began, and the crowd around him settled down to listen. How they enjoyed his stories about God's kingdom. He was the best teacher they had heard.

"He tilled the ground, and levelled the soil," Jesus continued, and the crowd nodded. Many were farmers, and they knew all about preparing the ground for a good harvest. "Then he left the seed to grow. But he had an enemy, who wanted to spoil the harvest. He came silently by night and sowed weeds secretly. Then he slipped away, and nobody knew what had happened until the plants came up."

The crowd shifted, whispering to one another, wondering what would happen now.

"The servants were very distressed. They rushed to the master, asking in bewilderment how weeds could have grown among the good seed sown.

"The master knew. 'An enemy has done this,' he stated. 'What shall we do?' asked his servants. 'Shall we go and pull up the weeds?'

" 'No,' said the master. 'If you do, you may root up the good seed with the weeds. They will have to grow together until harvest. Then you will be able to tell the difference very clearly. I will tell the reapers to gather the weeds first, bind them into bundles, and burn them. But the wheat will be gathered into my barn, unharmed.'

"God's world is like the field," Jesus explained. "Good and bad people live in the world. Some people look for God; others think only of themselves. Some people obey God; others do exactly what they want.

"The farmer had to be patient and let the weeds grow with the wheat. They were so thickly sown together that he would have ruined his crops if he'd tried to pull the weeds out before harvest.

"So you too must be patient with people," he warned his disciples. "For God is the only person who sees what we are really like. Don't do his work for him. Don't judge other people.

"I am the farmer," Jesus went on. "I have come among you to do my Father's work – that's what the tilling the earth, levelling out the soil is all about. And the enemy who tried out of hatred to ruin the crop is the devil who comes with his poisonous lies to keep people away from God. You know that at first it's hard to tell the darnel grass and the wheat apart. When the ears of grain show, then the difference is obvious. If the bearded darnel gets ground with the wheat into flour, well we know how poisonous that flour is. People are so sick afterward. It makes them drunk and then they die.

"So God must keep his crop pure when harvest comes," Jesus finished. "The harvest is the end of time. Then God's people, like the golden grain in the barn, will shine in the Father's kingdom."

Matthew 13

165

"Come to the feast"

"**T**ell us more about the kingdom," the people pleaded. "Who is welcome?"

Jesus responded with another story.

"What a flurry and a scurry there was in the palace that day! Through halls of gold, along corridors of ivory, servants rushed helter-skelter. And no one minded the hard work at all, for something very special was happening.

"It was the wedding banquet of the King's son!

"Of course, preparations had been going on for a very long time. In their stalls the prize calves and bullocks had been fattened up. The guests had been carefully selected. It was a great honour to be chosen for the King's feast.

"Now the invitations were being sent out by the King's servants.

"Imagine their dismay when they all returned with the same message. 'The guests had no time for us,' they told the King. 'One and all said: go away, we don't want to come.'

"The King was dismayed too. Of course he could have ordered the guests to come, but he was too gracious a monarch to do such a thing.

"'Go and rest now,' he told the servants who had been around all the guests. He chose other servants and sent them with a courteous message:

"'My bullocks and prize calves have been butchered. Everything is ready. Do come to the wedding feast!'

"But once again the guests paid no attention. They were all too busy! Some just went on with whatever it was they were doing, and ignored the King's message, but others grabbed hold of the servants. They beat them up and murdered them.

"The King was very, very angry. 'Go!' he ordered his commanders. 'Lead my armies against those murderers. Burn down their city!'

"Then he sent for other servants: 'The wedding feast for my son is ready,' he said. 'But the selected people have ignored my invitation. They've even murdered my messengers. Go now, up and down the land. Go to the busy main streets; go to the quiet country roads. Go to the dark narrow alleyways where little children play in filth and no one pays attention. Go to the thoroughfares where the sick and needy beg and the rich go trampling by. Invite to my feast as many people as you find.'

"So to the gold and ivory palace came a vast crowd of people, good and bad; poor and rich; sick and well; young and old, and the glistening wedding hall was filled with the sort of people you would never expect to find in the palace of a king."

Matthew 22

166

The purple... and the sores

"A slave only ever has one master at a time, doesn't he?" said Jesus. "He can't serve two people at once. It's the same with us. We must choose between God and wealth; we can't work for them both!"

Some rich Pharisees who loved their wealth sneered when they heard this, but Jesus had a story for them:

"Once," he began, "there was a very rich man. He wore the most expensive, most fashionable clothes. His tunic was of pure linen, his robe of richest purple.

"He lived in great luxury every day, eating sumptuously and enjoying a life of leisure."

"Now there was also a poor man named Lazarus," Jesus continued, and again the disciples exchanged knowing looks, for the name meant "God is my help".

"Lazarus was a beggar. His body was covered with sores. He couldn't walk, but each day friends would bring him to the rich man's door, and Lazarus lay outside in the street all day. He smelt the savoury food, he watched the man dip his fingers into dish after dish of food. When the servants swept the floor and carried away the empty dishes, they threw out the scraps of bread on which the man had wiped his fingers.

"Lazarus lived off these scraps. When they fell near him, he snatched them up before the scavenger dogs got there first. They, like Lazarus, lived off the rich man's food. They greedily gobbled up

the scraps and when they were done, they licked the sores on Lazarus's body."

"Oh!" some of the disciples shuddered, remembering the horrors they had seen in the filthy streets of Jerusalem.

"Then the poor man died," Jesus went on. "As we all believe, he went to heaven."

The Pharisees had to agree, for they too believed in a life that went on after death.

"Lazarus had always kept his heart fixed on God. Now at last he had an end to pain and starvation. He was received with honour and placed right beside Abraham, so that as they reclined together his head rested on Abraham's shoulder.

"Soon afterwards the rich man died. He went to Sheol, the place of departed spirits, and there he knew such torment! But the greatest torment was the sight of the beggar who'd lain with the dogs at his door, enjoying all the honour in heaven!

"He cried out to Abraham. 'Send Lazarus to bring me some water! I'm so thirsty!'

"'Do you expect Lazarus to wait on you like a slave?' Abraham demanded. 'You ignored all the commandments in your lifetime and enjoyed all the good things. Now Lazarus at last is at ease. He was a wretched beggar but he remained my dear son, for he followed closely the ways of our forefathers.

"'You both have the reward you deserve, and yours is pain.'

"'Oh, Father Abraham, send Lazarus to my five brothers who still live on earth and warn them so that they at least don't have to go to this place of pain!' cried the rich man.

"'My son,' said Abraham sternly, 'they have the writings of Moses and the prophets. Let your brothers read them and pay heed to what they say.'"

Jesus turned to the Pharisees. "That is the sign you seek," he said. "And that is my answer to you. But I'll finish the story."

"'Father Abraham,' the rich man cried out. 'The laws of Moses and the writings of the prophets aren't enough. But if someone were to rise from death and return to them from beyond the grave, then they would turn from their sins and believe.'

"'No,' answered Abraham. 'If they won't believe what Moses and the prophets say, they'll never be convinced, not even if someone were to rise from the grave.'"

The Pharisees turned their backs on Jesus and stalked away. Jesus sighed, and the disciples looked at one another with fear.

Luke 16

The lost sheep

Shepherds lived a hard, lonely life, high on the hills, out in all weathers. Sometimes they owned their sheep: sometimes they looked after rich men's flocks. The shepherd had to lead the flock to meadows where deep waters flowed slowly making the grass sweet and fresh. He had to keep special watch on the little lambs, and on the ewes who carried their young and were about to give birth.

Quite a lot of people owned small flocks. Their children used to help look after the sheep. Jesus told a story once about a man who had a hundred sheep.

"He and his children knew them all by name, of course," Jesus said, and the people in the crowd nodded. Yes, some of the sheep lived for many years and the family got to know them very well.

"One evening the children brought the sheep safely home to the fold. But, when they came to count them, one was missing.

"'Are you sure?' they asked one another, arguing a little about it. They counted again and again. It was a difficult job because of course the sheep didn't stand still, and even though they were in the sheepfold they butted each other and jumped over one another's backs. Ninety-nine they counted.

"How sad they were! They went running to their father. He checked the number once again.

"'I'll go out at once and look for our lost sheep,' he said, even though he was tired after a day's work.

"So the children went home for their meal while their father went out into the dusk.

"He hunted high and low. His hands and legs were torn by thorns. His feet were scraped and grazed by the rough rocks. The wind moaned in his ears. Then finally when he had almost given up hope he thought he heard a mournful bleat. He stood straining his ears above the rising wind and he heard it again.

"He hurried forward. The frightened sheep knew the shepherd's voice as he called and bleated over and over again, until at last the shepherd found it, lame in two hooves, a great sore in its side, stuck fast among thorns, and exhausted from struggling to free itself.

"It was a long difficult job to free the sheep, for the thorns tore the sheep's sides as the shepherd took it by the horns and tried to pull it free.

"In the end he laid the wounded, trembling sheep across his shoulders. Bent under his burden, he made his way home.

"Long before he reached his house the children who were out watching for him came running to him. They called all the friends and neighbours together.

How happy everyone was! The missing sheep was home again safe and sound!"

Jesus looked at them seriously. "I tell you there is joy like that in heaven when one outcast turns to God and says he is sorry for his sins. Remember that joy, because the Father has sent the Son like a shepherd to bring home the ones who were lost."

Luke 15

"It's the foundation that counts"

"What's the most important part of any house?" Jesus the builder looked round the crowd who had been listening as he taught them. They had much to think about, but this was an easy question.

"The foundations, of course!" several voices cried out.

"Right!" said Jesus. "We always try to build our houses on solid rock, don't we? Well, listen to this story.

"Two neighbours decided to build their houses side by side. Their harvest was gathered in, so it was a good time to begin work. They chose a good spot in a sheltered valley and set to work.

"One man was wise. He dug deep and went on digging until his spade struck solid rock. He straightened his back, sweating after so much hard work.

"But it had been worth it, for now his house would stand on a solid, sure foundation.

"He looked across at his neighbour. To his surprise the other man was already busy mixing his mortar. He'd collected shells and bits of broken pottery and had ground them to a powder. He was busily mixing them with clay.

"'You were quick,' the first man said. 'How did you get your foundations dug so quickly?'

"'Oh, I didn't bother going right down to the rock,' said his neighbour. 'That's too much like hard work! Besides it's not worth it. This ground's as hard as a brick. It will be a very good foundation. You'll see, just as good as rock.'

"But the first man shook his head. 'It may be hard now, but just wait until the rains come in October,' he warned his friend.

"So they went on building. The two houses looked just the same from top to bottom. Only the foundations were different. That's what showed, when the end of September brought the usual heavy rainfall and violent storms. The rain lashed down on the two houses. The valley was a dried-up river bed. It was soon flooded. The waters foamed around the base of the houses and the winds beat wildly around them.

"The house on the solid rock stood firm. Nothing would sweep its strong foundations away! But it was a different matter when it came to the house on the sand. The foundations that had been hard as a brick in June were soon washed away in October, and the house crumbled and tottered and fell with an enormous crash!"

People laughed. What a good story-teller Jesus was! He talked to them about the things they knew so well, the simple ordinary things of everyday life. He wasn't like the other rabbis who talked in such a learned way that no one else could understand. There was another difference, too, between Jesus and those other teachers. Whatever they said had always come from books. What Jesus said came straight from God. So now he explained to them seriously.

"You've all listened for a long time while I taught you many things about God. Well, let me tell you the meaning of this story. My teaching, the words you've heard from me, are like the firm solid rock. They'll never be washed away. If you obey my words, you'll be like the man who built his house on the rock. But if you go away and forget everything I've told you about the kingdom of God, you'd be like the foolish man. Your life might look just the same as your neighbour who obeys me, but it will have no firm foundation and when troubles come like a flood and disasters like a storm, beware! For you will suffer loss."

Matthew 7

A man who obeyed orders

Jesus often stayed at Capernaum where Simon lived with his wife and her mother. The main road from Damascus to Jerusalem ran through the busy bustling town. A garrison of Roman soldiers was stationed there.

Jesus sometimes taught on the lake shore in Capernaum. Sometimes the crowds gathered around Simon's house. Sometimes they flocked to the synagogue because Jesus was teaching there.

It was a fine synagogue, and it had been built by the Roman centurion in charge of the garrison. He had been brought up to worship many gods. He had come to love the independent Galilean folk, and to respect their God who was so different from all the pagan gods he knew. So he paid for a new synagogue to be built.

The Roman centurion had a servant, a slave whom he loved very dearly. One day the servant fell ill. All the best doctors were sent for, but nothing helped. The centurion sent for some of the Jewish elders. "Jesus is in Capernaum today," they said.

"Please go to him and ask him to come and heal my servant," the centurion requested.

The elders went to Jesus, pushing their way through the crowds to get to him.

"Do come, Rabbi," they begged. "He's a Roman but he really deserves your help. He loves our people. You know it's the very same man who built our synagogue."

Jesus went at once. Not far from the house some of the centurion's friends met them. They saluted Jesus.

"Sir," they said, "the centurion has sent us to tell you not to come all the way to his house. He says: 'I don't deserve to have this man come into my house!' He sent us to you, sir, because he didn't think he was worthy to come himself. He said: 'Just give the order and my slave will be made well, for I know you have come from God and heal under his authority. I, too, am a man under the authority of my superiors, and I have soldiers under me. Whatever order I am given, I have to obey and the same thing goes for my soldiers and my slave. When I give them orders, they have to obey. I tell one "Go away" and he goes, immediately. I tell another "Come here", and he comes at once. I order my slave: "Do this for me" and he does it'."

Jesus was amazed. He turned round and told all the people about him, "I have never found faith like this before, I tell you, either here in Galilee or among those who call themselves the Jews in Judaea."

The centurion's friends went running home to tell him what Jesus had said. The slave met them at the door, completely well.

Luke 7

"Don't stand so close"

The disciples didn't notice the poor man who stood at the roadside. A piece of rag was wound round his face to hide the marks of the terrible skin disease called leprosy.

They were so used to the sight of all the beggars and the sick folk who dragged themselves along the roads, calling out hoarsely for money. Everyone was. There were so many of them and no one could do anything to heal them or help them.

Except for Jesus! The man with leprosy was sure that Jesus wanted to help him.

As quickly as he could, he shuffled along on his crippled feet until he reached Jesus. He knelt down in front of him. The disciples noticed him then. They drew back falling over one another.

"Keep away!" they warned Jesus. "If we go near him, we'll catch the disease, too, and become just like him!"

The man held out two stumps that had once been hands. The rag had fallen from his face. His lips had been eaten away with the dreaded disease. He could hardly stammer out his plea for help, but they all knew what he wanted. His eyes were so filled with longing and hope.

"If you want to," he said, "you can make me better."

"Oh, Jesus, teacher, come away!" desperately Simon tugged at his tunic. "Don't stand so close."

"Of course I want to make you better," Jesus bent forward. His broad fingers that had hewn huge pieces of wood into well-made tools closed firmly over the man's ugly hands.

How amazed the disciples were as they saw the man's eyes light up with joy. His hideous face was transformed.

"No one has had pity on him before," murmured Andrew.

"And no one has ever come close to him or touched him," Simon said. "How wonderful of Jesus! He's braver than any of us," the tough fishermen went on and the others nodded.

"Be well again!" Jesus placed his hands on the man's raised head. Tears streamed down his face. With hands that could move properly he grabbed Jesus' wrists.

He jumped to his feet, "Oh Rabbi, thank you, thank you."

The disciples had crowded around now.

"This is the moment we've all been waiting for. Surely this is proof that Jesus is the Messiah!"

But to their surprise Jesus told the man, "Don't tell anyone about this. Go straight to the priest as the Law of Moses demands. Let him examine you, and when he decides that you're well you must offer the sacrifice laid down in the Law. Then everyone will have sure proof that you are healed."

But the man had already darted away, shouting his good news at the top of his voice. A great crowd gathered about him.

"Come," said Jesus to his bewildered friends and they slipped away into a lonely place.

Mark 1

174

"Stretch out your hand"

"**L**ook, here he comes!" a murmur of annoyance and surprise came from the group of Pharisees who were already in all the best places in the synagogue.

"I wonder that he dares show his face in our synagogue after the way he's openly broken our sacred Law about the Sabbath!" one of them said self-righteously.

"*And* he teaches his disciples to do the same!" another one raised his voice in hatred.

They were annoyed because Jesus and his disciples had been wandering through the fields on the Sabbath day. They were hungry, so they had picked some of the ears of wheat and eaten the grain. When the Pharisees had soundly scolded them for such a breach of the strict laws of the Sabbath, when no work of any kind could be done, Jesus had said calmly: "God made the Sabbath for the good of men. We mustn't be slaves to it." And as if that reply hadn't been outrageous enough, he had taken their breath away when he had added: "The Son of Man is Lord even of the Sabbath."

So now they all watched him closely to see what he would do.

Their heads reverently covered, Jesus and his disciples joined in the singing of the psalm.

But Jesus had already noticed the man whose hand was so bent and crippled that he would never be able to work in the fields or go out with the fishing boats. "Come up to the front!" Jesus called, striding forward so that everyone could see him. The man followed him. Everyone craned their necks to see what would happen next.

Jesus looked around them. His face was very serious.

"What is the real meaning of the Sabbath?" he said. "What does God's Law really expect us to do? Surely it's wrong to pass by someone who needs our help and not do anything for him just because it's the Sabbath? What do you think, shouldn't we help people even if it is the day of rest?"

Anger blazed in Jesus' eyes. "How far their hearts are from you, Father!" he thought. "They're so religious, but they don't know what their religion really means. They're still so stubborn in their beliefs, and so wrong too, aren't they, Father?" he thought.

"Stretch out your hand." His voice had the ring of authority that always set people's hearts beating. Everyone was staring expectantly.

But as Jesus healed the man's deformed hand, in front of them all there was a stir and a scuffle. The Pharisees stalked out of the synagogue.

Simon and Andrew, James and John looked at one another.

"They've gone to join with the people of King Herod's group, you may be sure," they whispered to one another.

They saw fear in one another's eyes. They knew that already Jesus had made powerful enemies. Already people were plotting to kill him.

Mark 2 and 3

"Who is this man?"

One evening Jesus and his disciples decided to cross Lake Galilee from Capernaum, on Simon's and Andrew's side of the Lake, to Philip's side.

They often crossed this way along the northern edge of the lake.

Other boats were there, too, bobbing on the waves.

As the disciples rowed, Jesus bunched his cloak up into a pillow and stretched out to sleep.

A tremendous storm suddenly blew up. The wind farther south whipped the waves furiously.

These storms were common during the day. The fishermen usually went out at night after their catch, in order to avoid being caught in such a storm, for the waves could easily capsize their small boats.

They hadn't expected a storm that evening. It took them by surprise and frightened them terribly. The wind whistled against them. The waves washed foaming over the sides of the boat.

Jesus was sound asleep.

Frantically they shook him awake.

"Teacher, teacher, don't you care that we're about to be drowned!" they shouted their complaints above the gale. "Do something, quickly. Save us!"

Jesus stood up. "Wind, be quiet," he commanded. "Waves, be still!"

Immediately the wind died away. There was a quiet calm.

Now the disciples were more terrified than ever. They clung together, sodden, shaking not from cold but from fear.

Jesus saw the doubt, the wonder, the hope and the disbelief in their eyes.

"Why are you so frightened now?" he asked them. "Haven't you any faith in me? Don't you recognise yet who I really am?"

But they still clasped each other tightly.

"Who is this man?" they whispered. They shook their heads. There were so many possible answers.

The question bored deep into their hearts. If they knew the answer they dared not give it.

"Even the wind and the waves obey him," Andrew sighed. "Everybody else is ruled by them. But not Jesus. Is he the Christ, the one whom God has specially sent to the world?"

Mark 4

The madman in the tombs

It had been so wild on the lake. Then Jesus had done that tremendous thing and calmed the storm. Now the disciples were very quiet as they got out of the boat.

"Who is this?" they just didn't know the answer.

As they were tying up the boat, they heard an uncanny cry. It sounded like the howl of a wild beast in pain on the mountains.

Yet it was the cry of a man, they realised, and they shrank back in alarm.

A raving lunatic came bounding out of one of the large empty tombs cut in the rocks nearby. Broken chains dangled from his wrists and ankles. They jangled together as the madman screamed again, waving his arms and tearing at his naked body with his long fingernails and the sharp stones from the hillsides.

The disciples looked at Jesus. They saw him pull his rough cloak over his head and knew he was already praying. His lips moved. He stretched out his hands.

The madman caught sight of him and fell on his knees.

"Jesus, Son of the Most High God!" he screamed. The disciples looked at one another.

"These are the words we've not dared to say," Simon said and some of the others nodded, while Judas sneered.

"They're the words of a maniac. He's possessed. How can you believe what he says?"

The man was jabbering on. "Jesus, what do you want with me?"

"Be healed! Be healed!" Jesus replied.

"Oh, swear by God that you won't torture me," cried the man. "Oh!" he screamed again.

"He's possessed by evil spirits," the disciples whispered in awe. "They're fighting with one another."

"What is your name?" Jesus asked.

"Mob! Mob!" the man yelled in a strange, high pitched voice. "There are mobs of them pulling me apart because of you, Jesus. Oh! Leave them in peace. Don't send them away from this place."

"Stop them! Stop them! Our pigs! Oh, come back! Grab them for us!" men were shouting close by. Frightened by the yells of the madman, an enormous herd of pigs suddenly stampeded.

They were owned by some wealthy Greek farmers who had big houses in the non-Jewish town of Gadara, seven miles away, and had been grazing close by. Now they were rushing madly past Jesus and his disciples, and before anyone could stop them the whole herd had charged over the edge of the cliff and were drowned in the lake below.

The swineherds rushed away to report the loss to their owners.

"We saw the madman who lives in the tombs kneeling in front of a Jewish Rabbi who'd just crossed over the lake with his disciples. The mad-

man was in a dreadful state, screaming and imploring the Rabbi to leave them all – he meant the spirits which possess him – in peace. The next thing we knew was that the pigs stampeded and they rushed over the cliff and were all drowned."

"What all of them! But that was more than two thousand pigs!" gasped the owners, wringing their hands at the loss of money that meant.

All the people who heard put down their tools and went off to see what had happened.

"There's the Jewish Rabbi and his disciples!" they pointed.

"But where's the lunatic? There's no sign of him at all."

"Where can he be then?"

"Here," a voice said, and all the people stopped short in amazement. The speaker was a quiet man, who was sitting so reverently at the Jewish Rabbi's feet that they had taken him to be one of his closest disciples.

"Yes, I am in my right mind now," the man said, "and the Rabbi himself has wrapped his mantle around me and tended the cuts on my body."

The crowd backed away in fear. They whispered among themselves for a while.

"Please, sir," one of them said to Jesus, "would you mind leaving our territory? We're sorry to ask you to go, but the loss of our masters' pigs has cost them much money and will cause us a lot of trouble. We really respect your powers. You certainly did heal this madman. It's really unbelievable, but, well, would you mind very much . . ."

Jesus stood up. "Of course we'll go away." He led the way back down to the boat. The man he had healed followed him, clinging on to him desperately.

"Please, please, let me go with you," he begged.

Jesus shook his head. He laid his hands on the man's shoulders. "No, you must go back home to your family. They'll be thrilled to see you after so long! Go and tell them what a great thing the Lord God has done for you. He's been so kind to you."

"I'll tell them, then. I'll tell everyone!" the man promised fervently. He stood for a long time at the edge of Lake Galilee watching the little boat, which looked as if it had weathered a bad storm, sail out of sight.

Then he went home. He travelled through the group of Greek cities called the Ten Towns and told everybody what Jesus had done for him.

Everyone who heard was filled with wonder.

Mark 5

"It's time to wake up now!"

As soon as Jesus and his disciples had reached their own side of the lake, a great crowd of people pressed all around them.

Thin crippled fingers were stretched out to him. These sick people clamoured on every side. The disciples, crushed together, turned hopelessly away.

Pushing desperately through the throng came a well-dressed man, a man with such an air of breeding and authority, that some people gave way to let him through.

It was Jairus, one of the leaders of the synagogue.

He fell down on his knees in the dust. His soft, jewelled hands touched Jesus' feet.

"Please, Rabbi, come to my house. My little girl, my only daughter, is dying. Come with me, Jesus, I beg you. Lay your hands on her and heal her."

Gently Jesus helped Jairus to his feet. "I'll come."

The great crowd of people still surged around him. Jesus and Jairus made their way forward with difficulty; it was as if they were wading against the tide. Suddenly Jesus stopped.

"Someone touched me!"

"Look at all the people pressed around us!" said the disciples, trying to hurry him forward. "Is it any wonder that someone has touched you?"

"Who touched me?" Jesus asked, looking all around him.

Frightened, and trembling, a pale-faced woman came out of the crowd.

"Sir," she said, "I touched you. I've been ill at home for twelve years. I spent all my money on doctors' bills. No one has helped me. Then I saw you in the crowd. I touched the hem of your cloak. I knew that was enough to make me well."

Jesus smiled at her. His face looked tired, drained of strength.

"My daughter, go in peace. Your faith has made you better."

The people around him cheered.

But Simon looked with concern at his friend's pale face.

"It must take a tremendous amount of strength from him," he suddenly thought, "healing people.

He was so exhausted last night that he would have slept all through the storm if we hadn't wakened him."

"Jairus, where is Jairus?" some people pushed their way through the crowd. "Oh, you've found Jesus. But, Sir, I'm afraid it's too late. Don't trouble the Rabbi any more. Your little girl died a few minutes ago."

Jairus gave a long shuddering sigh. He looked in despair at Jesus. Had he humbled himself before the carpenter from Nazareth just to hear this?

"Don't be afraid," Jesus' words strengthened him. "Have faith, Jairus. Have faith."

"Stay here," he told the crowd and all his disciples. "Simon, James and John, you come with me!"

Baffled, the crowd and the other disciples watched Jesus, Jairus and the three fishermen go off together into Jairus' house. What a commotion there was! All the women of the household and other mourners, hired for the occasion, were wailing their grief. They had ripped their clothing. They had ashes on their dishevelled hair. They beat their breasts, they tore their long hair and they yelled and howled

because they knew that the little girl had died.

"Hush!" Jesus said. "What's all this wailing? The child is not dead. She's just fallen into a deep sleep."

"Ho! Ho!" they jeered. "What nonsense! She's dead! That's why Jairus' servants sent for us. No one makes mistakes about death. A deep sleep? Yes, a very deep sleep!"

"Get out!" Jesus ordered. "Go away at once. I tell you she's asleep and there's no need for that noise."

"Come," he said to Jairus and his wife. Together they went up to the little girl. Simon, James and John followed.

She lay on a low bed, for this was a wealthy home and she had a room of her own.

The child could have been a little statue, life-like but without life.

Jesus lifted one of her hands and held it in his. "Little girl, it's time to wake up now," he said.

Her eyelids fluttered, then closed again. Under the rug that covered her they saw her legs move. She arched her back, rubbed her free hand across her face and sat up smiling.

Then she jumped up and ran across to her parents.

They hugged her and kissed her, laughing and crying and trying to find words to thank Jesus.

He shook his head. "I wakened her from sleep," he said. "Please, don't spread it around. Don't tell the people anything unusual has happened."

They nodded, but they did not know how they could keep their joy a secret.

"Get her something to eat," Jesus said, ruffling her hair as he went away, "or the girl will faint from hunger after so long and deep a sleep."

Mark 5

The hole in the roof

Bread was baking somewhere. The man lying on the sleeping mat in the corner could smell it. It was beginning to burn, but there was nothing he could do about it. He couldn't go and take it out of the oven. He couldn't stand up and walk.

For years he had been lying on the mat in the corner of the room. He had watched his family grow poorer without a father to work in the fields for them. He had watched his wife become careworn and cross.

He lay in the dark room, unless some of the neighbours carried his bed outside where he could at least feel the sunshine and look above him at the sky.

No one has been near him today. Where could they all have gone? Where was his wife? What were his children doing? They were never as quiet as this.

Then he heard the sound of eager feet running fast.

"Jesus has come back to Capernaum!" Four friends burst into the room.

"He's preaching in one of the houses just a few streets away. The whole town has left whatever they were doing and have gone into the house. They're packed together inside like the oranges in a basket on market day," one of them told the cripple.

Before he knew what had happened, his friends had each taken a corner of his sleeping mat and were carrying him carefully out through the door.

He bumped and swayed along the deserted streets but when they reached the house, the people outside, standing on tiptoe and pushing against each other to try to catch a glimpse of Jesus, said,

"It's no use. You'll never squeeze a bed into there. There's not an inch of room!"

The four men looked at one another in dismay, but they were determined to take their sick friend to Jesus. They soon thought of a way.

"Quick, the roof!" they told one another.

As carefully as they could, they carried the mattress up the stone steps outside the house. They laid their friend down and quickly got to work.

The roof was made of mud and brushwood dried and hardened. It was easy to make a hole in it.

Down below the people around Jesus looked up in surprise as twigs and crumbled mud came dropping down on to their heads.

Four faces, hot and sweating, peered through the hole.

They bound some cloth round the four corners of the mattress. Carefully they lowered the mattress into the room.

People were laughing now. "That's friendship for you!" they told one another and, although they were anxious to see what would happen, some of them backed away through the door so that there was room for the mattress to lie on the floor in front of Jesus.

Jesus and the lame man looked at each other. Then Jesus glanced up at the four eager faces peering in through the hole, just waiting for the word from him that would heal their friend.

"How full of faith you are!" he said. He looked down at the paralyzed man.

"Son, your sins are all forgiven," he said.

His words were like a flashing sword.

The religious folk, the scribes, looked furious.

"How can this man say such a thing?" they thought. "Only God has the authority to forgive sins."

Jesus knew what they were thinking.

"Listen," he said, turning in their direction. "Why are you harbouring such thought in your unloving hearts?" Jesus' eyes blazed. "Which do you think it's easier to do: tell a man, 'Your sins are forgiven' or heal a paralysed man?"

They couldn't answer him.

"Both are God's work and he has given me authority to do both!" Jesus said. His disciples read in each other's expectant eyes the excited thoughts they were all thinking. "I'll prove to you that I have power and authority from God both to heal a man's crippled body and drive away all the dark sins that warp and maim our souls," he said. He looked down at the helpless man on his bed.

"I order you now!" his voice rang out with an authority that amazed them all. "Get up at once. Roll up your mattress and walk home!"

There was utter silence. Slowly, fearfully, the man staggered to his feet. He looked at Jesus. The man hadn't bent his back for years. He stooped down, rolled up his mattress and in front of them all walked off home. His friends leaped from the roof and ran after him.

Everyone had burst into loud cheers. They praised God, laughing and shouting, "We've never seen anything like this!"

Mark 2

The picnic lunch

"Come," Jesus said. "We must go off to a lonely place where we can get away from all the people. We need to be by ourselves for a little while. Then you can rest."

The disciples got into their boat and rowed out across Lake Galilee.

But as soon as the crowd saw them going, they guessed where they were heading for.

"Come on!" they cried. "If we run fast, we'll get there ahead of them."

By the time Jesus and his disciples reached the shore they saw the lonely place thronged with a great crowd who sat around patiently on the hillside. The grass was fresh and green, for it was a day in early spring.

"I am grieved for them," Jesus said to his weary disciples. "They are like strayed sheep with no shepherd." So he taught them and laid his hands on the sick folk, curing them. All day long they hung on to his words, forgetting about the work they had left, the homes they had come from, the untouched food on their hearths.

But the disciples longed for rest and for food.

"It's getting late now," they said to Jesus. "Daylight is almost done. Send them away. They can go to the farms nearby and buy some food on their way home."

"Many of them rushed away after us without bringing any money," Jesus reminded them.

"Well what shall we do then, for they've been here for hours and had nothing to eat?" they asked.

Jesus looked at them seriously.

"You must give them something to eat yourselves!" he told them.

"What!" They couldn't believe their ears.

Judas was already counting out money from his pouch. Philip saw him: "There's no need to do that, Judas. Goodness, it would cost six months' wages to buy bread for so many people!" he said.

Andrew, Simon's brother, led a young boy to Jesus.

"This little lad has brought his picnic with him in his basket," Andrew explained.

The boy held open his basket. He took out his dinner wrapped up in a cloth, and shyly held it out to Jesus. "Take it, Jesus," he said.

"Thank you," Jesus said, unwrapping the cloth.

Five small flat loaves of barley bread (wheat was only eaten by the wealthy) lay in the cloth. The boy's mother had baked them at sunrise. She had packed them up for him to take when he had told her he was off with the crowd after Jesus. She had slipped in two small fish caught from Lake Galilee.

"That's not much for so many people," said Andrew, doubtfully.

"Ask them all to sit down in groups," Jesus said. So the people sat down in long rows and groups.

Jesus held the bread in front of him so they could all see it. He thanked God for it. Then he passed the little flat loaves to his disciples. They started to give them out amongst the people.

That was when everyone realised how hungry they were! They had all seen the loaves, five small very ordinary loaves, that had been in a small boy's basket all day.

Jesus held out the fish; two little fish, already cooked and looking a bit dry and shrivelled now. Again he thanked God for them. He gave two of his disciples the fish to take to the people.

And everybody ate and ate until they were full! The hungry people simply fell upon the food. There seemed to be no end of it. More and more bread and fish was passed round. The disciples borrowed empty baskets from a nearby farm and gathered up what was left. There was enough to fill twelve baskets.

The people were shouting now, cheering and laughing. "Let's make Jesus our King! Hooray! Jesus is the Deliverer. He's the one we've all been waiting for! Jesus, we'll march with you to the ends of the earth! We'll never be hungry again!"

But Jesus turned to them with sorrow in his eyes. "No!" he said. "I'm not that kind of King. Go away now, for my disciples are tired and must rest. I am going up into the hills alone. Hurry, go back to your homes before it is dark."

The crowd slowly melted away, puzzled, often looking back, deep in debate.

"Go now," Jesus told the disciples. "Row across to Bethsaida, Philip's town. The people there won't know anything yet about today's happenings, so you should be able to slip in quietly and get some sleep."

"What about you, Jesus?" they asked. "You look tired."

"I'm going into the hills to pray."

Mark 6

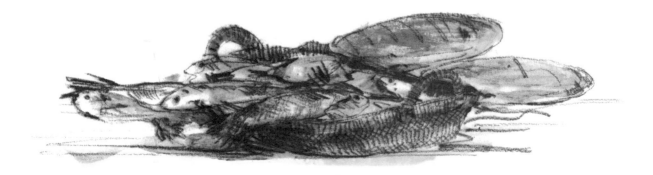

The secret follower

Nicodemus the Pharisee was puzzled. He had heard Jesus speak to the crowds. He listened with delight to his teaching.

Then reports went around of all his wonderful deeds; how he had made so many hopelessly ill people better; how a Roman centurion had not only sent for Jesus, but had also recognised in him the authority of God. The deeds that had set Galilee on fire were spoken of in Jerusalem, too, and Nicodemus found himself listening eagerly whenever anybody mentioned "Jesus, the carpenter from Nazareth". Nicodemus respected Jesus.

But there were other things about Jesus that puzzled Nicodemus. Everyone told stories of how he broke the Sabbath laws by healing people. At first Nicodemus, like the other strict Pharisees, found that very hard to understand. Nicodemus had his heart set on God. God would send his Messiah and he believed that Jesus had been sent from God.

"I think he is right to do good on the Sabbath," Nicodemus finally decided. "Only why does he break other rules? He eats food our Law says is unclean. He keeps company with sinners. Who *is* he?" the questions kept puzzling the pious Pharisee until one day he knew he would have to go and find out for himself.

Secretly, late one night, he slipped away from his house.

In the little room where Jesus stayed, his disciples were already dozing. They jumped up startled when they saw one of the leaders of the Pharisees standing in the room.

"Don't be alarmed. I'm alone. I've come to speak with Jesus."

He saw the fatigue leave Jesus' face as the smile of welcome which began on his lips spread to his eyes.

"Rabbi," he began respectfully, and Jesus knew the wealthy leader and learned teacher had a heart that was hungry for God. "I am perplexed about you. I know you are a teacher sent to us by God because no one could do all the wonderful things you do unless God were with him."

"You long for God, don't you?" Jesus said, and Nicodemus nodded slowly. "Listen, Nicodemus, I tell you the truth, no one will see the kingdom of God unless he is born all over again and becomes like a newborn baby belonging to God's family."

Now Nicodemus looked puzzled. "This is nonsense!" he exclaimed. "It's impossible for a grownup to become a little baby. How can anyone be born all over again?"

"Yet I tell you the truth," Jesus said. "You cannot enter the kingdom of God – no one can, unless you let God's Spirit work in your life. Don't you see? I'm not talking about the birth of a human baby. I'm talking on another level. I'm talking about the Spirit of God."

"Tell me something, Nicodemus," Jesus went on. "Have you ever seen the wind?"

The learned teacher shook his head, and the disciples from Galilee smiled. "The wind blows wherever it wishes. You can hear its sound. You can watch its direction, for as it touches the trees, they bend before it, but you cannot see the wind, Nicodemus, and God is like the wind. He sends his Spirit and our inner eyes are opened, the eyes of our mind, of our understanding, and we look up and see God. We understand his ways. That is something of what I mean by being born again."

"Oh Jesus, Jesus," sighed Nicodemus. "How can this be?"

"You're a great teacher of our Law," Jesus said.

"Can't you understand? I've spoken to you only of the things I've seen, and neither you nor any of the Pharisees can accept it. Well, if you don't believe when I talk to you about how God works on an ordinary human level, however will you believe when I talk to you about Heaven, for I came down from Heaven.

"Do you remember what Moses did when the people of Israel were being bitten by poisonous

people in the world. All you have to do is believe. Look, I have come like a light in the world." Jesus held the lamp high. Someone had swept the floor hastily before Jesus came, but they hadn't tidied away all the dust. It lay in a corner, and in another was a pile of odds and ends.

"You see," Jesus said, "light shows up all the dirt and litter, and so often people are like that. They prefer not to be exposed to God's pure light. They know they do wrong things, but it's easier to

snakes? He lifted up a serpent of bronze on a pole and held it up high. They only had to look at the bronze serpent and they were safe."

"Then they didn't die from the snake bites," said Nicodemus at once.

"Well, in the same way I must be lifted up, high above the people," Jesus said, and now the disciples looked puzzled and afraid. "Anyone who believes in me will live with God for ever. For God loved the world so much that he gave his only Son, not to judge the world but to save all the

blunder on in the dark. Whoever seeks what is true comes into the light, and the light shows up his obedience and faith in God."

Nicodemus went away puzzled still, but the words of Jesus remained with him and he became a secret believer. When Jesus died, Nicodemus and his friend Joseph went to the Roman governor and got permission to bury his body in a new tomb, one Joseph had bought for his own family use.

John 3

A rich man runs to Jesus

How fast he ran along the crowded road! He left his servants, left his beautiful cool house and rushed out into the heat of the day. He pushed past people whose smell offended his nostrils. He turned his face away from others whose deformed bodies offended his eyes.

He ran fast and he ran well, for he was rich enough to belong to the great stadium where the best athletes competed.

He ran to Jesus. He knelt on the dusty ground before Jesus.

"Good Master," he said. "Tell me what I must do to live the perfect life that God wants on this earth, and to live for ever with him after death?"

"Why do you call me good?" said Jesus. "Only God is good."

"I long for his goodness," answered the young man. "I am a leader among men. If I am not careful, I can use my power to hurt, not to do good."

"You know all the commandments," Jesus said.

"Yes," the young man said. "And ever since I was small I have obeyed them all carefully."

The disciples saw the love of Jesus shine out of his eyes and light up his face. How well they had come to know that look of love! They knew Jesus had seen in this rich young man a heart that longed for God.

"You need only one thing in your life," Jesus said.

Eagerly the young man listened. "I have so many, many things, Rabbi. One more thing will not be hard for me. What must I do?"

"Go your way. Sell all that you have," Jesus was looking straight at him, and love shone in his gaze. "Give away the money you get for all your things. Give it to the poor. You'll have riches in heaven then!" he added with a smile. "Then come and follow me."

But gloom had spread over the man's face. That one thing he still needed was too hard for him. He could not bear to part with his possessions.

Sadly, slowly, dejectedly he stumbled away to his beautiful house. He was a very rich man.

Jesus was sad too. He said to his disciples, "How hard it is for a rich man to unburden himself and enter the kingdom! You know the narrowest gateway into Jerusalem?"

They all nodded. It was called "the needle's eye" because it was so small.

"Have you seen a poor trader trying to get his loaded camels through?" Jesus asked, and they roared with laughter. It was such an impossible thing to do, but a stranger to Jerusalem might well try.

"Well, it's like that when a man still clings on to his possessions and wordly status and tries to enter the Kingdom."

"Look," Simon said. "We've left everything to follow you."

"Yes, I know," Jesus said. "And I tell you this: anyone who leaves anything to follow me will receive it all back a hundred times over. So don't worry; just put the kingdom of God first."

Mark 10

The man who climbed a tree

Zacchaeus was one of the smallest men in the town, but he lived in one of the largest houses. The Romans had given him one of the most important jobs in the town and he was one of the richest men in Jericho. But all the people of Jericho hated him more than anyone else, for he was the chief tax-collector.

He had heard all about Jesus, so when his servant mentioned one morning that Jesus was in Jericho, Zacchaeus said, "Oh, I must see him!"

"Well, hurry then, master, because a huge crowd has followed him," said the servant.

Zacchaeus rushed outside. He stood on tiptoe. He craned his neck. He even jumped up and down. It was no use. He was too small to see over their shoulders.

Suddenly he had an idea. He remembered that, a little farther on, a fig-mulberry tree grew by the roadside. People often stopped and rested in its shade.

Zacchaeus, who hadn't climbed a tree since he was a boy, clumsily scrambled up its trunk.

The leaves grew so thickly that, if he was lucky, no one would see him, clinging to one of the branches. But he could peer through the dark green foliage

and get a good view of Jesus. In fact, he was only just in time. For Jesus was coming along the road. Zacchaeus saw his broad shoulders, his travel-worn clothes. Now he could see his face.

The shadow of the tree fell across Jesus' path. Zacchaeus suddenly saw sorrow in his eyes – such sorrow! It made the little man shiver.

"Zacchaeus!"

He nearly fell out of the tree!

Jesus was talking to him! He didn't care that people round about were pointing up to him and laughing. He didn't care that the joke was going round: Jericho's chief tax-collector had climbed up a tree to see the prophet from Galilee!

"Hurry! Come down!" Jesus said. "Because I must stay at your home today."

Joyfully Zacchaeus scrambled down from the tree and rushed home to get everything ready.

But now the crowd was grumbling. "He's a scoundrel and a cheat. He's made himself rich at our expense. Don't you know that he's in the pay of the Romans, Jesus?"

"He's a descendant of Abraham like the rest of us," Jesus reminded them. "God has sent me to bring home the lost sheep."

Calmly he went on his way. He soon found Zacchaeus' beautiful big house.

"Welcome, welcome, Jesus," called Zacchaeus, joyfully running to meet his guest, while his slaves brought forward water to wash the feet of Jesus and his friends.

Zacchaeus welcomed each one of them with a kiss, as the custom was. He gave them costly oil which his slaves rubbed into their hair.

Then he led them to his table, and they lay on couches around it while the servants stood ready to give them whatever they needed. Furious, the crowd waited outside. They jeered at Zacchaeus and at Jesus. They spoilt the whole meal – until something happened that turned their jeers to loud cheers.

Servants were carrying out costly possessions: woven rugs, vessels of gold, the finest cloth and beautiful clothes.

"They're yours!" they shouted to the astonished crowd. "Come on, all of you poor people. This is what you've been waiting for! The master's giving away all his ill-gotten goods."

"Here you are!" cried Zacchaeus. "Forgive me! I'm giving you four times as much money back. Forgive me. I'm sorry I cheated you. It's yours, everyone! Jesus is my Master now. I'm not in the pay of Rome any more."

It was the talk of Jericho that day, but Zacchaeus turned back into his empty house and into Jesus' warm embrace.

"Salvation has come to your house today, Zacchaeus," said Jesus, as he hugged the little man.

Zacchaeus nodded. He was weeping now.

"That's because you stopped beneath the fig-mulberry tree and called me by my name!" he said. "Rabbi, I'll never forget the way you spoke to me! I'll follow your teachings from now on. I'll never cheat anyone again."

Luke 19

A blind man runs to Jesus

"How quiet it is today," the blind man thought to himself. He had been sitting by the roadside for hours, hoping someone would take pity on him and drop him a coin. Usually crowds of people flocked in and out of Jericho, but today there was not a step to be heard.

Bartimaeus soon tired of sitting there. He was about to give up and grope his way somewhere else when he heard the hubbub. Many feet were trampling in the dust. Leather sandals creaked and slapped against their wearers' soles. Bare feet walked almost noiselessly – but Bartimaeus, who had only his hearing to guide him, picked up the sound they made.

Perhaps it was a procession! He began to feel scared – supposing he was trampled on! No one else would worry. How lonely and wretched it was to be blind and a beggar! He felt very sorry for himself.

Now they were passing by. He tugged people's garments as they brushed by his face.

"Who is it? What's happening?" he asked, but no one heeded him and his voice was lost in the clamour of the crowd. At last someone who knew him said, "We're following the teacher from Galilee. Jesus of Nazareth has just passed by this way!"

Immediately Bartimaeus bellowed: "Jesus; Je-sus. Son of David, have mercy on me! Je-sus, help me!" His voice was hoarse; his throat was sore, and people all around scolded him. "Be quiet!" they said. "What a din!"

But he shouted even more loudly: "Son of Da-vid. Help me!"

Jesus stopped. "Who is that calling?" he asked.

"Oh, it's only the blind beggar," they said. "Old Bartimaeus, you know. He's always sitting there just by the gate, begging."

"Tell him to come to me," said Jesus.

"He wants you!" they shouted to Bartimaeus.

"Cheer up!" someone said. "Jesus is calling you."

At once Bartimaeus cast aside his shabby old cloak, leapt to his feet and ran to Jesus. How people laughed unkindly at the sight of the old blind man in his rags racing along the road, his thin knobbly fingers stretched out before him, in a vain attempt to guide him. He hadn't run like that for years!

But Jesus didn't laugh. He steadied the old blind beggar as he stumbled, panting, toward him.

"What do you want me to do for you?"

"Teacher, teacher!" begged Bartimaeus, breathlessly. "Oh, I want to see again!" Tears rolled down his hollowed cheeks, making channels in the dust that the crowd's trampling feet had blown into his face.

"Go on your way now," Jesus said. "Your faith has made you well!"

Bartimaeus blinked. The first thing he saw was the face of Jesus, and in his kind eyes the man who had been blind saw the love of God. Many in the crowd who had eyes to see were blind to what Bartimaeus saw.

Crying with joy, Bartimaeus followed Jesus along the road giving thanks to God. Some people in the crowd joined him. So they walked along, praising God with all their hearts as they followed Jesus on toward Jerusalem, twenty miles away.

Mark 10

"You must keep this a secret"

The disciples felt tired and disappointed. Jesus had done so many marvellous things, but he just didn't fit the picture everyone had of the Messiah – the Deliverer who would do miraculous things to bring the people wealth and power over all the nations. He kept going to the outcasts, to the beggars and tax-collectors. The Pharisees and Sadducees were just waiting for the right moment to seize Jesus and kill him.

So now Jesus and his followers went like outlaws into another part of Galilee, to the beautiful city which King Philip, one of Herod's three sons, had made into a summer capital.

They were unknown here. They climbed into the hills where the River Jordan had its source.

It grew out of the melting snows of the great towering mountain, Mount Hermon.

There in the quiet Jesus turned to them.

"What does everyone say about me?" he asked.

"Who do people say that I am?"

It was the very question they themselves often asked, but never aloud. Jesus' words were like a sword in their conscience: did they really believe him to be the One sent from God, the Anointed One specially chosen, spoken of by Moses and all the prophets? So they answered hesitantly.

"Well, some people think you're John the Baptist come back to life again," they began.

"Others say that you're Elijah. You know we all believe he will come back one day when our land needs him . . ."

"Other people say that you're another of the prophets. They all think you're someone special, Jesus," they added.

He looked straight at them. "What about you?" he asked. "Who do you say that I am?"

They didn't know where to look. Certainly not at one another in case each should see the other's doubt. Certainly not at Jesus, in case the costly words they dared not say sprang to their lips at the sight of the love and sorrow in his eyes.

It was Simon who said it, brusque, burly Simon, the impulsive fisherman. He put into words what they all thought.

"You are the Messiah, the Anointed One sent from God. You are the Son of the Living God!"

They saw joy like fire light up Jesus' face. He flung his arms around Simon. "Oh, Simon, son of Jonas, how favoured you are! For it was my Father in heaven who put those words in your heart. Now I am giving you a new name. You are Cephas, Peter, the name which means rock. My church will be built on the rock you have described, that I am the Christ."

They were all smiling now, caught up in joy. Yet still they did not understand. They thought simply that things were going to be all right now. Jesus *was* the Messiah. He would establish his kingdom of power. They envied Peter, the one who would hold such an important position in it.

Jesus sighed. How hard it was to make them understand! He had learnt the lesson so clearly alone, hungry in the desert, and during all the nights of prayer.

"Look," he said. "You must keep this a secret!" His eyes searched their faces. "I can see I must teach you the things about the Messiah that everyone is too blind to see — yet they're written so clearly in the Scriptures."

He began to teach the disciples what the prophets foretold about the Messiah. He would bring peace and love; abundant riches, but not in the sense of money. The riches were the things of God that Jesus had tried to explain in his parables: forgiveness, a new family to belong to, joy that no trouble could take away.

"These are the things I bring," Jesus said. "But first, as the Scriptures plainly say: I shall be rejected by everyone; people will spit at me, turn their backs on me. They will kill me and my body will be laid in a new tomb. And then after three days I shall come back from the dead."

The disciples couldn't understand. They listened in horror.

"No, no, no!" Peter cried. "You must be wrong. It can't be like this."

But Jesus spoke very sternly to him. "That is the way the devil spoke to me in the wilderness," he said. "And that is the way everybody wants to think, but it's not God's way!" Patiently he taught them. "You will all have to bear your cross, too, if you want to be my followers," he said. "Every day you must trample on your selfish longings. That's carrying the cross. You must give up your lives and you will have a life that's really worth living. For you will be following God's way."

Mark 8

The cloud on the mountain

One day Jesus took Peter, James and John with him further into the quiet hills. They climbed higher and higher until their footprints were crunching through the untrodden snow. The sun shone across the snow, dazzling their eyes.

The fishermen were not used to the cold loneliness of the hills, but Jesus strode ahead of them tirelessly, gladly.

"He is going ahead to pray," Peter whispered. "He will meet his Father."

"I'm frightened of him," John murmured. "He's suddenly become so different from us, as though he walks into a light which would overpower us. He's going beyond us, somehow. I don't want to lose him, but I'm afraid to follow."

The sun had grown brighter than ever. The three disciples shaded their eyes. They were tired; Jesus was striding ahead of them and they did not try to follow. The sun was very warm against the rocks. The weary men huddled together and fell asleep.

Perhaps it was the glory that woke them! Startled, they looked up, rubbing their eyes. They saw Jesus far ahead. His rough homespun robe gleamed white against the snow-covered mountain side. He seemed to be clad in light that shone through him and in him and all around him.

"No dye on earth could make cloth so clean and pure," Peter whispered.

"Look, Jesus isn't alone. Two others are walking with him."

Awed, they watched and saw Jesus talking freely with the greatest of all the prophets: Moses and Elijah.

Low over the mountain hovered a great cloud. It was not a cloud of snow or of rain. It was a cloud of light. God's glory flooded it. The cloud's shadow fell over them. It was not a dark shadow. Such a cloud could never reflect darkness! Light poured out of the cloud. They felt themselves soaked through and through in this downpour of glory.

Then they heard a voice. What they heard thrilled them beyond their wildest dreams. It terrified them, and gave them great peace.

"This is my own dear Son," said God in the glory that danced before their eyes, that rejoiced their innermost spirit. "Listen to him."

And then they did not know what to do or say. They fell flat on their faces in the wet shining snow and Jesus came to them. His touch comforted them.

"Don't be afraid. Get up now."

When they stood up they were alone with Jesus in the snow.

"Don't tell anyone what you have seen," begged Jesus. "Say nothing until the Son whom God has given out of his love for the world, dies and has been raised from death."

But still they didn't understand.

"What does this mean: raised from death?" they wondered.

"Rabbi," they asked Jesus, "why do the teachers of the law tell us that Elijah has to come back first before the Messiah comes?"

"They are right. Elijah must come back. Then the Son of Man can come. But I have a question for you," Jesus said. "Why do the Scriptures tell us that the Son of Man will suffer terribly and be rejected and cast out by everyone?"

But they shook their heads, unwilling even to think of such a terrible thing.

"I tell you," Jesus said, "Elijah has already come back." And they knew he meant John the Baptist. "People treated him exactly as they wanted. He was locked up in a dungeon and killed. The Scriptures tell of that, too."

Fearfully, they glanced up at him. They saw what Zacchaeus had seen: there was sorrow in his eyes, so controlled and restrained that they realised its source was in suffering far beyond their understanding.

Mark 9

"Shout now Jerusalem! Here is your king!"

As Passover time drew near Jesus made his way south to Jerusalem. The city was already thronged with pilgrims from Judaea and Galilee, and countries near and far, wherever Jewish people had settled throughout the centuries.

All the small villages around Jerusalem were crowded, too. Jesus and his twelve disciples stayed in a small village called Bethany. There they had good friends; two sisters called Martha and Mary, and their brother whose name was Lazarus.

After they had rested, the small group made ready for the short, final stage of their journey.

Jesus sent two of them ahead. "Go into the next village. There you will find a young donkey. It hasn't been broken in yet. No one has ridden it. Untie it and bring it here."

"Suppose someone tries to stop us?" they asked.

"Just say, 'The Master needs to borrow it'."

The two men went ahead. They found the foal, tied to the door of a house. They started to untie it.

"Here you two," people standing by started. "What do you think you're up to?"

"The Master needs it," they said.

"The Master, eh? Oh, all right then." The people let them lead the donkey away.

They brought the foal to Jesus, and then their hearts were happy. Gladly they laid their heavy cloaks on the little foal's back for Jesus to ride in comfort. Smiles spread over their faces. The other ten were starting to cheer, for to their minds came the words of one of the prophets, and Jesus was fulfilling the Messiah's triumph.

"Daughter of Zion, rejoice and be glad!
Shout now Jerusalem, here is your King!

He is triumphant, though humbly he's clad
Riding a donkey; what peace he will bring."

They chanted the words together. Other pilgrims from Galilee saw what was happening.

"It's Jesus. It's our great Prophet! Look, they're cheering! Hear what they're saying!"

"Shout now Jerusalem, here is your King.
Hosanna! Hosanna! His praises we sing!"

The pilgrims joined in. Like the disciples, they pulled the young, fresh green branches from the palm trees at the roadside, and waved them as they marched singing behind Jesus. Other people strewed the road ahead of the donkey with branches. Carefully, delicately, the unbroken foal stepped along. And Jesus fondled his coarse woolly mane and encouraged him with gentle words when the young animal started in alarm at the cheers and singing.

People even laid their cloaks on the road in front of Jesus, and everyone, those who ran on ahead and those who followed, joined the singing. "Praise God! Blessings upon the Son of David who comes in the name of the Lord! Blessings upon the one who has come to set up the kingdom of David. Praise God! Hosanna!"

People bustling through the busy streets stopped to stare. A few joined the song.

"Shout now, Jerusalem, here is your King.
Hosanna! Hosanna! His praises we sing."

But the Pharisees turned on Jesus. "Teacher from the country!" they said scornfully. "Order your followers not to make such a din!"

"If they keep quiet," Jesus answered, "I tell you, the very stones of Jerusalem will shout."

The crowd cheered and sang the louder at his reply, but when they came close to Jerusalem, Jesus held out his arms. Tears came to his eyes. Alone in the cheering, happy crowd, he wept.

"Oh Jerusalem!" he mourned. "If only you could really see what I have come to do among you! I come in the name of the Lord, but it is not David's mighty kingdom I will establish within your walls. You cannot see that. You don't understand what real peace means!" His grief broke from him and he sobbed openly so that the crowd looked on amazed, but he knew what lay in the future and they didn't.

"Because you didn't recognise the time when God came to save you, your enemies will destroy your people entirely. You'll be besieged and captured. They'll not leave a single stone in its place."

So Jesus came into Jerusalem blinded with tears.

The pilgrims went up to the Temple and then, baffled and bewildered, they disappeared into the crowds, and the tired, disappointed disciples trailed after Jesus through the oncoming dusk back to Bethany, to the warm welcome of Martha and Lazarus and their sorrowing sister, Mary.

Luke 19
Mark 11

The market in the Temple

Noise, noise, noise! The Outer Court of the Temple was teeming with activity. Pilgrims from many different countries thronged the courtyard. They lined up at the bankers' tables to change their money. For they had to buy doves to offer as sacrifices, and the only money that was accepted was a coin from Tyre. It was exactly like the old Hebrew shekel. The priests gave the money-changers their licence. They did a thriving business and, although the money for the offerings went to the Temple, the bankers were wily enough to make a good profit.

Doves in their cages beat their wings, traders set up their stalls and hawked the doves to worshippers. Outside, since it was Passover time, sheep bleated and oxen stamped and lowed.

It was like one vast market, rowdy, bustling . . . and wrong. How wrong! The prophet had said how wrong it all was. He had said that the Messiah would make the worship of God pure and clean again.

Crash! One of the heavy tables went tumbling. Coins rolled jingling in all directions. Furious money-lenders shouted in protest, but no one paid any attention. Jesus sent another and yet another

table flying. He toppled the stalls of the dove-sellers. With a wild shining of their wings the caged doves flew free, soaring high into the sunlight above the Temple.

Confused, people didn't know whether to cheer or to run.

Jesus picked up the bits of rope that lay with all the other rubbish, and knotted them together as a makeshift whip. He drove away the sheep and the oxen. Out into the narrow hilly streets that led to the Temple they ran, oxen bleating and lowing, mingling with the crowds that flowed unceasingly up and down to keep the Passover.

"Listen!" Jesus cried. "Don't the Scriptures tell us that God has said, 'My House shall be called a house of prayer for all peoples'? A house of prayer! You've turned it into a robbers' den! I am making it clean."

The Temple was quieter now. Jesus began to teach the people, who had gathered around in amazement. The Pharisees, the chief priests and the teachers of the Law were furious.

"We must kill this man," they fumed. But they dared not arrest him during the day because he was surrounded by people who hung on to every word he taught them.

Mark 11

Questions and answers

The day after Jesus had cleared the Temple courts of all the bankers and traders, he and the disciples went back to Jerusalem.

As they were crossing the courtyard of the Temple, the chief priests, the teachers and elders came to him.

"What right have you to do things like this?" they asked. "Who gave you the authority to overthrow all the religious traditions of our people?"

Jesus looked at them. He knew that if he said,

"I am the Son of God. He has given me the authority to set up real worship in his Temple," they would have killed him on the spot.

So Jesus didn't give them a direct answer. He said, "I'm going to ask you just one question. Answer that and I will tell you who gives me the right to do all these things."

"Ask then," they said.

"John baptized people and told them that God's kingdom was at hand, that the Messiah was here. Who gave John the right to do this?"

They muttered together, heads close. "Whatever shall we say?" they debated. "If we say 'God', Jesus will ask us – 'Well, why didn't you believe John and accept God's kingdom?' But if we say, 'Oh some person must have given John this authority . . .' no, we can't say that. The people are convinced that John was a prophet straight from God."

So they answered lamely, "We don't know."

"Then neither will I tell you who gives me the right to do those things," said Jesus, and the disciples smiled triumphantly. All except Judas.

"Why didn't Jesus say openly who he was?" he brooded.

Once again the religious leaders tried to trick him with more clever questions. Some Pharisees addressed him respectfully, flattering him. "Teacher, we know you are honest. We know you're ready to teach the truth no matter what people think about you. Tell us then," they went on, "is it against our Law for us to pay our taxes to the Roman Emperor? Should we pay them or not?"

If Jesus said it was right to pay taxes to Rome, not one person in that crowd would have followed him any more. They hated paying taxes so much. But if Jesus said, "Oh, it's wrong for Jews to pay taxes to earthly powers. We must pay our taxes to

God, to his Temple," he could have been arrested as a rebel against the Roman government. The leaders waited eagerly for his reply.

The crowd round about waited anxiously to hear what Jesus would say.

"Why do you try to trick me with such questions?" Jesus answered. "Fetch me a coin, a Roman denarius." Someone went off for one, because they were in the Temple where foreign coins were not allowed. He tossed it to Jesus. Jesus held the coin out to the Jewish leaders. "Whose head do you see stamped on it?" he asked.

"The Emperor's," they answered.

"Well then," Jesus said, "pay to the Emperor what belongs to him and pay to God what belongs to God."

The leaders were left with nothing more to say and the crowd stared at him in wonder.

Nearby was the Temple treasury, where there was a row of thirteen boxes shaped like rams' horns. Worshippers came by in long rows, dropping their offerings into the boxes. The disciples noticed how much money the rich men dropped in.

Jesus noticed a poor widow. She came along quietly and slipped two small copper coins into one of the boxes. They were worth very little. But Jesus called all his disciples together. "Look at this," he said. "That poor widow put more in the box than anyone else."

"Did she!" they marvelled. "However much did she put in, Teacher?"

"Very little," said Jesus. "But all the others who have put in large amounts of money have still got plenty more to live off when they go back home. She, poor as she is, put in everything she had. She gave God all that she had to live on."

"Does God really want us to live like that?" they wondered. But Judas turned away in despair. This sort of talk would never set up the kingdom he wanted Jesus to rule.

Mark 11 and 12

203

The price of a slave

Judas trailed through the streets of Jerusalem. "Jesus must declare himself soon!" he thought. The days were slipping away with so many fine opportunities lost. "Perhaps he is just waiting to be arrested and then he'll surprise everyone," Judas thought.

That must be it! He'd wait until the Roman soldiers, the followers of King Herod, and all the religious leaders had him in their power. Then he'd break the fetters from his hands and make his captors captives. Then he'd hand over their wealth and power and privileged life to the poor and the oppressed. Then, oh, then the wonderful empire that they'd dreamed of through centuries would come . . .

Judas pressed his hands to his aching head. He was always so alone! He despised all the other disciples, knowing well that they thought he was a thief because he looked after the money bag, which was empty as usual.

Judas strode purposefully on to find the chief priests.

They concluded a business deal. "What will you pay me if I hand Jesus of Nazareth over to you?" he asked.

"We'll pay you thirty silver pieces," they agreed. It was the price of a slave.

In return, Judas promised that he would lead them to the place where Jesus could be found at night. Then they could arrest him secretly with no crowds around to start a riot.

"Tomorrow night then," Judas promised, as he slipped away. "I'll come to you again tomorrow night."

Mark 14

The new covenant

"**W**e will celebrate our Passover meal tonight." Jesus called two of his disciples together. They made their plans secretly.

"Look," he said. "Go into the city. A man carrying a water jar will meet you."

"A *man* carrying a water jar?" they asked in surprise. Only women carried water.

"This is the secret sign," Jesus explained. "Follow him to his house. Ask the owner to show you the room where we will eat the Passover meal. He will show you the room upstairs. There you must make the meal ready for us."

The disciples slipped away. The man carrying the water jug met them in Jerusalem. He led them to the house which one of Jesus' followers had offered him. Her name was Mary. She had a son called Mark. Young Mark watched and listened with mounting excitement when he realised that someone very special was going to use the upstairs room that night.

When evening fell, Jesus and the rest of his disciples came to the house. They found everything ready. Quietly, they took their places and ate the Passover meal.

Then Jesus got up from the table. He took off his seamless robe and tied a towel around his waist. He took a basin and poured some water into it.

"My friends," he said, "no one has washed your feet." He went to each one of them and knelt before them on the floor. He slipped off their sandals and washed their feet, drying them with the towel he had tied round his waist.

It was Peter who protested. "Lord, you're surely not going to wash my feet. That's a slave's job!"

"Perhaps you don't understand why I'm doing this for you now, but you'll understand one day!" But Peter couldn't bear to see Jesus, their Messiah, serving them like that. It was only when Jesus said, "If I don't wash your feet, you'll not be a disciple any longer," that Peter gave in.

When he had finished, Jesus put his seamless robe back on and sat at the table again. "Do you understand what I have just done?" he said. "You must serve one another as I have served you. No one must lord it over the other. That's not the way

of the Kingdom of God!" Then he cried out in distress: "But one of you will betray me!"

They were very upset. "Lord, surely not me? Oh Lord, you don't mean me, do you?"

Jesus broke a piece of bread, dipped it in sauce and handed it to Judas.

"Quickly, go and do what you must!" he urged him.

Judas took the bread. His eyes glinted. How stupid the others were, and how clever Jesus was! The Master had understood at once! He left the table at once and slipped outside into the night.

Jesus took the bread. He thanked God for it, broke it and passed it around to his disciples. "Take it. Share this bread, for this stands for my body which will be broken for you."

In silence, bewildered they shared the bread.

Then he took the cup of wine. Again he thanked God and passed it around to them. They all drank from it.

"The wine stands for my blood. It will be poured out for many. For this is the new agreement. God gave us our first Covenant through Moses. They sacrificed an animal to seal the agreement. This time I am the sacrifice to seal the *new* agreement. I will die so that others may come into God's kingdom. I tell you, I will never again drink wine until I drink the new wine in the kingdom of God."

Mark 14
John 13

The new commandment

For a little while longer Jesus spoke to them. He told them beautiful, deep, hidden things about God and about themselves. Their worried, upset minds couldn't take it all in then, but afterward they remembered and they understood.

Patiently he dealt with their questions.

Thomas, the twin, said to him, "Lord, we do not know where you are going. You tell us you will take us to be with you where you are. Where is the place? What is the way to go?"

"I am the way, Thomas, the only way to the Father," answered Jesus.

"Oh, Master," sighed Philip. "Show us the Father, that is all we need."

"Have we been together for such a long time, Philip, and still you ask me to show you the Father?" Jesus answered. "Don't you believe yet that I am in the Father and the Father is in me? Anyone who has seen me has seen the Father. My Father and I will love the person who loves me. I shall show myself to him."

Jude said, "Lord, how will you show yourself to the person who loves you?"

Jesus answered, "My Father and I will come and live with the person who obeys my words. I have told you this while I am still with you. . . ."

"Lord, Lord," interrupted Peter anxiously, "you're not going to leave us, are you! Where are you going?"

"You cannot follow me now where I'm going," Jesus told him. "Later on you will follow me."

"Why can't I follow you?" Peter asked. "You mean that you're going to die, don't you? Oh Jesus, I am ready to die for you!"

"Are you really ready to die for me, Peter?" asked Jesus. "I tell you the truth. Before cockcrow tomorrow, you will have sworn three times that you don't know me."

Then there were no more questions. Something was happening that was too big for them, and they were afraid.

Jesus was grieved for them. "I have told you all these things so that my joy will be in you, and your joy will be complete," he said. "Listen! I'm going to give you a new commandment. Love one another, just as I love you. Now listen again. The greatest love a man can have for his friends is to die for them, and you, oh, you are my friends if you love me and obey me. You call me Master, but I call you friend. You didn't choose me, I chose you. Just love one another."

Puzzled, they sang the Passover psalms and then they followed Jesus outside. They left Jerusalem, crossed the brook called Kidron and went up the hillside to the Mount of Olives.

They came to a garden where the olive trees that grew higher up the hill were pressed to make olive oil. It was called the garden of the oil press: Gethsemane.

Judas knew that Jesus loved this place. He knew that he would be going there.

In the darkness the young lad named Mark followed the disciples to the garden.

"Stay here," Jesus said. "I am going to pray." He took Peter, James and John with him. "Oh," he cried, "I am crushed by the sorrow inside me. It is too great for me. Stay here and keep awake with me and pray."

He moved through the moonlit garden. Tired and dejected, the three disciples slumped to the ground and watched Jesus fall to his knees. He was only a stone's throw away from them. He bowed his face to the ground.

"Father, my Father," he prayed. "Oh Father, all things are possible to you. Oh, take this bitter cup from me."

In an agony he stretched out his hands; they were distorted by the pale light.

He stood up and went over to his three closest friends. He found them sleeping.

"Can't you keep watch with me?" he asked them. Once he himself had slept like that, exhausted in the midst of a storm. Now he was tossed in a tempest. There was no one who would come and rescue him.

Mark, watching in the shadows, saw Jesus go back again and pray. The boy shivered. The night was cold, and he was only wearing a thin linen cloth which he had wrapped around him. He could see sweat run off Jesus as he groaned in an agony of prayer.

"Don't let me drink this cup of pain," Jesus sobbed. "Yet my Father, your will be done. Your will be done," he repeated. "Father, Father, your will, not mine, be done."

There was silence in the garden, but from somewhere Mark could see that comfort came.

Jesus stood up. He went to his disciples and wakened them. "Are you still resting? Get up now, it's time."

Startled, the disciples jumped to their feet. Lanterns glowed in the dark. Marching feet came nearer, relentlessly nearer. Armour jingled, metal weapons flashed.

Mark shrank back against a tree. He heard Judas whisper: "The man I kiss is the one you want."

The disciples stood like statues, too terrified to move. Calmly Jesus stepped forward, waiting.

Judas hurried to him, "Rabbi!" he said, kissing him. At once the soldiers surrounded Jesus. Two of them wrenched back his arms and held him, but he did not flinch.

A sword flashed. Someone cried in pain. Peter, mad when he saw Judas betray their Master, drew one of the two swords the disciples possessed and struck one of the slaves of the High Priest. He cut off his ear. The slave reeled back, stunned and bleeding.

"Put up your sword, Peter," Jesus commanded. "This cup of suffering has been given to me by my Father. I must drink it."

He wrenched free from the soldiers, and touched the wounded slave, healing him.

"Day after day I sat openly in the Temple and you didn't lay hands on me. Now you have come with spears and swords as though I were a bandit, a wanted man."

Then he let them lead him away.

All his disciples fled away.

Mark remained in his hiding place. One of the soldiers tried to arrest him, catching hold of his linen cloth. He wriggled out of the man's grasp and fled away naked, leaving his cloth behind.

John 13 and 14
Mark 14

By the charcoal fire

They took Jesus to the High Priest's Palace.

Secretly, Simon Peter followed and hung around the courtyard, shivering and rubbing his hands for the night was cold.

A servant girl saw him. "Hey, you're one of that prisoner's friends, aren't you?" she said shrilly.

Peter looked up in alarm. "No, no I'm not, you're completely mistaken," he lied.

Slaves and sentries had lit a charcoal fire, and were standing around warming themselves, chatting idly. Peter went and joined them, holding out his hands to the warmth, while inside, bound and held, Jesus was being questioned by the High Priest.

"I never did anything secretly," Jesus said. "Why do you ask me all these questions about the things I taught? Plenty of people heard them. Question them instead."

One of the guards hit him. "Be quiet, don't you know who you're talking to – the High Priest."

"Have I told a lie?" Jesus asked. "And if I haven't why hit me?"

"Look," the High Priest said. "We've got to get this finished before the Sabbath. Come on, let's have some witnesses."

Hastily they summoned some people they had paid to make false statements about Jesus. They all came forward with their lies, but none of the stories agreed.

Jesus said nothing in his own defence. The High Priest became impatient. "Look, haven't you got anything to say for yourself?" he demanded, but Jesus made no reply, so the High Priest questioned him directly.

"Are you the Messiah, the Son of God?"

Firmly Jesus answered, "I am."

Then the High Priest tore his robes. "Blasphemy! You've condemned yourself with such sinful talk. What is your verdict?" he asked the councillors.

"Stone him! Stone him!" they shouted. It was the punishment for blasphemy; for taking God's name in vain. Then they spat at Jesus. Some of the soldiers blindfolded him and they rained blows upon him.

"Come on, Messiah!" they jeered. "Prophesy! Who hit you?" But Jesus made no answer.

"At dawn take him to the Roman governor," the High Priest ordered. "He'll confirm the death sentence. We can't pass it ourselves; it's not in our power."

So the soldiers had a little while yet to make fun of their prisoner.

Peter was still warming his hands at the fire. The servant girl saw him. "He *is* one of the prisoner's followers," she said.

"No, I'm not," Peter muttered.

"You're from Galilee, your accent gives you away!" one of the slaves exclaimed. "Besides, I recognise you." Peter swore and cursed, denying that he knew Jesus.

Just then a cock crowed, raucously announcing the new day. And Jesus was brought out of the High Priest's Palace. He looked at Peter as he passed. Peter broke down and stumbled outside, weeping bitterly.

They led Jesus off to the Roman governor to be tried again and because they knew Pilate, the governor, being a pagan, wouldn't worry in the least about someone who claimed to be the Son of God, they brought false charges against Jesus. Pilate met the religious leaders outside the Roman headquarters, the Castle of Antonia. The Jewish leaders would not go into a non-Jewish place, especially just before the Passover meal.

Mark 14
Luke 22

Pilate and Jesus

"What do you accuse this man of?" Pilate asked them. The Roman governor looked at Jesus in surprise. He didn't look at all like the brigand from the hills that Pilate had been expecting, openly defiant, rebellious and cursing. Jesus stood quietly, almost as though he didn't quite belong to what was going on around about him. It almost seemed as if he were saving his strength for the ordeal to come – or perhaps more likely, thought Pilate, he didn't have any fight left in him.

"He's a dangerous criminal," the religious leaders insisted. "He must be, or we'd never have sent for you so urgently. Oh, he's a fanatic, you know, a visionary who says he's the King of the Jews. But the poor people listen to his empty talk. We've heard him stir them up and tell them not to pay taxes to the Emperor."

Pilate had to take notice of that. He went back into the Castle and sent for Jesus.

"Are you the King of the Jews?" he asked, curiously.

"My kingdom doesn't belong to this world," Jesus said, and Pilate thought, "Oh, one of those foolish dreamers, more than half-mad."

"If the kingdom I set up were an earthly kingdom, don't you think my followers would have fought for me?" Jesus asked. "They'd never let me be handed over to my enemies without a blow being struck for me, would they?"

"Quite right," Pilate admitted. "Well then, are you a king?"

"I have one purpose," Jesus said. "I have come to speak about the truth."

Pilate turned away at these words. "What is the truth?" he asked, as he went outside to the Jewish leaders.

"I cannot condemn this man to death," he said. "He's a dreamer, talking about truth and things of another world."

"But his teachings stir up rebellion in people's hearts," they insisted. "He turned Galilee upside down and now he's coming here!"

"Galilee, eh!" Pilate seized on his solution. "That's Herod's department then, not mine. He's in charge of Galilee. He'll try your prisoner."

They led Jesus through the awakening streets

to Herod's palace. Herod was so pleased to see the miracle worker at last that he didn't even take exception to his sleep being disturbed.

"Come on then," he said, "do a marvellous thing for me."

But Jesus stood in silence, and Herod started to probe him with questions. "What, no answer at all!" he said finally, annoyed now at being dragged out of bed. "You'd better go back to Pilate then. I don't want anything more to do with you."

Herod's soldiers mocked Jesus before they took him back to Pilate.

"Herod can't find him guilty either," Pilate said to the Jewish leaders. "He wouldn't have sent a guilty man back. This man has done nothing to deserve death. I'll have him beaten, if you like, and then we'll let him go."

The religious leaders had gathered a crowd of their followers.

"Kill him," they shouted. "Kill him."

Pilate still tried to save Jesus. "Listen," he shouted. "You have a custom and I always do my best to respect your customs. I always set a condemned man free at Passover. Do you want me to free Jesus for you?"

Urged by the leaders, the crowd yelled back, "Not him! We want the other Jesus, Jesus Barabbas. Barabbas."

"Barabbas! Barabbas!" they shouted. Barabbas was a rebel and a murderer who had been sentenced to death for his crimes. "Set Barabbas free."

"Then what shall I do with Jesus who calls himself your King?"

"Kill him! Nail him to the cross! Nail him to the cross."

So Jesus was cruelly beaten, scourged with leather whips with pieces of metal at the tips. That was the custom before a condemned man was led out to die. Then the soldiers gathered round to have some fun at the prisoner's expense. They put a purple robe on his wounded, bleeding body.

"You're a mighty monarch now," they said.

"We worship you!" Some of them went up and hit him, while others mockingly bowed before him.

"He's a crownless king!" someone said, so they tore down some thorny branches and bent them into a crown which they thrust on his bent head. They put a stick in his hand and knelt before him. "Long live the King of the Jews," they jeered at him. Then they beat him with the stick.

Pilate went out to the crowd again. "Look, I'll bring him out to you. Then you'll see why I can't find any reason to sentence him to death."

He led Jesus, still wearing the robe and the crown of thorns outside.

"Look," he shouted. "Here is the man!"

"Nail him to the cross!" they shouted.

"You take him then and nail him to the cross," Pilate shouted back, desperately. "I can't find any reason to condemn him."

"He says he is the Son of God!" the Jewish leaders shouted. "Our Law says we must kill him for that."

Pilate went pale. "Where do you come from?" he asked Jesus. But Jesus said nothing. "Won't you speak to me?" Pilate pleaded. "I have the authority to free you or kill you."

Then Jesus answered: "You only have this authority because it was given to you by God."

Pilate was more frightened than ever. "I'm going to set him free!" he shouted to the crowd.

"If you set him free, that means you're no friend of the Emperor's," they shouted back. Pilate looked helplessly around him. There was nothing more he could do. His whole future was at stake now. He, himself, was on trial. If he supported Jesus, he'd be in trouble with his superiors. He would lose his job, even his life perhaps.

"Here is your King," he pointed to Jesus.

"We have no king but the Emperor," the crowd yelled back. In front of them all, Pilate washed his hands with water a slave had brought. "I wash my hands of this. I am innocent of the death of this just man," he said, signing the order for Jesus to die.

The soldiers led him out to the religious leaders and people of Jerusalem, who gladly took charge of Jesus.

Matthew 27
Mark 15
Luke 23
John 19

The woodworker's yoke

Across his torn and bleeding shoulders they laid the heavy bar of his cross. He had to drag it through the crowded streets out to the place which the Jews called Golgotha, and the Romans called Calvary. It was a hill outside the city and its name meant "Skull Hill".

Jesus fell. They forced him to his feet. He stumbled on, blinded by blood and weakness. A pilgrim from Africa, up in Jerusalem for the festival, was ordered to carry the cross for Jesus.

Women, seeing what was happening, wept and wailed but Jesus told them, "Don't cry for me! Save your tears for yourselves and your children."

They took two other condemned men, both of them criminals, up to the hill where the crosses were ready.

Jesus, the woodworker from Nazareth whose skilled hands had smoothed many a yoke for oxen to bear, lay bleeding on the rough splintered wood, his body tensed, awaiting the blows that would press sharp iron through his flesh, nailing him to the cross till he died.

Jesus said, "Forgive them, Father, they don't know that they are doing!"

They raised him high and fastened his feet. He hung between two criminals.

Some people watched, others mocked, some soldiers offered him a drug, laughing, "Save yourself, if you are who you say you are!"

He refused the drug, which would have eased the pain.

Other soldiers sat by, idly throwing dice for his clothing.

"Aren't you the Messiah?" shouted one of the

criminals beside him, writhing in agony. "Save yourself and us."

"Don't you fear God!" gasped the other man. "We've been justly sentenced, but this man has done nothing wrong." With difficulty he turned his head toward Jesus.

"Remember me, Jesus, when you come as King!" he said.

"Truly, today you'll be with me in Paradise," Jesus answered.

The slow agony went on until noon, when a great gloom began to spread over the hill and the city beyond.

His friends had abandoned him, but the women who loved him stood weeping at the cross. Fisherman John, Zebedee's son, his cousin on his mother's side, was there, too. And so was Mary herself, distraught, weeping, suffering shame for her son who died the cruel death kept for the worst criminals.

"Mother, here is your son," Jesus said, and he meant John. "John, here is your Mother," he said, and John from that time took Mary into his care.

Then he said nothing for a long time. For the pain was great and he was dying, slowly.

Out of the darkness Jesus suddenly cried in despair to his Father, "My God, my God, why have you forsaken me?"

No voice answered him, yet he knew now that his task was almost finished. He had faced the suffering that he had dreaded. He was about to die.

"I am thirsty," he gasped.

A soldier ran and soaked a piece of sponge in a bowlful of cheap wine. He stuck it on a branch and held it up to Jesus. Jesus felt the wine moist on his cracked lips.

"Father," he cried loudly, "it is finished!" And there was gladness in his voice.

Heartbroken, the people who believed that their Messiah had died went home beating their breasts. John supported Mary, who seemed to be in great pain.

The army officer in charge of the execution praised God. "He was a good man!" he cried. "I've never seen a man die like that!" At sundown the soldiers made sure that all three men had died, since the bodies could not hang on the crosses on the Sabbath.

Joseph, a wealthy man and a secret follower of Jesus, went to Pilate and asked him if he could take Jesus' body and lay it in the tomb he had bought for himself. Nicodemus, the Pharisee, who had come to Jesus at night, went with Joseph. He

took spices, myrrh and cloves for embalming the body. They wrapped the body in a linen cloth and laid the spices between the folds. There was no time to do more, for when the sun set, the Sabbath began and they could do no work.

The women watched them lay Jesus' body in the new tomb. A heavy, round stone was rolled securely in front of the entrance and they went away, weeping, through Jerusalem, where families gathered to eat the lamb killed for the Passover meal.

Matthew 27
Mark 15
Luke 23
John 19

The sad Saturday

What a sad Sabbath the disciples spent, while everyone about them celebrated the Passover with joy!

Their feast had been celebrated already with Jesus, who had washed their feet and passed to them broken bread and poured out wine.

Now it was all over. Secretly, behind locked doors, fearful lest every footfall bring their arrest and killing, they sat in despair.

Night brought the end of the Sabbath and the women got to work, preparing the spices for their last act of love. They would embalm his body properly.

The man in the garden

Very early in the morning, while it was still dark, the women set out for the tomb.

"We will have to wait till the gardener comes by. He will roll away the stone for us," they said.

In the dim light they made out the tomb. But it was open. The great circular stone set in grooves in front of the entrance had been rolled back already.

Frightened, they ran back to the disciples.

"They have taken the Lord away!" they gasped.

Peter and John sprang to their feet, while the others questioned the women. They were puzzled and fearful.

Heedless now of their own safety, Peter and John dashed through the streets to the garden. John ran faster than Peter. Yes, it was true! The stone had been rolled back. He bent down and looked into the tomb. It was certainly empty! He could see the linen cloths that had bound Jesus' body lying there. But there was no body.

John waited outside the tomb, but Peter ran straight in.

He saw the linen cloths there, and the cloth that had been wrapped around Jesus' face. It was not lying with the linen cloths but was rolled up by itself.

John followed Peter in.

"It's true! It's empty," they agreed, but they did not understand what had really happened. They went back to tell the others.

Mary from Magdala, Mary who loved the Lord, had come back to the garden.

"Why are you weeping?" a man's voice asked. "Are you looking for someone?"

"They have taken his body out of the tomb and I don't know where they have laid it," she sobbed. She dried her eyes and looked up. The sun had risen now. It dazzled her eyes, tired and full of tears. She thought the man was the gardener. She couldn't make him out properly. "Oh, sir," she begged, "if you took his body, tell me please, tell me where it is."

"Mary!" the man said.

"Rabbi! Rabbi!" her heart was pounding. Tears

flowed down her cheeks, but now she was smiling with the tears. She flung herself before him, the Lord who had come back to her out of the tomb, and tried to embrace his feet, but he stepped back.

"Mary, don't hold on to me, for I have not yet gone back to my Father. Now, go to my brothers and tell them I am going back to my Father, who is your Father, to my God who is your God."

Joyfully she ran back and rushed into the room.

"I have seen the Lord," she said. "I have spoken to the Lord!" They found it hard to believe her.

"Your tears blinded you, Mary. Your grief has disturbed your wits."

But she stood there laughing, and went singing about her daily tasks.

That afternoon two of the followers of Jesus went sorrowfully home to their little village of Emmaus, seven miles from Jerusalem.

"Why are you so sad?" a stranger asked them. "What are you talking about together as you walk along?"

"You must be the only person from Jerusalem who doesn't know what's been happening these last few days," Cleopas answered.

"What's been happening?" the stranger asked.

"Why, they've killed Jesus, our wonderful prophet," Cleopas told him. "But some women of our company went early this morning to the tomb and found it empty. One of the women said she actually spoke to Jesus."

"And don't you believe that's possible?" asked the traveller. "Don't you know what the scriptures tell us about the Messiah?" Then, as they walked along, he explained to them what the prophets had written so many years ago about the one who would come and suffer and then enter his glory for evermore.

They listened eagerly, nodding their heads as this piece and that fitted in with what they knew about Jesus. Before they knew it, they reached Emmaus village. The traveller was walking on, but they begged him to stay.

"It's getting dark now," they said. "Do have supper with us and spend the night here."

He sat at table with them, took the bread, gave thanks and broke it. As he gave them the broken bread, they knew who he was.

"Jesus!" they cried, but at that moment he disappeared.

Heedless of the oncoming night, they hurried back to Jerusalem to tell the others.

"Why didn't we know him earlier?" they asked each other as they rushed along.

"A fire burned in my heart as he spoke to us," one commented.

"Yes, it did in mine too," agreed the other. "Yet we didn't trust our hearts to guide us."

"We have seen the Lord," they told the others as they hammered on the locked doors.

Then Jesus came and stood among them. "Peace be unto you," he said.

But Thomas, the twin, was not with them when Jesus came. When he heard of it, he said, "You're imagining things: I won't believe until I see him for myself. Not only see him either," he added. "I'm going to touch his hands and put my fingers right where the nails were."

A week later Jesus came again.

"Peace be with you!" he said. Then he turned to Thomas, "Come, Thomas, don't doubt any longer. Here are my hands. Put your fingers here into the scars of the nails." But Thomas didn't need such evidence now. The sight of Jesus was enough. "My Lord and my God," Thomas answered fervently, worshipping him.

For forty more days Jesus appeared to his disciples. He promised that when he left them his Holy Spirit would come. Then they would always have Jesus with them in the spirit, helping them in the task he now gave them to do.

"The whole world is ready and waiting for the good news," he said. "You must go and tell them that God has sent his Son to die for all mankind.

Go and teach them everything I have told you. Heal the sick, make disciples for me everywhere and teach them to obey all the commandments I have given you. And remember! I am with you always, right to the end of time. Wait in Jerusalem for the Holy Spirit to come to you."

He climbed the hills behind Bethany. They followed him and he blessed them. They fell on the ground before him.

When they looked up, he had gone.

But now their hearts were happy. They stayed in Jerusalem, praising God in the Temple with all

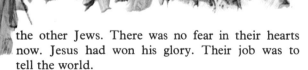

the other Jews. There was no fear in their hearts now. Jesus had won his glory. Their job was to tell the world.

He went to reign on high, the King of Kings. They met in the upstairs room in Mark's house and they waited for Jesus' promise to come true. They waited for the Holy Spirit to come.

Luke 24 Matthew 28
John 20   Mark 16

The body we share

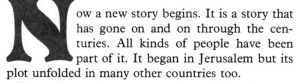

N ow a new story begins. It is a story that has gone on and on through the centuries. All kinds of people have been part of it. It began in Jerusalem but its plot unfolded in many other countries too.

It carries on in our own day and in our own country, wherever we are living.

We are part of it.

This is the story.

A man's body was broken. A man's body was shared. The man went away. He left behind power and he left behind love. The power was not the kind that powerful people ever recognise.

The power came like fire. The power came like the wind. The power came like a dove.

It is the power that was there when God made light out of darkness. It is the power that was there when Jesus stilled the wild winds and tamed the madman's heart. This power is still at work in the world.

It is the power of the Holy Spirit.

The love is the love of Jesus. The people who were left behind to use both the love and the power are the church of Jesus.

The church of Jesus is not a building. The church of Jesus is not made of stone or wood or mud. The church of Jesus is all the people who follow him, serve him and obey him. The church of Jesus is people.

That is why the story hasn't finished yet.

That is why we are part of the story.

Fire and thanksgiving

It all began in Jerusalem.

For ten more days after Jesus had left them, Peter, James and John and the other eight disciples stayed in Jerusalem. Every day they went to the Temple, but they also met in the upstairs room at Mark's house. There they prayed and they were joined by the women who had loved Jesus so much. About a hundred and twenty people were there, including his mother and his brothers. They believed that Jesus was the Messiah, the Son of God. They were all waiting for the gift he had promised them: the Holy Spirit.

During those ten days they chose another man to be one of the twelve special messengers, the apostles whom Jesus had first chosen. For Judas was dead, buried in a field he had bought with thirty silver pieces: the price of a slave, the price they paid him for Jesus.

Twelve was a special number for the Jews. There had been twelve tribes of Israel. That is why Jesus had chosen twelve men to be his close followers. That is why they now chose another man from the 120 believers. They prayed together and chose Matthias. So he was added to the group of the apostles.

Quietly they spent those days; they spoke together of Jesus. They waited for the coming of the Holy Spirit, and they praised God.

Meanwhile the streets of Jerusalem became more and more crowded with pilgrims from all over the world. Fifty days after the feast of the Passover, the Jews celebrated another very important festival. It was called Pentecost in Greek, because it came fifty days later. The Hebrew name was the feast of Weeks: seven weeks after the Passover they celebrated the feast for seven days. It was important because it was the thanksgiving for the harvest of the wheat crops. But it also celebrated the time when God gave the Law to Moses on Mount Sinai. That's what made it such an important feast that pilgrims came from all over the world for that day. In fact, the crowds that gathered in Jerusalem came from as far west as Italy and as far east as the boundaries of India.

It was on the day of Pentecost that God gave his Holy Spirit to the disciples.

They were all gathered together in the upstairs room, built on the flat roof of Mark's house. As they prayed, God himself swept through their midst and they were filled with joy and praise.

"It was like a rushing, mighty wind," the fishermen afterwards said.

"It was like being warmed and lit up by fire," said Simon the patriot who had fought in the hills against Rome.

"It was like the breath of God," the women whispered. "Like the coming of a dove," they added, remembering the beauty of that moment.

It filled the whole house and filled each one of them. Suddenly they all praised God together, but not in the rough accent of Galilee. They all cried out to God in foreign languages. It was the Holy Spirit who put on their lips the words they didn't understand.

Excitedly, transformed by joy, they rushed out into the street still praising God; telling him that they loved him and were no longer afraid of him, as they had always been before.

A great crowd gathered. Pilgrims from fifteen different countries in and outside the Roman Empire found to their amazement that these simple, uneducated Galileans were each pouring out in all the languages of the world the wonderful story of God's love.

"What does this mean?" they asked each other. "They're from Galilee, aren't they? Yet we hear them telling us in our own languages the wonderful things God has done."

But there were some who jeered. "Drunkards! That's all the good that comes out of Galilee! They've been drinking!"

"No!" Peter said, stepping forward, with the other apostles around him. "We're Jews in Galilee too, you know, and no Jew drinks wine before the time for morning prayer. So listen to me all of you, whether you come from Jerusalem or from far away places. This is what the prophet wrote:

'This is what I will do in the last days, God says;
I will pour out my Spirit upon all men;
Your sons and your daughters will prophesy,
Your young people will see visions,
And your old men will dream dreams.

Yes, even on my slaves, both men and women,
I will pour out my Spirit in those days,
And they will prophesy . . .
And then whoever calls on the name of the Lord
will be saved.'

"Listen, then," shouted Peter. "God has brought Jesus back from the dead. He freed him from the grave, for how could the tomb keep him a prisoner? Didn't David himself say about him: 'You will not leave my soul in the world of the dead. You will not let my body rot away.' "

They nodded. Yes, they all knew those words so well.

"Then listen," Peter said. "David died and was buried. His grave is still here in Jerusalem. But he believed God's promise, and he spoke about the resurrection of the Messiah in those words."

"Yes," they nodded again.

"We are witnesses to the fact that God raised Jesus from the dead. He is at the right hand of the Father. What you see and hear now is his gift. It is his Holy Spirit which he has just poured out on us. All you Jews are to know for sure that this Jesus who was nailed to the cross is the Lord, the Messiah, the Son of God."

"Oh, what shall we do, brothers?" they asked.

"Turn from your sins," Peter said. "Be baptized in the name of Jesus; then you will receive the forgiveness of sins and the gift of the Holy Spirit, God's promise."

About three thousand people believed that day and went gladly into the water to be baptized. Then the apostles laid their hands on them so that they, too, might receive the Holy Spirit.

Wonderful fellowship grew up among Galileans, Judeans, Jews from civilised parts of the Empire, Jews from far away, more backward countries. They shared meals together and prayed together and listened to stories of Jesus.

They shared their belongings with one another too. They sold everything they owned and shared the money among them. Every day they met together in the Temple and worshipped God there. But they also shared a common meal which they called their love-feast.

As they shared bread and wine together, they felt joined to Jesus. As they ate they praised God.

The love they shared marked them out so that all the people spoke well of them. Every day more and more believers joined their group.

The Church had been born and was growing.

The Acts of the Apostles 1 and 2

225

"I will give you what I have"

"Oh, please give me a coin! Spare a half penny piece for a poor lame man. I've never walked in my life. Give me a coin so that I can eat."

The lame man sat as usual by one of the eight gates into the Temple. He was carried there every day, and he begged for money from the people who were going to worship God.

Two strong, burly men walked up. How lucky they were, sighed the lame man! How wonderful to be so strong and to stride along like that!

"Spare a penny. Oh, spare a penny!" he cried.

Peter and John stopped beside him.

"Look at us!" said Peter.

Surprised, he looked up and held out his hand for them to drop a coin in.

"I've got no money at all," said Peter. "But I will give you what I have: in the name of Jesus the Messiah from Nazareth I order you to walk!"

He bent down and seized the beggar's right hand. His strong grip tightened. He helped the lame man get up. Immediately strength flooded into the man's feet and ankles. He jumped up, stood on his feet alone and then started to walk around.

"Oh, thank you!" he cried. "Oh, thank you, Jesus. Oh, praise God! Look, look everyone! I can walk. I can jump too!"

Peter and John walked on towards the Temple. The man they had healed followed them, leaping alongside, praising God. Worshippers turned their heads in surprise; the crowd that thronged the outer courtyard started to point and exclaim:

"Surely that's the lame man, the one who's always sitting on the steps of the 'Beautiful Gate'?"

"Of course it is! He's been there for as long as I remember," they said to one another.

"Look, those followers of Jesus, the fishermen from Galilee, are with him."

The crowd flocked over to them.

"Why are you so surprised?" Peter asked them. "Do you think our own power or godliness made this man walk? Our God has given his power to Jesus. You had Jesus killed, even though Pilate wanted to set him free. But God raised him from the dead – we saw him afterward. We know it for sure. It was the power of his name that gave the lame man strength. You see him leaping there? That was done because we believe in the name of Jesus.

"Now, my brothers," Peter went on. "You had Jesus killed out of ignorance, I know. You didn't know that he is our Messiah. But God told us long ago through the Scriptures that the Messiah would have to suffer. Believe this now, turn to God and he will wipe away your sins."

Peter and John were still speaking to the people, showing them from the Scriptures that the Messiah had to suffer for them, when the priests, the haughty Sadducees and the Temple guards surrounded them.

"Arrest these men!" the Sadducees ordered. "Don't listen to their empty talk," they told the startled crowd. "They teach you that Jesus has been raised from the dead. Everyone knows that such a thing is impossible!"

They marched Peter and John away and put them in prison.

Many of the people in the crowd who had seen the lame man jumping around and heard Peter's words believed what he had said.

By now about five thousand Jews believed that the Messiah had come; that Jesus was the Son of God.

The Church was growing, but trouble was in store for the body of people who had been left in the world to spread good news around.

Acts 3

227

All the Jewish leaders and the High Priest gathered together to question Peter and John, who stood in front of them.

"So you made a lame man walk?" they asked them. "You're just ordinary men, aren't you? You've no authority to address great crowds of people. You've caused a public disturbance. How did you do it? What power do you have, or whose name do you use?"

Peter spoke up: "Leaders of Israel!" The fisherman's Galilean accent grated harshly on the cultured aristocratic ears of the members of the Council. "You are questioning us about a good deed done to a lame man, aren't you? Well then, you must know that this man stands here before you completely healed by the power of the name of Jesus, the Anointed One from Nazareth. You had him killed, but God raised him to life!"

"The man was executed as a criminal," they protested. "How can you claim that he is the Messiah?"

"Don't you know the Scriptures?" Peter asked. "They say: 'the stone that you builders despised turned out to be the most important one'. I tell you salvation is to be found in Jesus alone. No one else has a name which can heal and save."

The members of the Council were amazed at Peter's boldness.

"You were his companions, weren't you?" they asked, and Peter and John nodded.

There was nothing the Council could say. The man who had been lame was standing there, perfectly well again.

"Leave the Council room," they ordered.

"Look," they debated when Peter and John had been taken away. "What can we do with these men? Everyone in Jerusalem knows by now that these rough, uneducated fishermen have performed this amazing miracle. We can't just deny it."

"But we can stop it from spreading," someone said and several of them nodded in agreement. "We must warn them never to do such a thing again. They must never speak to anyone in the name of Jesus."

Peter and John were brought before them again.

"Under no condition are you to speak or teach in the name of Jesus!" the Council ordered.

Peter and John answered: "You must judge what is right in the sight of God. Should we obey you or should we obey God? We can't stop speaking about the things we've seen and heard."

"It's got to stop!" the Council warned them.

They had to let the two Galileans go free without any punishment, because everyone was praising God for the healing of a man who had been lame for more than forty years.

As soon as they were set free, Peter and John returned to the believers and told them what the Council had said.

At once they started to pray: "Give us boldness, Lord God," they begged, "so that we may speak your message and heal and help people." When they finished praying, they felt again the coming of the Holy Spirit.

The church was beginning to taste trouble just as Jesus had done. They drew upon his power as he had drawn on the power of God, and they continued to preach boldly.

Every day they went to the Temple. All the believers met together in Solomon's Porch, but now it became harder for people to join them, even though people still spoke highly of them.

Yet daily their numbers grew. People came to Peter and John from all over Jerusalem and from the surrounding villages. They brought sick people with them and they were all healed.

Then the High Priest and the Sadducees decided to take action. Peter and John were arrested and put in the public jail.

In the night God spoke to them: "Go and stand in the Temple and tell the people about this new life!"

They obeyed and found themselves walking right out of prison as dawn broke. They went straight to the Temple and began to preach.

A full meeting of the Council was ordered. Everyone was summoned, including a strict Pharisee, a student of the law, called Saul from Tarsus; he was a Roman citizen who spoke Greek as his everyday language, but he knew Aramaic, the language of the Jews of Palestine. He had come to Jerusalem to study under the famous teacher Gamaliel, a tolerant, open man who was also on the Council.

They sent for Peter and John.

"They're not in prison," the officials reported.

"Not in prison! But we put them in prison yesterday!"

"They're in the Temple," someone told the Council. "They're teaching all the people."

"Arrest them at once," the High Priest ordered. He questioned Peter and John when they stood before the Council for the second time.

"We gave you strict orders not to teach in the name of that man who was executed not long ago. But see what you've done! You've spread your teaching all over Jerusalem, and beyond. And you blame us for his death."

"We must obey God, not other men," Peter and John answered. "God raised Jesus to life, though you had him nailed to a cross. He is on God's right hand now, the Saviour of Israel. We are his witnesses – we and the Holy Spirit who is God's gift to all who obey him."

They were so furious they had only one thing to say: "Kill them."

Gamaliel got to his feet.

"Take the prisoners away," he ordered, and spoke to the Council. "Be careful what you do with these men. Don't start a persecution. These troublemakers come and go. Their followers soon melt away. If you take action now, you'll certainly start a riot. Besides, you might find yourselves rebelling against God!" he added. "So, take my advice. Just wait and see. If they're not genuine, the whole thing will have died away in a matter of months. If they are . . . we don't want to fight against God."

Gamaliel was so highly respected that the Council followed his advice. They sent for Peter and John and had them beaten. "Never speak in that man's name again," they said, setting them free.

Peter and John left the Council full of joy that God had allowed them to suffer punishment and disgrace for the name of Jesus. Back they went to the Temple; there, and in people's homes they carried on telling everyone about Jesus.

Acts 4 and 5

Hurling stones at Stephen

The people who were the church in those early days were all Jews. But some had been born and brought up in Jerusalem. They stuck very rigidly to every small detail of the law, whereas the Jews from other countries were not so strict about all the small points. Not only that, but they spoke Greek. They read the Scriptures in Greek and in their daily lives they lived in a Greek way.

The differences between them were tremendous. The love that was part of the power of Jesus brought them together. The strength and wisdom of the Holy Spirit helped them overcome all the barriers.

But tensions arose. The Greek-speaking Jews complained that when food and clothing and money was given out to all the needy people, their poor widows weren't getting their fair share.

Everyone met together to discuss the problem. They chose seven men, all of them Greek-speaking Jews, all of them strong believers and full of the love of Jesus. These men were to look after all the practical jobs of caring for the growing group of believers.

One of them was a young man whose name was Stephen.

There were very many synagogues in Jerusalem. At least 480 small meeting-places were built in different parts of the city. Some of these were specially for Greek-speaking Jews. One of them was for a special group of Jews; freed slaves. It had been built by a Jew called Theodotus whose family had been slaves in Italy. They had been given their freedom there and had eventually resettled in Jerusalem.

Stephen went to the synagogue of the freed men, where there were Jews from Africa, from Egypt and from the east.

"These things just can't be true," they argued with Stephen.

"Oh, but they are!" Stephen said, and helped by the Holy Spirit, he spoke so powerfully that they could find no answers for him.

"It's no use. We can't outwit this man," they complained. "See how the people love him. He heals many sick people and yet there's just nothing we can say against him."

So they paid some men to make false charges against Stephen:

"This man teaches everyone that Jesus of Nazareth is going to pull down the Temple, and do away with the whole way of life we've all been following since the days of Moses," the paid men told all the leaders of the synagogue.

So Stephen was arrested and brought before the Council. Saul, the strict Pharisee, sat glowering at the prisoner.

"He deserves to die," he thought. "How can he say things against our sacred Law?"

But Stephen joyfully faced the men who could condemn him to die. There were those who said that Stephen's face was as radiant as that of an angel whose work is to adore God.

"Have you said this?" the High Priest asked him. "Have you said that we don't need a Temple?"

Stephen was on fire now! How he longed for the High Priest and all the Council members to believe in Jesus too! Already many priests in Jerusalem had come to believe in Jesus. Perhaps this was the moment when they would all believe.

So he stepped forward and fearlessly talked to these important men. With burning conviction he talked to them, the experts in the Law, about their history.

"God chose our people; yet we have always rejected his prophets," he said. "Look how our ancestors kept wishing that they could go back to Egypt instead of following Moses to the Promised Land. In those days they carried a special tent around with them. In the tent was the Ark, the sign of God's presence. It was only after the time of David that we came to the Temple to worship God. It was Solomon who built him a house.

"But how can God live in houses built by men? Our own Scriptures tell us that he has no need of such a thing."

They listened in fury as Stephen went on:
"Heaven is glittering; suns and moons gild
God's splendid palace there; heaven's his throne.
Earth is his footstool; then why do you build
Dwellings for him? Heaven and earth are his own."

There was nothing they could say. Stephen was quoting Scripture. They gnashed their teeth in rage.

"You have murdered God's Messiah!" he said. "You haven't obeyed God's law; look, look, oh look!" he cried with joy. "For I see the highest heaven open wide and all God's glory shines on Jesus, who is sitting at the Father's right hand."

They bellowed with rage at this, stuck their fingers in their ears and they all rushed on him. "Stone him!" they shouted.

They didn't wait to take him to the Roman officials to be tried by them as Jesus was. They threw Stephen out of the city, and there his accusers who, according to the Law, had to be the first to throw the stones, laid their bulky outer clothing at the feet of the young Pharisee, Saul, who stood by, in charge of these garments.

Then they hurled boulders at Stephen.

As the stones hit him he called: "Lord Jesus, come and take my spirit!"

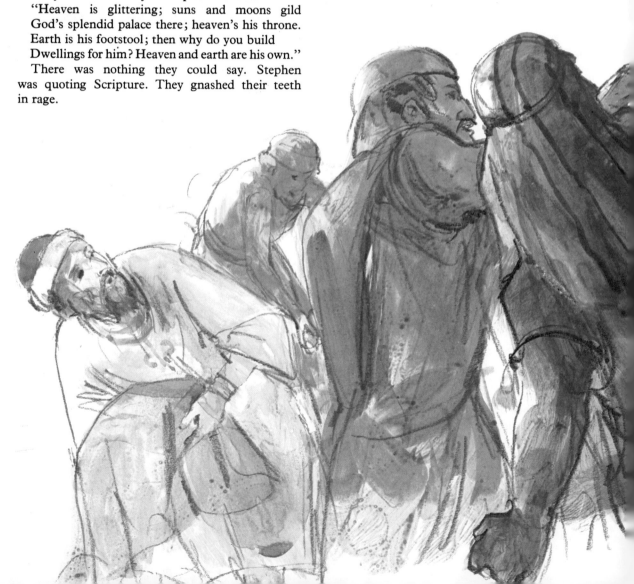

Bruised and bleeding he fell to his knees. "Lord, don't hold this against them!" he cried. He toppled over and lay dead amongst the boulders.

Saul watched him die. "He deserved this penalty for saying that Jesus was God's Messiah," he muttered. "I entirely approve of this killing," he said to the men who came to collect their cloaks. "From now on we must treat all followers of this new, false Way with the utmost severity. These Nazarenes hold beliefs which are impossible for true Jews to hold. We must stamp out this new faith."

But still the church grew. Now it was being hunted and hurt. The body of believers became scattered. Wherever they were scattered, the church

grew. So the hunting could not destroy it and the hurting brought it strength.

Saul the Pharisee tried to destroy the church. Throughout Jerusalem he searched thoroughly through the houses, dragged all the believers out and threw them in prison, where they sang praises to God.

But still the church grew up wherever the hunted believers fled. Saul could not stop it. It was stronger than he.

Acts 6 and 7

On the road to Damascus

"Kill them all. Don't let one of them remain alive," declared Saul, the young student of the Law who had come from the thriving, busy trading town of Tarsus about 500 miles north of Jerusalem to study under Gamaliel.

As he strode back and forth across the room, some of the other students stared at him admiringly.

"Truly, there's no one more zealous than Saul of Tarsus!" they said. "He's really stamping out this false faith in Jerusalem."

"Only to let it grow up everywhere else," someone muttered behind his hand, and one or two people laughed. They were students of Gamaliel too, and they followed the advice of their master: if this thing is of God, better leave it alone, it will grow anyway. They swung outside, leaving Saul, the fanatic.

Saul, a little man, brilliantly educated, headstrong, energetic and utterly determined, made his way to the High Priest.

"We've stamped it out in Jerusalem. At least, all the Greek-speaking Jews who followed this false way have either been put in prison or have fled elsewhere," he told the High Priest. "I want to go to Damascus, to visit all the synagogues. If there are any followers of this Nazarene there, I'll arrest them and bring them back to Jerusalem."

"Saul! That's a journey of 140 miles. It takes about six days," the High Priest said.

"Give me a guard of soldiers and a letter of introduction to all the synagogues," said Saul. "I'll bring back as many of these dangerous heretics as I find."

"There's no one as determined as you," the High Priest said. "But are you sure you are strong enough to undertake the journey, Saul?"

Saul clenched his fists. "I'll succeed!" he said.

So, with an armed guard, he set off along the sandy road, sweltering under the hot sun. The soldiers could hardly keep up with the little man.

The gruelling journey was nearly at its end, and they would soon glimpse the ancient trading city. Damascus had grown up in a fertile plain beside a beautiful river at the intersection of three main caravan routes. It had been rebuilt by a Greek planner five hundred years before. Now a long straight street ran right through the city. It was called "Straight Street" and was lined with shops where many Jewish traders sold their wares.

Spurred on by the thought of the mission of killing he was soon to begin, Saul pushed forward under the blazing sun. His thoughts were in turmoil, for he had seen Stephen die, asking God's forgiveness for his murderers. He had seen him give his spirit to his Lord. He had seen other followers of Jesus, dragged off from their families, look up and sing.

Questions had been churning in his mind all the

time he'd forced his puny body along the baking road. Now he could stand it no longer. The voice within him, the voice he had been trying to stifle, grew louder and louder. The question he had not wanted to listen to resounded in his ears. But now it was not the voice of his conscience.

The power that was the Holy Spirit mastered Saul. A great light dazzled him and he fell on his knees to the ground.

"Saul, Saul, why do you persecute me?"

"Who are you, Lord?" Saul cried, knowing but not able yet to bear the answer.

"I am Jesus. You are arresting me, putting me in prison, yes and killing me over and over again."

Saul groaned. Yes, he was guilty. He'd separated mothers from their children. He'd marched them away in chains. Was punishment coming to him from God, he wondered?

But now the other voice spoke, the voice of the one he had called Lord.

"Get up. Go into the city. There you'll be told what you must do."

The puzzled soldiers helped Saul stand.

"A voice spoke to him," one of them said.

"No, it was the great light. Look, it's blinded him."

Shocked and shaking, Saul let the armed guard lead him into Damascus where he lay, not eating or drinking, and completely blind, for three whole days.

Everything he had lived for had been destroyed.

There was a knock at the door.

"Brother Saul," a man's voice spoke gently. It could not lift Saul from his despair, but the next words amazed Saul.

"The Lord himself has sent me to you to help you."

"Oh, come in," Saul struggled to sit up. "Does he care for me so much then? Aren't you frightened of me?"

"I was!" the man admitted. "The Lord spoke to me as I was praying. He said, 'Go and lay hands on Saul of Tarsus so that he may see again.' I said, 'Oh no, Lord, don't you know? That man's done terrible things to our people and that he's come here to arrest all your servants.'"

Saul felt the man's smile. It warmed his heart.

"Of course the Lord knew all about that," the man said. "So I came. My name is Ananias."

"Lay hands on me, Ananias," begged Saul.

Ananias put his hands on Saul's eyes and on his head.

"See, Saul!" he said. "And be filled with the Holy Spirit."

Saul rubbed his eyes. "I see!" he cried. "Come, Ananias, baptize me now in the Name of Jesus."

With joy Ananias baptized Saul. When Saul had eaten, his strength returned.

He went straight to the synagogues.

"Jesus is the Son of God!" he declared.

But now neither the Jews nor the believers in Jesus could accept him. They were all astonished. The followers of Jesus feared it was all a trick. The Jews became more and more angry.

"I must get away," Saul said to Ananias. "It's still hard for me to see that the Lord has come to save everyone, Jews and pagans alike. I want to take time to think through what I believe."

So for three years Saul remained alone with God. He read the Scriptures and thought and prayed, strengthening his faith, so that he might strengthen others.

Acts 9

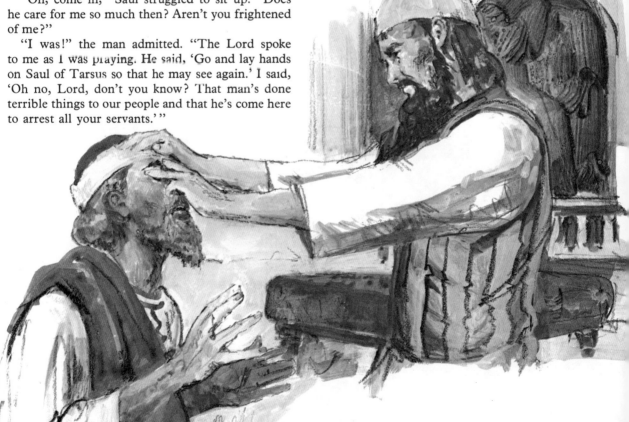

Two harbours

Ever since the days of King Solomon, the city of Joppa had been the Jewish harbour. It was the only natural harbour on the coast, but the sea there was so shallow that no deep sea ships could use it. Only the small ships that plied their trade along the coast could load and unload at Joppa. Even so, their cargoes had to be brought to shore in small rowing boats. The surf was strong and the breakers boomed.

But Joppa was important until the days of the Roman Emperors. Then, thirty miles away, Herod the Great built an artificial harbour. Skilled engineers built a breakwater of solid stone. Now the water was 120 feet deep, and ships could sail straight in and unload their cargoes at the quay.

Not only that, but the new town called Caesarea – in honour of the Roman Emperor, or Caesar – was such a beautiful city that all the leading Roman officials – men like Pontius Pilate – lived there and ruled from there. It became the more important city, and was exactly like all the other pagan cities, with an amphitheatre bigger than the famous Coliseum in Rome. It was oval in shape, and crowded with people who came to watch men armed with only a net or a short sword fight against wild beasts.

Five hundred Roman soldiers were stationed there.

No wonder the Jews in Joppa especially hated the rival pagan city and would never go into it if they could avoid it.

Yet in Caesarea there were people who loved God and wanted to know more about him. One of them was a soldier, a centurion who was in charge of a hundred soldiers. His name was Cornelius.

Cornelius and his family worshipped God in the Jewish way, because it seemed to them a much better way than that of the pagan gods, who used people as tools and did cruel things – or that's what many of the myths said. Cornelius helped poor people and he spent a lot of time praying. He longed to know God.

One day at three o'clock Cornelius felt that God was speaking directly to him. "Send some men to Joppa to fetch Simon Peter from Galilee. He is staying with his friend Simon who lives in the leathershop by the sea."

Cornelius at once sent two servants and another soldier who also worshipped God to fetch Peter.

As the centurion watched them go, he wondered if Simon Peter would come. No practising Jew ever went into a pagan's house. He would make himself unclean according to the teaching of the Jewish law. Yet Cornelius was sure that God had something special to tell him, so he invited all his relatives and close friends to come in two days' time.

It took Cornelius' servants a whole day to travel to Joppa. They arrived at about noon and came to the gate of a house by the sea.

"Is Simon Peter from Galilee staying here?" they called out.

Peter was up on the flat roof at prayer. He had just had a vision from God. He saw an enormous sheet being lowered from heaven. In it were all kinds of food. Peter was ravenous. It was hours since he had eaten, and they were cooking a meal for him in the house. He looked longingly at the food in the sheet – and then realised that it was all food forbidden to Jews by their law.

"Get up Peter, have a good dinner," he heard a voice.

"Certainly not, Lord!" Peter answered indig-

nantly. "I've never eaten anything unclean in my life."

"Don't call anything unclean that comes from God and has been made clean," the voice said. This happened three times, and Peter was still wondering what it all meant when he heard the men shout his name down below.

"I have sent them," the Holy Spirit told his innermost mind. "Go with them."

Peter went down and greeted them.

"Please come to Cornelius in Caesarea," they said. "He worships God, and he felt God telling him to send us here to you."

"Come on in then," Peter said. "Spend the night here. We'll start tomorrow."

They set off in the morning, taking some of the believers from Joppa with them. It took them another day to reach the famous pagan city.

When they arrived at Cornelius' house, the centurion fell to his knees at Peter's feet and bowed low to the ground.

"Oh, no!" Peter said. "Get up," he bent forward and helped him up. "I'm only a man after all."

So they went into the house together. Peter was surprised to see so many people gathered together, but that did not prevent him from speaking.

"You all know, I'm sure, that we Jews are forbidden to mix with people from different races. We're just not allowed to visit them at all, but God showed me a vision and I understand now what it

meant. I mustn't think anyone is unclean or set apart from me. That's why I've come here. But tell me, how did you know where to find me and what do you want me for?"

Cornelius looked at him and they both smiled, knowing the answer. "God told me to send for you," he said. "So I did, and you've been kind enough to come. Now here we all are, and we're in the presence of God. We're waiting to hear you say whatever the Lord tells you to."

"I know now that God loves us all," Peter said. "It doesn't matter what country we belong to. As long as we respect him and do good we are equally acceptable to him and he doesn't have any favourites at all.

"You all know about the great things that happened in Judaea? You've all heard about Jesus?"

They nodded. "Did you know that even though he had been nailed to a cross, God raised him to life? We ate and drank with him, and he told us to go everywhere and tell people that if they believe in him their sins will be forgiven."

Even as Peter spoke, the Holy Spirit swept powerfully through the house. It was like Pentecost all over again!

The Jewish believers who had come from Joppa with Peter stood by in utter amazement.

"See. God has poured out his gift of the Holy Spirit on these people too, even though they're not Jews!" they cried. "Listen, they're all praising God in strange languages, just as it happened at Pentecost."

"Let us baptize you all in the Name of our Lord Jesus Christ!" Peter spoke joyfully. "For you are already his, linked to us and to him by the Holy Spirit."

He stayed with them for a few days more, telling them everything about Jesus.

The news reached the Jewish believers and the other apostles in Jerusalem. These followers of Jesus, who had been brought up so strictly by their Jewish traditions not to have anything to do with non-Jews, were horrified that Peter had not only gone to Caesarea, but had actually stayed in a Roman soldier's house.

"It's God's doing, not mine," Peter said when he arrived back into Jerusalem. "How could I refuse to baptize people to whom God had given his Spirit?"

So the others stopped being critical and praised God too.

Acts 10 and 11

The answer to their prayers

"These Nazarenes are still making trouble, are they?" King Herod Agrippa sat in his palace in Jerusalem. "Well, their leader's dead and buried. My uncle asked him to do a miracle, I remember."

Herod's mind was troubled. His uncle had done his best to stamp out the new belief that God's messenger had come with a new kingdom of peace and joy. Yet there seemed to be no ending to this tale. The Baptist was beheaded. Jesus from Nazareth had been nailed to a cross, but their followers had increased. In Herod's dreams a little girl danced; a sword flashed and to a banquet was borne a bleeding head on a dish. Sometimes the dreams changed. A silent figure stood bound before a king. The prisoner was silent, but his eyes spoke, and Herod, the nephew of the man who had tried Jesus, heard in his dreams the wordless message of sorrow and love and pity. He cried out in his sleep.

Perhaps if he killed all the followers of that mute captive, dead and buried at least ten years ago, he would lay to rest these ghosts that haunted his reign.

"Arrest them! Kill them!" he ordered.

The first apostle to die was James, the brother of John; James who had seen Jesus bring a little dead girl back, warm and glowing, to her happy parents. James, who had climbed the snowy mountain slope with his brother and with Peter, and had seen Jesus transformed, and heard the voice of God; James was led off to be executed.

"Lose your life and you will save it," Jesus had said.

James was killed, and when Herod saw that the leading Jews were pleased, he had Peter arrested too.

It was Passover time. Herod planned to bring Peter out in front of all the people when the Passover celebrations were finished. Meantime he was kept in chains, closely guarded, but people still met in Mark's house, and prayed earnestly for Peter.

The night before Herod was going to hand him over to the people, Peter slept peacefully in the prison. His hands were chained to the two soldiers who were on guard duty at that time. There were other guards at the prison gate.

Suddenly a light shone in the dungeon. "Hurry, get up!" God told Peter, who woke up at once. Immediately the chains fell off his hands. "Put on your sandals, Peter, tighten your belt. I'm setting you free," said God.

Not knowing if he was awake or dreaming, Peter walked out of the prison past the first four sentries; past the second four sentries, until at last he came to the iron gate leading out to the city. The gate opened by itself and Peter walked down a street.

The cold night air convinced him that this was no dream.

Perhaps he remembered the Passover night that had been so cold the sentries and servants had lit a fire. That night a man had been bound and no one had rescued him. A man had been tried . . . and had been three times denied.

He went stealthily now through the dark streets to Mark's house. Many people had gathered there. Peter's knock disturbed their prayers. A servant girl called Rhoda ran to open the door.

"It's Peter!" he said, hearing her fumble with the bolt.

"Peter!" she cried and in her hurry to tell the others she forgot to open the door.

"It's Peter!" she said.

"You're crazy!" They were white-faced and weary after their night of prayer for him. "Peter's in prison, about to die. That must be his ghost at the door!"

Peter kept knocking. At last they opened the door and found, to their amazement, that God had answered their prayers. Excited, their tiredness forgotten, they all talked at once, asking him what had happened. He raised his hand and they were quiet as he told them how God had rescued him.

"Tell everyone else what has happened," he said, and slipped away to hide somewhere safe.

Herod's soldiers looked for him, but they couldn't find him. Soon afterward Herod died.

Acts 12

"Send Paul and Barnabas into the world"

"There's famine in Judaea," the news spread around the Christians in Antioch.

"Then we must send help. We're all part of one body, aren't we?"

So Barnabas and Saul returned to Jerusalem with a generous gift for the needy believers there.

"Imagine, non-Jews are giving us gifts," the grateful believers exclaimed.

"It's the love of Jesus that binds us together," Barnabas said. "It overflows. The Christians in Antioch want to spread the good news still further."

When Saul and Barnabas returned to Antioch, the leaders of the church prayed and went without food. As they did this God spoke to them: "Send Saul and Barnabas out into the world. I have work for them there."

That was how the story of Jesus was spread even farther afield, this time by men who had been chosen especially for the job.

The journey took a year. They took Mark with them.

First they travelled sixteen miles to the port of Antioch, where they went on board a ship bound for Barnabas' home, Cyprus.

There were some Christians in Cyprus. Saul and Barnabas and Mark went to the main cities. In Salamis they went to the synagogue and spoke about Jesus. In Paphos the most important man on the island, the Roman Governor Sergius Paulus heard them preach. He was very impressed by the message about the Lord Jesus and by Saul, who now used his Roman name, Paul. Paul's fervent preaching made the Governor listen with great interest. He received Paul's message gladly.

But hard times came upon Paul and Barnabas as they crossed from Cyprus to Asia Minor, to low marshy land, where the climate was bad for Paul's health. It was in this fever-stricken countryside that Mark deserted them and went back to Jerusalem.

Paul and Barnabas travelled on for 100 miles over the mountains of Galatia, where the simple folk of the hills treated them with wonderful hospitality. Paul was very ill now; he preached fervently to them in spite of his weaknesses. They nursed him, as he afterward said, as though the Lord Jesus himself had come to them, weak, exhausted and needy. And they accepted his preaching with great joy.

On they journeyed to the large towns where it would be easier for their preaching to spread. They went to another town called Antioch; Antioch

in Pisidia, the capital of the Roman province of Galatia. Here, as usual, Paul and Barnabas went to the synagogue and explained to the people how Jesus fulfilled all the teaching in the holy Scriptures. The Jews were very interested and invited them to come back next week. They followed them out into the street asking more questions. Paul and Barnabas spoke encouragingly to them.

Next week a great crowd flocked to hear the news. Suddenly some of the strict Jews became frightened. They spoke out against Paul, but he and Barnabas shouted out: "If you reject God's offer of ever-lasting life, we shall go to the Gentiles, for God is using us to tell the whole world the news of his salvation."

How happy the non-Jewish hearers were! Many of them believed. The Church grew and the message spread all round the area, which annoyed the strict Jews still more.

They stirred up trouble for Paul and Barnabas and had them thrown out of the city.

Paul didn't care. The body had been shared again. It had started to grow, a body of people filled with joy, filled with the Holy Spirit; a church

which would spread the news farther around.

On they travelled for another sixty miles to an important trade centre called Iconium. Here there were orchards with plums and apricots. The people were weavers, which was the trade Paul had learnt during his childhood in Tarsus.

Paul and Barnabas stayed for a long time in Iconium. Soon the whole town had heard the news. They became divided. Some people supported the Jews, others the apostles, who not only preached boldly but also did many wonderful things which helped people believe. When Paul and Barnabas finally had to run for their lives from Iconium, they left a growing church behind them there as well.

Twenty-five miles further away was the small town of Lystra. Here, in the crowd, a lame man listened to Paul's words. Paul noticed him. He could see that the man believed. He healed him and for the first time in his life the man jumped up and started to walk around.

What an uproar this caused. The people all shouted: "These are not men, but gods in human form." The priest of the god Zeus led bulls garlanded with flowers to the gate, and wanted to sacrifice them to the apostles. In despair, for the people spoke their own dialect that was hard for the strangers to understand, Paul and Barnabas tore their clothes. "No," they cried, running through the crowd. "We're just ordinary human beings like you. The reason why we've come to you is to tell you the Good News: turn away from stupid beliefs in lifeless gods to the living God. He made the whole world – and how well he looks after it: your food comes from him and every time you're happy, it's God's work."

But now strict Jews from all around: from Antioch in Pisidia and from Iconium, arrived. They stirred up the crowd against Paul and stoned him and dragged him away, leaving him for dead.

The believers gathered around him and helped him regain consciousness. He went back into the town with them and they looked after him. The next day Barnabas and Paul travelled on. It was too dangerous for them to stay. Once again, they left a new church behind, and not only a church. A young man called Timothy came from Lystra. He was very young then. When he grew up he travelled with Paul and became a leader in the church.

A small church was started at the next town, Derbe, twenty miles away from Lystra. Here too a disciple of Paul grew up. His name was Gaius and he, like Timothy, would later travel with Paul, plant churches and lead them.

Their journey had finished. Now they retraced their steps, although they could have gone back an easier and quicker way through Tarsus, where Paul might have rested. But they went back to all the new churches, encouraging them, reminding them that they must be ready to suffer for their faith. With each little group of believers they had a special time, when they asked God to help them choose leaders. They prayed, going without meals, and chose good men to care for the new body that had begun to grow.

They stopped at Perga this time and preached there. Then they sailed to Antioch. But they didn't forget the new Christians. Paul visited them as often as he could. He wrote to them, too, and he also remembered to the end of his days the hardships he had suffered during that year of travelling. "But the Lord rescued me from them all," he said.

Acts 13–15

245

A man from Macedonia

"No, I'm not taking Mark!" Paul stated firmly. "I'm sorry, Barnabas. I know he's your nephew but he left us last time. Remember Perga? Remember how ill I was? We could certainly have done with his help then, and I'm afraid he really let us down."

"I know, but he's older now. I want him to come. He's been in such close contact with all our believers ever since the earliest days. Why, he was with the Lord in the garden of olive trees, as neither you nor I were, brother Paul."

But Paul and Barnabas, great friends though they were, had a quarrel and parted company. Barnabas took Mark with him and sailed off to Cyprus, while Paul chose Silas. Silas had been a leader of the church in Jerusalem before the persecution there. He was a good preacher and a Roman citizen and, like Paul, he longed to take the teaching of Jesus to the non-Jewish world.

On they travelled. Now Timothy from Lystra joined them. He was half-Jewish. Paul loved his family dearly, and looked on Timothy as his own dear son. A little farther on, a doctor joined the party. He came from Macedonia.

Paul had a vision. A man from Macedonia seemed to be calling for him. "Come and help us in Macedonia!"

Immediately the little group prepared to travel to Macedonia, but now the doctor travelled with them. His name was Luke, "Luke, the beloved doctor," as Paul called him. He served Paul devotedly, and he wrote down the story of all their travels, their successes and their failures, the hardships they experienced and the kindness they found.

They sailed to Greece, where they immediately travelled along the great Egnetian Highway, bound for Philippi, a Roman city, the chief town of that part of Macedonia. There were few Jews there and they had no proper meeting place.

After spending a few days in the city, the group went down to the river side, a mile away from the town. Here, beside the swift flowing waters of the Gangites, devout Jews met for prayer. They sat down and talked to the women there. One of them was called Lydia . . .

Lydia was wealthy and independent. She ran a prosperous business, for she sold the beautiful purple cloth that rich people wore. How lovely her welcome had been!

"This is just the news I have been waiting for. I have worshipped God for some time, but now that you tell me of Jesus, I feel that through him I have come to know God. Can you baptize me now?" she asked. She and all her household were baptized.

"Now if you are sure I'm a true believer in the Lord, come and stay in my house," she had invited them.

But trouble lay ahead for Paul and Silas in Philippi. Paul healed a poor slave girl whose masters made their fortune out of the strange powers she possessed. She could tell the future. But when Paul healed her, the magic went. Her masters were furious that they could no longer make money out of her, and they dragged Paul and Silas before the magistrates in the public square. "These Jews are causing trouble," they said. What a riot there was! The crowd joined in the attack without knowing the cause. The magistrates tore Paul's and Silas' clothes off their backs and ordered them to be flogged.

"Lock up these men," the magistrates ordered, and roughly the jailer threw them into the inner cell. Their hands were chained. He clamped their feet between two heavy blocks of wood that were hollowed out so that a prisoner's legs would fit tightly in the holes.

But Paul and Silas took their punishment joy-

fully. They sat there singing hymns and praying to God while the evening wore away. The other prisoners listened in amazement. About midnight there was a violent earthquake. The stone walls of the prison trembled and shook. The doors burst open and the chains which bound the prisoners to heavy iron rings in the walls fell loose.

But no one ran away.

The jailer, wakened by the noise, tried to kill himself. "The prisoners have escaped. They'll kill me for this," he said and drew his sword.

"Stop!" shouted Paul. "Stop that at once! Don't do yourself any harm. We're all here! No one has tried to escape."

"A light! A light! Someone get me a light!" called the jailer. He rushed in and fell trembling at the feet of Paul and Silas. "Sirs, Sirs, tell me please," he begged as he led them away. "What must I do to be saved?"

"Believe in Jesus," they said. "Trust him and you and your family will be safe for ever." There and then, wounded and sore though they were, they preached from the Scriptures to the jailer and his startled family. Even though it was so late at night, the jailer washed their wounds and then asked

them to baptize him and all his family. Then he gave Paul and Silas a meal.

Luke came from Philippi. He knew the jailer. He smiled to himself as he remembered the change that had taken place in the whole family.

The next day the magistrates came to the prison and apologised to Paul and Silas for having beaten and arrested them. They were really afraid when they heard that the two men were Roman citizens. As soon as they were set free, Paul and Silas went back to Lydia's house where they spoke words of encouragement to all the believers and told them that the jailer and his family would be joining them to worship the Lord and share their love feasts.

"You must shine out like stars lighting up the sky," Paul told them. "We all belong to Jesus, don't we? Well, we must love one another and share with one another."

The little church grew, happy and warm-hearted, helping Paul by sending money for his expenses. One of them called Epaphroditus became a soldier for Jesus, with Paul helping him to spread the story of love.

Acts 16

The people who turned the world upside down

Seventy miles on from Philippi, they journeyed with two overnight stops until they came to Thessalonica, the chief seaport of Macedonia.

As usual, Paul went to the synagogue, where for three Sabbaths he argued with the people, proving from the Scriptures that Jesus is the Messiah. As usual, the non-Jews who worshipped God listened eagerly and many of them believed. A few of the Jews and many of the leading women of the city became Christians.

As usual, trouble followed.

"These men have caused trouble everywhere. They've turned the whole world upside down!" their opponents shouted. "Now they've come to our city. They break all the laws saying that there's another King, King Jesus."

Paul and Silas were nowhere to be found, but the magistrates arrested Jason at whose house they stayed. They released him when he had paid them some money. Paul and Silas slipped away secretly, so as not to trouble the believers any more. The church they had started grew, with Jason as one of their leaders.

Fifty miles farther on, Paul and Silas stayed at another town called Beroea. Once again Paul went to the synagogue and spoke to all the Jews. But here the people listened eagerly. They studied the Scriptures every day to see if the things Paul claimed about Jesus were really true. Many of them believed and so did many of the Greeks, both men and women.

"Now we all share one body," Paul and Silas taught them. "Now Jews and non-Jews can eat together and pray together. For we all belong together since God has shown us that Jesus died for us all."

How wonderful those days were. But unfortunately the Jews from Thessalonica heard where Paul had gone. They sent trouble-makers there and stirred up a mob against him.

"Paul, this can't go on," his friends urged him. "They'll kill you."

"I'm ready to die for the sake of the gospel," said Paul and they knew that he meant it.

"Yes, but think how much the young churches need you," they said. "There are so many people who haven't heard the good news."

"Look, we'll make it seem as if you're going to the coast, but instead some of us will take you on to Athens," the new believers said. "Then Silas and Timothy can join you after they've taught us more about the Christian way and all the excitement has died down."

Beautiful Athens! Its many marble buildings turned pink when the sun set. Dead stones seemed alive.

Paul had been brought up in Tarsus where there was a Greek university. He knew Greek thought and wisdom. But as he wandered through Athens, he sorrowed to see the empty worship of so many people. The city was thronged with idols; statues to a whole host of gods and goddesses. One altar was built to honour "the unknown god".

So Paul made God known. In the synagogue he argued with the Jews and the Greeks who followed

the Jewish way. In the open squares where philosophers and students, idlers and thinkers endlessly debated questions as to the best way to live, Paul spoke to them about Jesus and about the Resurrection.

"What's this ignorant show-off trying to tell us," the philosophers sneered.

"He seems to be talking about foreign gods: well, let's hear him out. We're always ready to hear anything new!"

They took Paul to the slopes of a hill in the northwest of Athens. It was customary for the city court to meet here in the open to decide legal matters or discuss religious or political things. Paul summoned all his wisdom, all his gifts as a thinker and public speaker in order to convince the intellectuals of the world of his day that Jesus is Lord.

"Men of Athens, I see from all the altars and shrines round about how religious you are," he began. "You even worship the unknown god. Then let me make this God known to you, for he is the Lord who created the world and life itself, yet he is not far from any one of us. In fact it is because God lives that we live and are the human beings that we are. Even some of your poets have said 'we are his children'."

They nodded, pleased that this Jew knew their writings and beliefs so well.

"Why then do you worship idols of stone or silver or gold? We are not made that way; we, the children of God, must bear the family likeness. Now God has shown us what he is like. Now he tells everyone all over the world to turn to him. For one day he will judge the world and his Judge will be a man who was specially chosen. His name is Jesus and he was raised from the dead."

"What a joke!" they shouted him down. "A man raised from death."

But some people said: "We want to hear you speak again."

Disappointed, Paul went away, but some men joined him and became believers. One of them was a council member called Dionysius, another was a woman named Damaris.

From Athens Paul went to Corinth. It was a city famed for its wickedness, but there were many there who were glad to hear about God's love for them and the power he could give them every day in their lives. They believed Paul's message, and another group of believers became linked to the body of the church.

Acts 17 and 18

"Great is Diana of Ephesus"

Ephesus was a very important city, one of the greatest along the shores of the Mediterranean. A married couple called Aquila and Priscilla, who were friends of Paul, and tent-makers by trade, had settled there. They were believers in Jesus, and a little church soon started in their home. It was some time before Paul could spend any time with the group, though he was very anxious to see the church there grow up as a body of people who loved Jesus and would go and tell others about God's love.

In Ephesus, the main street was paved with marble. The roadway was broad, thirty-six feet wide, and lined with shops. Magic signs and spells were written on the walls of many of the buildings. People came to Ephesus from all over the world and brought their gods with them.

Above all else, Ephesus was the city of the goddess Diana. By this time, people had been worshipping this Mother Goddess for eight centuries. A great burning stone had fallen from heaven. Men had built an altar and planted a sacred tree where it fell. Later, they built temples, beautiful temples.

Above them all towered the statue of the goddess. To the Greeks she was Artemis: the Romans called her Diana, the slim maiden with her bow, the huntswoman whose sandalled feet could outrun the deer. Diana was the great Mother, the Mother of life, the Mother of the dark mysteries. Men had worshipped at her shrine since the beginnings of time, for they believed she was the one who gave life.

Men flocked from all countries to worship her in her temple. In little shops in the city her images could be bought. Some were of gold, others of silver, some were of ivory, others simply of wood and many men made their living from the making and selling of those images.

At first Paul spoke in the synagogue at Ephesus, but later he went daily to the lecture hall of the schoolmaster, Tyrannus. During the hottest time of the day, when the hall was not being used, he would stop his tent-making and for five hours he would teach the way of Jesus to anyone who was willing to listen. Many people heard him and believed in Jesus. Others were healed by Paul, and finally all the Christians burned their books of magic in front of a huge crowd of people.

Paul stayed two years in Ephesus. Then he began to talk of going back to visit the other churches that had grown up through the work he and his growing band of helpers had done during the last years.

"You go on ahead of me," he said to Timothy and Erastus. Erastus had been the City Treasurer of Corinth, a very important man in the city, but he had given up his job to go with Paul. "Tell the churches that I will be coming soon. Encourage men to hold on to Jesus, no matter what troubles come."

Paul had never stated that the worship of Diana was wrong, but so many people believed in Jesus that the silversmiths were losing money and customers.

Before Paul left Ephesus he had to face more trouble because of this.

The Festival of Diana was celebrated each year and the city was already filling up with pilgrims from all over the world. Paul wanted to stay and preach Jesus to them.

But the silversmiths were furious. "All our money is going, the faster this faith spreads," their leader Demetrius said. "Besides, Ephesus is the centre of the great goddess. We can't see her name dishonoured like this. She's worshipped by everyone in Asia and the whole world."

"Great is our goddess Diana. Great is Diana of Ephesus!" they shouted. Crowds of pilgrims, not understanding, took up the shout.

"Let's get Paul!" they shouted. They couldn't find him, but they found two other Christians called Gaius and Aristarchus who travelled with Paul. They dragged them off to the public meeting place, the vast round theatre that could seat 25,000 people.

It was packed that day. "Great is Diana," the shouts went on.

"Let me go!" Paul said. "I must go and help Gaius and Aristarchus."

"No, no," the believers said. "The mob won't hurt them, but they'll lynch you."

"Don't come to the theatre; we'll handle this," a message came from some of the friendly Roman officials.

For two hours the crowd in the enormous theatre shouted their slogan: "Great is Diana of the Ephesians."

At the end of that time they were tired enough to listen to the town clerk, the chief man of the city. "Everyone knows that Ephesus is the keeper of the great stone that fell from heaven. Everyone

knows that we honour and worship Diana here. No one can deny these things – and no one has tried to. Now, tell me, which of these two men has tried to rob any of our temples or spoken any word against our goddess. There's no need for this riot. If Demetrius and his friends have any cause for complaint against anyone they can bring it to the court at the proper day and the right people will sort it out. If there's anything else anyone of you wants, why it can all be handled by the legal meeting of all the citizens. That's the way we handle things in Ephesus, not by this sort of rabble and noise. If it gets to the ears of the Roman authorities, they'll accuse us of rioting. We wouldn't be able to give them any good reason for it and we'd lose all our privileges of self-government."

The crowd saw the sense of this. They'd all struck a blow for the honour of Diana. No one had said anything against their goddess. Now they could go and enjoy the rest of the festivities.

But Paul realised his life was in danger. He didn't want to bring trouble to the church. He left soon afterward and went on to Greece.

Acts 19

"A prisoner because I served the Lord"

Paul left Macedonia to travel back to Jerusalem. He was in a hurry to get there before Pentecost. He had decided not to stop back at Ephesus, so he sent a message asking the elders of the church to meet him at Miletus, his next port of call.

The elders wept openly as they met him. Paul encouraged them, telling them to be shepherds of the little flock of believers who were in Ephesus. They were reluctant to let him go, and came with him to the ship, standing on the shore until they were no longer able to see him.

Paul had been told in a prophecy that when he reached Jerusalem he would be bound. Some of his companions feared for his life, but Paul said, "Don't break my heart with your sorrow. I am ready not only to be bound, but to die for my Lord."

When they arrived in Jerusalem, the Jewish Christians there told Paul of some of their difficulties. The only way the little church had survived there, under severe persecution, had been to observe all the Jewish customs, which Paul had told the non-Jewish believers were not a necessary part of the Christian way of life. James, the brother of Jesus, pleaded with Paul to show that he was still a follower of the Law of Moses. He asked him to take part in the Temple ceremonies during Pentecost. It would mean staying another seven days in Jerusalem.

Paul agreed, because he had always said that he would do nothing to cause other people difficulty. So he spent the time in the Temple, even though it meant staying longer than he had planned.

The trouble came when Jews from Asia saw Paul with some of his friends from Ephesus in the outer courts of the Temple. Then later, they saw Paul taking part in the religious ceremonies, right in the innermost courts, where only Jewish men were allowed: no woman, or non-Jewish man might go there. The penalty was death.

"Men of Israel!" the Asian Jews shouted. "Grab that man! We've seen him with a non-Jew from Ephesus right in our innermost courts!"

At once they closed the Temple doors. Paul was arrested and dragged out into the street. He was turned over to the furious mob that had gathered. They tried to kill him. The Roman troops were brought in to stop the riot. The Commander rode through the dense crowd and took charge of Paul.

"What have you done?" he asked, but no one could give him a proper answer. No one really knew.

"Kill him!" they all shrieked. The soldiers had to carry Paul over their shoulders to protect him from the savage attacks by the mob.

Luke and the others stood by helplessly, as Paul was carried away, battered and stunned, above the heads of the crowd.

He was taken to the Fortress of Antonia, the head-quarters of the Roman troops, where Jesus had also stood and been mocked and scourged.

The crowd followed.

"May I say something to the people?" Paul's fluent Greek amazed the Army Commander.

"Do you speak Greek? I thought you must be that Egyptian rebel who persuaded 4,000 guerilla fighters when the walls of Jerusalem tumbled down at his bidding they could rush in and plunder the city," the Commander said.

"I am a Jew from Tarsus, the great city of Silicia," said Paul. "Please let me speak to the people."

Paul raised his hand, and the mob fell silent. In Hebrew he cried out, "Brothers and fathers, listen to my defence." The crowd became even quieter as they heard his fluent beautiful Hebrew, and Paul told them his whole story. He explained how he had hated the followers of Jesus, how the Lord had appeared to him on the hot road to Damascus, but as soon as he started telling about his mission to tell the non-Jews that God loved them as well, the crowd broke into an uproar. "He's not fit to live! Kill him!"

So the Commander ordered his soldiers to take Paul inside and beat him, hoping that the leaden whip would make him give away the real reason for the crowd's hatred of him. As they stripped him and tied him up, Paul explained proudly that he was a Roman citizen, and that to beat him would be breaking the law! The officer-in-charge was very impressed with his statement and kept him safe in the Roman fortress until they could find out what the real trouble was.

Acts 21 and 22

"The Lord stood by me"

Claudius Lysias, the officer-in-charge, was determined to find out why the Jews wanted to kill Paul. So he unchained Paul, and called for the chief priest and the whole Council. Paul was brought before them.

"Brothers," he began, "I am a Pharisee. I am on trial here because I hope that there is a life after death."

At once the two groups, the Pharisees who believed in the life after death, and the Sadducees, who did not, started to argue. They became so violent that Claudius Lysias was frightened that Paul would be torn to pieces. His soldiers dragged Paul to safety and took him back to the fortress.

Bruised and sore, and very discouraged, Paul tossed and turned on his prison bed that night.

"Will your people never hear, Lord? Will they never understand your way?" he thought in despair.

Then the Lord stood by him, and comforted him. "Don't despair, Paul. You have given all the evidence about me here in Jerusalem. You must go to Rome, too, to be my witness in the capital of the world."

Acts 23

256

"Like me, except for these chains"

ore than forty Sadducees took a vow that they would eat no food or drink until they had seen Paul killed. Their plan was overheard by Paul's nephew, who reported the information, first of all to Paul, and then to Lysias.

So, with an escort of two hundred foot soldiers, seventy horsemen, and two hundred spearmen, Paul rode out of Jerusalem late at night when everyone was asleep. They took him along the military road to a town 39 miles away, where they camped for the rest of the night. Then the foot soldiers returned to Jerusalem, while the others escorted Paul the rest of the way to Caesarea. He was being sent to the Governor of Judaea, a man called Felix.

Felix read the letter from Lysias, which said that in his opinion, Paul was not guilty of any crime.

"You must stay under guard in Herod's palace until your accusers arrive," said Felix.

Five days later, Paul was on trial again. This time the Jews had hired a professional lawyer who made a very bad case against Paul. He argued that Paul was guilty, not of offences against the Jewish religion, but against the Roman law.

Paul was then allowed to defend himself. "I know you're well informed about our nation and our beliefs, including the way of the Lord," he told Felix. "I admit freely that I follow the way of Jesus, but in fact what I am being tried for is my belief in life after death. The Council themselves believe in that, in any case."

Felix heard the evidence of both sides, and then said, "I'll make a decision later."

Two years later Paul was still in prison. He was given a certain amount of freedom, and his friends could visit him. Luke came often, full of stories he had learnt from the Christians in Caesarea about the early days of the church. Best of all he was hearing more and more stories about Jesus, about the things different people had seen him do, or heard him say. These he safely wrote down, and they formed the basis of his gospel.

Paul's hard-working assistants came and went with reports from the growing churches. They took back letters from Paul to the new Christians, encouraging them and helping them to sort out the problems they met.

Felix himself hadn't forgotten about Paul. He came several times. He enjoyed hearing Paul preach, but when Paul's words pricked his conscience too much, he left him. Finally, a new Governor, whose name was Festus, was appointed. Festus was a good man who wanted to see justice done. Three days after his arrival, he started to sort out Paul's case. So Paul stood on trial for the third time.

"I've done nothing against the Law of the Jews, the Temple, or the Roman Emperor!" he declared.

"Listen, Paul," Festus said. "Would you like to go to Jerusalem and be tried by your own people there, or stay here to be tried by me? I'm new, as you know, and I'm still fairly ignorant about the whole situation."

"I'm standing before the Emperor's court," Paul replied. "I will not be handed over to the Jews, as I've done nothing wrong. I have a right to appeal to the Emperor for justice. I make that appeal now."

After a quick word with his legal advisers, Festus said, "That is the right of every Roman citizen. Since you appeal to the Emperor, I'll arrange to have you sent to Rome."

But before he was sent to Rome, Paul spoke once more in his own defence. This time it was in front of King Agrippa, the great-grandson of the cruel King Herod, who had killed the baby boys in Bethlehem, in a mad, jealous search for the baby who had been born a King. Paul seized his chance. He spoke clearly and well, telling Agrippa everything about himself and his encounter with Jesus.

"King Agrippa," Paul ended, "I can tell you about these things, because you know all about our beliefs. You've read the Scriptures. Do you believe the prophets? I know you do."

"Really, Paul," joked Agrippa, "you'll be making a Christian out of me next!"

"Indeed, I pray that you and everyone who has been listening today would become a Christian like me," Paul said. "Except of course for these chains," he added, holding up his hand in one of his gestures that spoke so much.

"If he had not appealed to the Emperor, we could have set this man free," said Agrippa to Festus.

But Paul had appealed to the highest power, and so they had to send him to Rome. He set out gladly even though he was still a prisoner, for his Lord had told him that he was needed there.

Acts 23–26

And so Paul came to Rome

"It's getting late in the year to travel," centurion Julius told Luke. "And of course, there are no direct sailings to Rome," he sighed a little. Rome was so far away. He was an Italian and he hoped to be able to snatch a visit home if they got to Rome early enough.

"So what do you plan?" Luke asked.

"We'll sail along the coast of Asia as far as we can." He showed Luke a map. "From somewhere near Myra here, in the south-west, we should be able to get a corn ship. They go across to Rome from Alexandria, and sail even when other ships don't dare to risk the voyage."

Luke nodded. The emperors had to supply plenty of free grain to the Roman people – otherwise there would be riots.

"You'll let us go with Paul, Aristarchus, a fellow-Macedonian and myself?"

"Yes, but you're not meant to be with him, you know. You'll have to pretend you're his slaves. I'll be glad to take you both. I can see he's an innocent man, not like the others." He jerked his head in the direction of the other prisoners, who were all bound for the great Roman amphitheatre where crowds would gape as wild beasts tore the men to death.

They sailed away, and the next day called at Sidon, where Julius kindly allowed Paul to see his friends. Then the winds blew against them so they sailed on the sheltered side of the island of Cyprus, the eastern side. After fifteen days sailing they reached Myra. There Julius found a corn ship. It was a big ship, for it held 276 passengers, the crew and all the cargo.

For several days they sailed slowly, heading for the coastal town of Cnidus, but the wind would not let them land. They struggled on, hugging the coast of Crete until they came to a place called the Fair Havens.

There they landed, but the going had been so slow that winter had now come upon them. Sailing was dangerous.

"What can we do?" asked Julius.

"This harbour's no use to winter in," said the captain.

"Yet if we sail it will be with loss of our cargo and damage to the ship. It's too late in the year."

They turned in surprise. The speaker was Paul, the experienced traveller.

"Well, we'll ask the crew what they think," they decided.

"Put out to sea. We'll head for a safer harbour."

"Let's make for Phoenix in Crete. We could spend the winter there."

So they planned to sail, especially as a gentle southerly breeze had started. They pulled up the anchor and sailed on, but not for long. Soon the ship was tossed off course by a strong wind blowing right down from the island.

"The 'Northeaster's' got us," the sailors groaned.

"Head her into it!" roared the captain.

"We can't keep her on course!" they shouted back.

"Let her run with the wind," the captain decided. "There's shelter in the lee of the island. We'll pass it to the south."

There they strengthened the ship, passing strong ropes around the planks.

But once past the island the sailors' fears grew.

"The quicksands off Libya," they groaned. "She's running straight for them! They stretch for 300 miles."

They lowered the mainsail and tried to steer westwards.

"There's no sun by day and no stars by night, nothing to guide us," the captain held the useless rudder in his hand. "We've nothing to steer by and the wind is as strong as ever. We'll have to throw the cargo overboard."

The precious boxes of grain bobbed away on the waves. They tossed over equipment and furnishings. No one ate anything. They all gave up hope.

"I beg you," Paul, the little man who had endured so much, stood cheerfully in front of them all. "Take heart. Cheer up! I know God will bring us safely to Rome. The Lord to whom I belong, the God I worship, came to me in a dream last night and said: 'Don't be afraid, Paul. I'm going to get you to Rome to stand before the Emperor.' And God in his goodness will save us all. I'm entirely convinced of that since he told me so."

It was now the fourteenth night of the storm. About midnight a sudden hope seized the sailors. They sensed land was near. They took soundings with a long rope which had a lead weight at the end of it.

"Twenty fathoms deep!" they cried, pulling it in.

A little later they tried again and this time the depth was fifteen fathoms.

But now they were afraid of the rocks so they lowered four anchors from the stern to keep the ship's high prow facing land.

There was nothing else to do except wait for daylight; some of them prayed for it.

"Do eat something," Paul said. "You've all been so long without eating anything. You must eat if you're to survive. I tell you, you'll all be saved." He took some bread, and in front of them all gave thanks to God, broke it and began to eat. Then the sailors cheered up and ate their fill. Afterwards they threw the rest of the grain overboard.

"The ship must be light for the wind to drive her to shore," Julius explained to Luke, who knew nothing about sailing.

Day came at length, but now no one recognised the coast. They spotted a bay ahead and decided to let the ship run aground there. They cut off

261

the anchors and hoisted the sail to catch the wind. But the ship ran on to a sandbank. The bow was stuck while the stern broke to pieces in the stormy sea.

"Kill the prisoners!" said the soldiers. "We'll answer with our lives if any of them escapes."

"No," Julius wanted to save Paul. "Everyone who can swim jump overboard now and swim for the shore. Everyone else is to follow holding on to planks of broken pieces of wood from the ship."

Everyone came safely ashore. It was raining but the friendly islanders – who told them they had landed on Malta – lit a fire for them. Paul helped to gather sticks.

They spent the rest of the winter there and Paul healed many sick people, including the father of the chief man of the island, who had given them such a hospitable welcome.

After three months they sailed away on another corn ship from Alexandria. The kindly Maltese showered presents upon them.

Thereafter they made smooth sailing and landed at the busy port of Puteoli, 140 miles from Rome. To Paul's joy a group of believers met them and Julius, as sympathetic as ever, allowed Paul to spend a week with them.

"And so we came to Rome," wrote Luke. They travelled by road. Forty miles from the capital a group of Christians from the church in Rome came to meet them at a small village. Ten miles further on, another group greeted them. Once again Julius and the soldiers stood by as slaves and humble folk flocked round Paul, hugging him and welcoming him with joy.

Paul stayed for two years under house arrest in Rome. During that time he wrote letters to the churches and won new followers of Jesus even amongst the Emperor's slaves. Soldiers, wealthy people, a certain runaway slave and many others found themselves welcomed by the prisoner Paul and found that there was a place for them in the kingdom of God.

Acts 27 and 28

A rich man and
a runaway slave

The light burned late that night in a house in Rome. It had been a busy day, with many people coming and going, humble folk mostly, many of them slaves. The soldier on guard in the room was used to this by now, but he could never get used to seeing them all sitting talking so freely together: the Greek doctor, the half-Jewish man, the high ranking official and the slaves. All the differences that mattered so much everywhere else didn't seem to matter here. They seemed to share something that went deeper with them than anything else, something that spread and glowed like lamp-light in the quiet room.

Now there were only a few people left. Paul, the prisoner had been dictating a letter. Timothy, half-Jewish, half-Greek, had been writing for hours now. The soldier who guarded Paul, linked to him by a long chain, had been dozing in the corner. Every now and then he jerked awake, and his ears caught the sound of words so filled with love and gentleness that when he dreamt again a smile softened the hard lines of his face.

"How could this man be convicted of wrong-doing?" he thought as he listened sleepily to Paul's voice.

"Don't tell lies to each other. You've thrown off your old self like old clothes, and you wear a new self, which God made and keeps on remaking inside you, so that you come to know him better and better. Now there are no more Jews or non-Jews, barbarians

or savages, slaves or free men. It doesn't matter what race you belong to, or what sort of education you've had. Jesus is everything to us and Jesus is in us all!"

"That was why they showed so much love to one another!" thought the soldier listening to the lovely words. "These are your new clothes: love, kindness, peace and thankfulness."

The soldier must have slept a little, for when he awoke Paul had nearly finished his letter. "I am sending our dear brother Tychicus to you. He'll cheer you up by telling you how we are all getting along. With him goes Onesimus, the dear and faithful brother who belongs to your group."

The slave Onesimus was sitting on the floor beside Paul. The soldier saw him take Paul's bound wrist and press it to his lips.

Paul was smiling at him. "How I'll miss you, Onesimus!" he said, but there were tears in the slave's eyes and he did not answer.

"He's a runaway slave," the soldier thought, "and Paul's so fond of him, yet he's sending him back to the place he escaped from. Aren't they frightened? He's bound to be put to death."

"Are you ready then?" Paul asked.

Tychicus nodded. "We'll leave at daybreak, Paul. Oh! It will be good to be home again! We'll tell everyone about you. They'll hang on to every word. I know they're all waiting for you to return to them, especially Philemon."

"Dear Philemon!" said Luke. "Everyone says how kind and generous he is."

Onesimus nodded. "Perhaps that's why he gave me my name," he said, ruefully, and everyone smiled. His name meant "helpful", but Onesimus had not been helpful. He had run away from his kindly master.

"My heart was so full of bitterness," he said. "My chains chafed and hurt. I did not know how to wear them as you wear yours, my father," he turned to Paul.

"But it is different now," Paul reminded him. "We all serve one another because Jesus is our Lord. Look, Onesimus, here is a letter for you to take to Philemon.

"To our friend Philemon and the church that meets in your house . . ." Onesimus nodded, remembering the lovely big hall that his wealthy master had used, not for big dinner parties as other rich men did, but so that believers should meet freely with one another there. He hadn't understood then what that had meant.

Paul read on: "Philemon, I am sending you back your helpful one! True, he was once useless to you, but he has been very helpful to me while I have been a prisoner here. Indeed, he has helped me as you would have done if you had been here. He is my own son in Jesus, and now not just a slave of yours, but much more than a slave: a brother in Christ."

The soldier leant forward, hardly able to believe his ears. No runaway slave would ever dare go back to his master! And what master ever treated a slave like a brother?

"I know the welcome you would give to me," Paul read. "I ask you to welcome Onesimus as you would welcome me. And if he owes you anything or has stolen anything, charge it to my account." He broke off and turned to Timothy: "Have you the pen? I'll write this in my own handwriting." The pen scratched across the parchment. "There!" Paul said. "I, Paul will pay you back." He read on. "I am sure as I write this that you will do this favour for me for the Lord's sake: in fact I know you will do more than I ask."

Onesimus interrupted. "No, Paul, no! You must not write like that! It's more than I deserve. Besides, how could I be freed and you still wear a chain? You have shown me the meaning of freedom. In Jesus I am already free."

At dawn the two men set out. Months later and a thousand miles away there was great joy in a gracious lovely house, where a rich man held out his arms and welcomed back a runaway slave.

The letter, already travel-worn, was read and re-read and passed around from hand to hand. It was treasured by Philemon and by all the believers in the town where he lived. Centuries later, in many different languages, people still read the letter that brought Philemon and his escaped slave together into one family, whose story is still being told; one body, which many, many share.

Philemon

"Bring the books, Timothy, and my cloak"

ow that Paul was in prison, a lot of care and work with the growing churches had fallen on the shoulders of his helpers. Timothy, the half-Jewish boy from Lystra in Asia Minor, whom Paul looked on as his own son since Timothy's own father was dead, and who had followed Paul through many dangers for more than ten years, looked after the churches in and around Ephesus.

Paul wrote two letters to him, encouraging him, for he was young and alone and often sick. He urged Timothy to be like a soldier who wants to please his commanding officer, and who keeps himself from getting too mixed-up in the happenings of everyday civilian life; to be like an athlete who obeys the rules when he runs the race and to study

the Scriptures and remember the times he and Paul had shared.

How anxious Paul was for Timothy! It was just as a father always feels worried when his grown-up son sets out on his own in the world. He was sure the boy just wouldn't be able to manage on his own. Paul was lonely too, and a little cold, for even in Italy the winters were cold for the prisoner from Tarsus.

"Do your best to come to me soon," he urged. "Do you remember how Demas drew apart from us when you were with us here? He has forsaken us now, fallen in love with this present world. It's so easy to be snared! We have to be ready to endure suffering.

"I am ready, Timothy! But now the time of my departure has nearly come. I have done my best in the race. I've run the full distance and finished the entire course. I have kept the faith. Now I am on the finishing lap leading around the stadium, and I know the prize of victory is waiting for me; but my Lord has no garland of green boughs of bay and laurel, which wither and fade. He will put on me the crown of righteousness when the race is over.

There will be many prize-winners then, and many cheering people to acclaim their King.

"Meantime I am almost alone. The other workers have all gone their ways to look after the churches. Only Luke is with me. Pick up Mark and bring him with you. Once, long ago, he deserted me, but that is far in the past and we have both forgiven each other. I need him for the work here. When you come, bring my cloak. I left it in Troas. Bring the books too, Timothy, and especially the parchments. There are so many letters to write!

"No one stood by me the first time I defended myself. But the Lord stayed with me. He strengthened me so that I was able to tell everyone the story of Jesus and his kingdom. Now all the world knows: Jews and non-Jews. I was rescued from all harm and hurt and the Lord will rescue me from evil and take me safely to his heavenly kingdom."

His letter was almost finished. He sighed. If only he had Timothy here with him! He picked up his pen again.

"I send greetings to my dear friends in Ephesus: to Priscilla and Aquila. Oh, Timothy, do your best to come before the winter sets in and no boats sail!

"All the brothers here in Rome greet you.

"Timothy, my son, the Lord be with you and God's grace with all the churches."

Paul laid down his pen. There was nothing more to write. Luke came into the room.

"I am longing to go to Jesus, Luke," Paul said. Suddenly he smiled. "It's been a great race," he said, "for either way we win. To me, living is Jesus. He is everything. And to die – why that's gain! We can't lose!"

In the quiet room the Jewish prisoner and the Greek doctor laughed softly together.

So, thirty years after the body of Jesus Christ was stretched and broken on a cross, the church that he had left behind had spread all over the world from Jerusalem to Rome.

Three years later came times of terrible persecution, when the mad pampered Emperor Nero massacred as many Christians as he could find. Peter and perhaps Paul died during those days.

The church did not die. The church went on growing. There will be an ending, but it will be a beginning: the beginning of joy that will never have an ending; the story of people who live happily ever after.

1 and 2 Timothy

Jesus, royally reigning

The next two chapters tell how the Apostle John, in exile on the island of Patmos, encouraged the churches of Asia by telling them of visions he had seen.

There was One high and exalted, seated on the throne. In his hand he held a scroll, rolled and sealed. An angel cried out, loudly. I heard his voice and saw that he was mighty. He challenged God's creatures: "Come and open the scroll. Come if you are worthy. Who is worthy to open and unseal the scroll? See, there is writing on both sides. Let someone come and read."

His voice rang through the arches of heaven.

The stars caught the sound. His voice vibrated over the earth. The mountain tops sent the message down to the deep vales. Under the earth, the depths of the underworld heard the cry.

I listened and trembled, wondering who would come and open the scroll. He would have to come to the throne of God. All in front of the throne was a crystal sea, many faceted, all shining, rainbow hued. I knew my footsteps would shatter that pure lovely shining glass, nor dared I, John, approach the glorious winged creatures who stood before the beautiful throne, worshipping God.

So I waited, wondering, but no one was worthy: no one in heaven, nor in all the earth, nor in the lands of mist half-dreamt-of by mortals. No one was worthy.

I wept then. Do you wonder why I wept? I wept because tears were all I could offer. I wept because God could not now entrust his love to any one. I wept because music beyond desiring would not now be heard. I wept because man's dearest dreams are never fulfilled. I wept because love is lost and grows cold. All the sorrow of the world was before me because there was no one to open the scroll.

"Why worry and weep?" The joyful voice spoke to me. It belonged to one of the elders of heaven and he comforted me: "Do you not know that the Lion of Judah, the One who was born of David's House in Bethlehem, the Lamb that was slain has triumphed. He is worthy. He will open the scroll."

He comforted me with the words spoken in our Scriptures by Jacob as he, dying, blessed his sons: Words long ago by Jacob, dying were spoken: "Judah, by great strength shall your foes be broken; Lion are you, Judah; now climb back from your kill:

Lion-like he crouches, lies down watchful and still. Take sceptre and mace: now reign. Your brothers shout praise.

God plants his new shoot in you, a green branch will raise –

From afar flock all peoples, pay homage, acclaim The Lion, the young slaughtered Lamb. Worthy his name!"

Then I saw him, the Lamb that had been slain, he came forward and when he took the scroll the elders and the wonderful winged creatures bowed down to the ground. From golden bowls the prayers of God's people rose like incense. How fragrant the incense! I did not know that prayer is so precious to God in his glory. Then they sang a new song to worship the Lamb. I heard with my heart. I heard all creation worship our Jesus who laid aside his glory and came like light into our darkness. My heart sang silently, vibrantly with them.

"You are worthy to take the scroll
And to break open the seals.
For you were killed, and by your death
You bought men for God,
From every tribe, and language,
and people and nation."

Then for the honour that he had gladly shed, counting it a greater thing to do his Father's perfect will, all heaven gave our risen Lord honour. I heard the sound of angels and animals and men, glorified, and beautiful, an immense crowd, dense and radiant, beyond counting. I heard them praise Jesus. Then I heard all the living things in creation lift their voices: the wind on the mountains; the waves of the sea; the silent green springing of grain; the flight of the seabirds and the soft scurry of small wild things; the sound sleep of a newborn babe: all things great and little gave Jesus praise and heaped on him their honour. Then the lovely winged creatures, whose beautiful reflection was broken into a myriad sparkling pieces in the crystal sea around God's throne, cried: Amen. The depths of heaven resounded and the whole of heaven bowed in worship before the One who bore on his body the sorrows that torment mankind.

Revelation 5

"Come!"

Do you cry now, my brothers and sisters? Your homes are plundered; your belongings are thrown out on the street. You are imprisoned, impoverished and mocked.

You weep, yet it seems to you that no one hears. No one comes to comfort you, to dry your eyes and wipe away your tears.

Weep no more; there will be no more crying. Loud, loud cried a voice: "Here, oh here, God lives with men for ever. He makes his home among us. We are his guests for always. Once we were like nomads, always moving on, glimpsing God as thirsty shepherds glimpse the oasis in the desert, but moving on. Now God is with us, and with us for ever. There is no death now; no sorrowing, no sadness."

My brothers and sisters, my little ones who sob alone, God has begun a new age, a new heaven and a new earth. The old world has gone and God himself stoops down to you and wipes away all tears from your eyes.

For I saw this in a vision. Let me tell you what I saw.

From out of heaven came a bride. How beautiful

she was! Oh, but no wonder she was beautiful, for she came straight from God and all his radiant glory shone in her face and sparkled from her wonderful robes.

An angel spoke to me, the one who had shown me the visions of heaven. "Come, John, I will show you the husband who has married this lovely bride."

He showed me the young slaughtered Lamb; he showed me Jesus, who fought for his love until his hands were red with his own blood and his feet sorely torn.

Then I understood that the bride is the church. We shall all share the marriage feast and we will see our God face to face.

No need now of Temple or church building! God is with us in the streets of Jerusalem. The new Jerusalem, the holy city that will stand for evermore.

The angel showed me the holy city, the bride of Jesus. Its walls were of pure diamond: the city was made of gold, shining like newly-cleaned glass. There were twelve gates and each gate was a single peerless pearl. I saw foundation stones of diamond, of lapis lazuli, of turquoise and crystal, of agate and ruby, quartz, malachite and topaz, of emerald, sapphire and amethyst. On each precious stone was written the name of one of the twelve apostles.

So shone the beautiful city, lit with the glory of God, drawing all the pagan nations to it. Its gates are always open; for it is always daytime there. It will never be night again; black night with its shadows of sorrow and despair has been chased away for ever, vanished with the past age.

So come, my little children, come to your beautiful city. Time will end one glad morning. Jesus will come.

I hear voices in heaven. They say: "Come!" The Spirit and the lovely bride, her arms held wide, say: "Come!"

I, John, who write to you heard and saw all these things. When it was over, I knelt at the feet of the angel who had showed me them, but he said: "It is God you must worship. I am just a servant like yourself, and like everyone who treasures the words you have written in your book."

Then I heard the voice of Jesus himself. "I have sent my angel to you, John, to show you all these things for the sake of the churches on earth who suffer. I repeat to you all my promise: 'I shall indeed come again soon'."

I cried to him then: "Oh yes, oh yes, come Lord Jesus."

It is our hope through the ages: Jesus will come.

Revelation 21 and 22